Elementary Statistical Methods

Elementary Statistical Methods

REVISED EDITION

HELEN M. WALKER

Teachers College, Columbia University

JOSEPH LEV

New York State Education Department

Holt, Rinehart and Winston · New York

PREFACE TO THE REVISED EDITION

While this book is presented as a revision of the book under the same name published by the senior author in 1943, it is actually a completely new piece of writing. Only an occasional paragraph and a few graphs and tables from the earlier book have been incorporated in this one. Nevertheless, it resembles the earlier book in many respects.

Like its predecessor, this book is intended as a text for a one-semester introductory course. The authors have attempted to provide an introduction to statistical inference which is modern, intuitive, and nonmathematical, although the coverage is limited by the scope of the book. An effort has been made to present the material with such simplicity and clarity as to make it almost self-instructive. The treatment is nonmathematical, formulas being presented as economical descriptions of computational procedures and, in some instances, as a means of clarifying concepts. The formulas are not derived, but the underlying assumptions are stated when those assumptions limit the conditions under which a formula may properly be used.

The range of activities involved in the entire statistical enterprise has been indicated as far as seems possible in a one-semester text. The purposes of statistical studies, and the collection, summarization, and presentation of data are discussed in the first four chapters. In the earlier book, and in many of the other current texts, these matters are more or less taken for granted, on the assumption that students understand these principles without instruction.

Most of the book is concerned with statistical frequency distributions in one and two variables. These distributions are analyzed by direct examination of their contents and by the use of such summary measures as percentiles, means, standard deviations, and correlation coefficients. It should be noted that in every instance measures which describe the distribution of the group are presented first. Later considerable attention is given to measures such as percentile rank, standard score, normal deviate, and deviation from regression value, which describe the placement of individuals with reference to the group.

Chapters 13 to 16 deal with such topics as point and interval estimation, tests of hypotheses, and power function, in situations where these can be dealt with by the use of the normal probability distribution or Student's distribution. The authors have not felt it wise to thin down the explanatory material in order to make room for the binomial, chi-square, and F distributions. However, by including the z transformation for r, the correction for continuity in tests of proportions, certain facilitating tables, and certain non-parametric tests, the range of applications has been considerably extended. The Appendix contains a number of useful tables, one of which has not been published previously.

The exercises in this text are intended to serve two purposes. Some are the usual types of practice exercise, presenting applications of methods under discussion. Other exercises are intended to classify meanings, to encourage the student in an active search for relationships, and to extend the development of concepts already presented. Because the sets of exercises are timed to come at particular stages in the expository treatment, it seems desirable to place them immediately after the exposition of particular topics rather than at the end of chapters or in a separate manual. Answers to questions in the exercises appear in the Appendix.

In preparing exercises the authors have made repeated use of the same two sets of data, so that the same data may appear in exercises in tabulation; graphing; computation of percentiles, means, and standard deviations; and determination of relationships between pairs of variables. The decision to use the same sets of data in many types of problems is based on the belief that it is easier for a student to comprehend a statistical concept if he is familiar with the subject matter of the data. It should be pointed out, however, that a great variety of additional data are included in the book to enrich the reader's experience. In the interest of emphasizing statistical principles, a new idea is often introduced with a miniature problem in which the arithmetic is so simple that computation requires little attention. These short problems have been specifically planned to facilitate the development of meanings. Short problems are also used occasionally to test the student's grasp of principles.

The discussion of tabulation and graphing has been greatly expanded. In Chapter 6 the discussion of percentiles has been separated from that of percentile ranks to emphasize the difference in the role of the two concepts. The treatment of regression and correlation has been greatly revised to clarify the role of these concepts in applications. Perhaps the greatest change has been the expanded treatment of statistical inference, from one chapter in the earlier book to four chapters here.

New York   H. M. W.
March, 1958   J. L.

How to Use This Book

This section is addressed in part to teachers and in part to students. Since the students in this case are adults, however, no important distinction need be made.

Physical Features of the Book. Before studying any text the wise student familiarizes himself with its physical structure. Among the features of this book which help economize student time and energy are the Lists of Tables and Figures, which follow the Table of Contents in the front, and the List of Formulas and Glossary of Symbols in the Appendix. If the text is read selectively rather than sequentially, unfamiliar terms or symbols may be encountered. The page on which these are introduced and explained can be discovered by consulting the Glossary of Symbols or the Index, or both. The manner of numbering tables, figures, and formulas identifies the chapter in which they are placed.

Reading Habits. Some students who have consciously trained themselves to read very rapidly and are not accustomed to the study of scientific or mathematical material may find it necessary to revise their patterns of study. Until they come to understand that in a work of this nature one cannot read a page at a gulp, they may feel a sense of frustration and that progress is slow because the number of pages covered in a given period of time is far below their average. Students must learn to gear themselves according to the subject matter. While some material may appropriately be covered at high speed, other material calls for thoughtful perusal — for continual comparison of the section under consideration with earlier sections. As Chrystal, a great English teacher of algebra in the nineteenth century, once said, "Every mathematical book that is worth anything must be read 'backwards and forwards'." His advice is still valuable.

The following pattern of study is suggested as likely to produce the clearest understanding for a given expenditure of time. (1) Read a chapter rapidly to get a general impression of the material contained and the purpose of the discussion. In this rapid preliminary reading try to keep a chapter or two ahead of the class discussion. (2) Just before a section is taken up in class, go over it in detail, comparing, rereading, solving problems, verifying numerical statements, and making note of all points that are not fully clear. (3) As soon as possible after a section has been studied in class, read it once more to consolidate the understandings gained from the class discussion. (4) Several weeks later, reread the chapter once more. The practice of rereading material studied previously not only clarifies one's thinking but tends to improve morale. Points that seemed completely obscure on a first reading now seem so obvious that one experiences a real sense of growth. On the other hand, some points which seemed quite simple on a first reading now, in the light of further knowledge, have new implications which raise new queries. That, too, is a mark of growth.

Students unaccustomed to scientific or mathematical work are often discouraged by their need to read statistical material many times. They should realize that this is a characteristic of the type of material.

Abstract Imagination. The purpose of statistical method is to abstract from a mass of individual observations certain information which will enable one to comprehend the whole. Therefore, statistical measures are essentially *abstractions*. An understanding of such abstract concepts has to be built up by experience, just as one builds up the concepts suggested by the words "quaint," "patriotism," "irresponsibility," "nevertheless," and "implication," for which no photograph or diagram can suffice. These concepts must grow in the imagination. To stimulate such imagination is the purpose of certain sets of artificial data used throughout the text and of certain developmental exercises, both verbal and numerical. The building of concepts is a more important undertaking than any other aspect of the course, because without a clear comprehension of concepts all skills are useless.

The beginner does not know which concepts can be clarified graphically and which cannot, and sometimes he is needlessly troubled by his inability to "see" a statistic (e.g., the variance) for which he can obtain no satisfactory visual image. If a student is uncertain about the existence of a useful visual symbol, he might well take the responsibility of asking his teacher before he indulges in too much worry.

Mathematical Preparation. The extreme diversity of mathematical background usually found in a beginning class creates problems for both the teacher and the student. This text is written primarily for the person whose study of mathematics ended when he left high school. At points where such persons are likely to experience difficulty, either special explanations are provided or references are made to Walker's *Mathematics Essential for Elementary Statistics* (Holt, Rev. Ed., 1951). Teachers who use this book may want to require each student to take the self-scoring tests with which each chapter begins. Students who make no errors on a test need do nothing further with that chapter. Those who make errors should study the explanatory material and the practice exercises, then take a second self-scoring test parallel to the first one. Each student can go through the book at his own speed, reporting each week on the chapters he has studied and the number of errors made on each test. A student with good mathematical background can finish the book in a few hours. The student who cannot needs the help he will secure from its use. By this method practically no class time is taken up with difficulties that relate to the simpler aspects of mathematics.

Order of Topics. The sequence of development followed in this book is not the only one which might successfully have been adopted. However, if a person should attempt to study *this* book in a different sequence, rearranging the topics in some new order, he will almost certainly suffer the frustration of encountering the use of technical terms and concepts before he has studied the basic explanation clarifying them. The authors have devoted a great deal of thought to the arrangement of topics and have consistently used the earlier sections to prepare for later ones. Most of the accruing advantages will be lost if the sequence of topics is drastically revised. However, the ensuing confusion can be somewhat mitigated by consistent reference to the Index and Glossary of Symbols.

Minimum Course. Not all classes will be able to complete this text in the time at their disposal. If some material must be eliminated, we suggest that Chapters 1, 2, and 4 be rapidly skimmed, and that the following be eliminated altogether: the last ten pages of Chapter 12; the last part of Chapter 14 beginning with "Power of a Test," and all of Chapters 11, 15, and 16.

TABLE OF CONTENTS

LIST OF TABLES

LIST OF FIGURES

1

The Role of Statistics

Statistical method is one of the devices by which men try to understand the generality of life. Out of the welter of single events, human beings seek endlessly for general trends; out of the vast and confusing variety of individual characters, they continually search for underlying group characters, for some picture of the group to which the individual belongs. This group picture is not merely a summary of the individuals which form the group. It transcends the individuals. It has meaning of its own not to be discovered through the most intense contemplation of any single individual. Such group trends are sometimes apprehended subjectively and almost intuitively by a person of penetrating insight, who observes, without the aid of numerical computations, that "this group is more variable than that" or "these two characteristics are not likely to occur in the same individual," or the like. Such statements are fundamentally statistical in nature, because they relate to tendencies of a group as a whole which either have no meaning with reference to a single individual, or may not be true of a particular selected individual. That such a statement is vague, subjective, debatable, quite possibly false, and inefficiently arrived at does not keep it from being statistical in nature. Controlled, objective methods by which group trends are abstracted from observations on many separate individuals are called statistical methods.

Statistics in Modern Life. To a very striking extent our culture has become a statistical culture. Even on the most elementary level it is impossible to understand psychology, sociology, economics, finance, or the physical sciences without some general idea of the meaning of an average, of variation, of relationship, of sampling, of how to read charts and tables. Even a person who has never heard of an index number is affected in the intimate details of his daily living by the gyrations of those index numbers which describe the cost of living. Perhaps the clearest indication of the extent to which statistical ideas pervade modern life is provided by the use which advertising firms make of such ideas. Quoting statistics in favor of almost any product they wish to popularize, even if those statistics have little relation to the quality of the product, and making liberal use of graphs, they tacitly assume that the American people are accustomed to thinking in statistical terms or that if they do not understand they may at least be impressed by a statistical argument.

Let us look briefly at some of the ways in which statistical facts and statistical ideas impinge on the life of an ordinary person. This business begins early. The parents of a newborn baby are soon asking how his rate of development compares with that of the "average" child, and are perhaps quite unaware of the large amount of statistical research required to furnish the norms needed to provide an answer for their queries. For the baby's ills as well as their own, they expect the doctor to have available tested remedies. But such testing is the outcome of the statistical analysis of data obtained from large-scale experiments. They expect to be able to buy clothing and shoes accurately sized for children of various ages. But how could a manufacturer get the information which makes such sizing possible unless measurements had been made and statistically analyzed for large numbers of children at each age level?

Perhaps the parents take out an insurance policy to provide for the eventual college education of the new baby. An insurance policy actually represents a gamble in which the individual bets that he will not live a specified number of years or that some stated disaster will happen to him, and the company bets that the disaster will not occur. Rates that will permit the company to stay in business but not to make excessive profits can be set only by a very large-scale continuing analysis of mortality data, accident data, and the like. It is impossible to foretell or control the chance factors in life, but it is possible statistically to estimate their group impact and by spreading costs over many people to mitigate the effect of calamity on any one person.

In our "average" family, money is probably not plentiful and they watch the cost-of-living index anxiously, although they may have no idea of how the Bureau of Labor Statistics works year in and year out to gather the statistical data on which that index is based. Or they may watch apprehensively the published figures on unemployment, without knowing anything about the enormous sampling project conducted by the Census Bureau and the Bureau of Labor Statistics in order to obtain current information on the extent of unemployment in various industries and various regions.

When the erstwhile baby is of school age, his parents expect the school to obtain and make proper use of information about his aptitudes, abilities, progress. Yet without the psychological and statistical labor of many people over many years, there would be no tests of reading readiness, of intelligence, of achievement, of vocational preference.

Just as parents expect the medical profession to have reliable information about the effects of all kinds of drugs and treatments, old and new (information that can be secured only through large-scale experiments, statistically analyzed), just so do they take it for granted that the teaching profession will have tested information concerning how children learn; how they develop physically, mentally, and emotionally; which school practices are beneficial to children's development. Such knowledge requires the observation of *many* children, with statistical analysis to extract meaning from the observations.

Population increases or population shifts will affect the living arrangements and personal comfort of our "average" family. Statistical information concerning population changes is essential to the long-range planning of such agencies as housing and traffic authorities, public utilities, and school boards. Thus the "average" person reaps the benefit of statistical studies or suffers when they are not properly made.

The legislator is faced with many decisions which are essentially statistical in nature, relating to such matters as proposals to revise the social security program, to authorize programs of slum clearance and public housing, to extend or withhold foreign aid, to change the pattern of unemployment compensation, to encourage or discourage prepayment for health services. To reach a sound decision on such matters requires a thorough statistical analysis similar to the analyses which permit the successful operation of insurance companies, but all too often the debate on such bills appeals more to emotion than to statistical fact.

Persons who hold managerial positions in industry must be able to interpret statistical studies of the quality of the manufactured product and the efficacy of the manufacturing process — studies which involve drawing inferences from samples. Business men are often concerned with studies of consumer preference and the effectiveness of an advertising campaign, which are also based on samples.

The teacher who does not understand certain basic statistical ideas is in a position to do real harm to pupils because of his ignorance. If he is not aware of the universality of human variability and of ways of measuring it, he may use a test norm as a standard to which he tries to make all pupils conform. If he does not understand the approximate nature of all measurement, the conventional measures of test reliability, the qualities to be sought in selecting standardized tests, and methods of determining the reliability of teacher-made tests, he may place too much faith in unreliable measures of pupils. If he has never studied correlation and regression, he may confuse correlation with causation and thus propose irrelevant action, or he may assume that the child with the highest intelligence quotient in his class should be expected to stand highest in other desirable traits and therefore be censured if he does not excel, thus demanding the impossible of some pupils and giving insufficient challenge to others.

The student majoring in education, psychology, sociology, or economics soon discovers that, unless he has at least a minimum acquaintance with statistical vocabulary and statistical method, much of the important literature of his field is incomprehensible to him. Often he discovers that he himself has become interested in working on some project to which statistical methods are basic.

Everyone who reads the newspapers is now familiar with the various opinion polls and so has some vague idea about generalizations based on samples. The educated person needs to understand something about the practice of drawing samples and making inferences from sample data, and to become sensitive to sources of bias in any sample on which he is depending for important information; he needs to know that sampling has become a highly technical matter and that, if he plans to make an important investigation utilizing sampling, he must either study the literature on sampling methods or consult an expert, preferably both.

Persons who do not feel confident of their own ability to interpret a statistical statement usually resort to one of two extreme positions, each unsatisfactory to the well-educated man. One extreme is the uncritical acceptance of any statement buttressed by statistical data, however fantastic. The other extreme is uncritical suspicion of *all* statistical reasoning. Aside from these two extremes, the only alternatives appear to be either reliance on authority or some comprehension of what statistical reasoning is and on what principles it depends for validity and cogency. One cannot count on having a satisfactory authority always at hand, however, and the person who wishes to make judicious decisions in regard to personal matters, business matters, or public policy will often need to base those decisions on information that is essentially statistical in nature.

Choice of Action. A very important use of statistical information is to furnish a basis for choice between two or more courses of action. A statistical study can throw light on the probable consequences of each of the alternative actions, but it does not pretend to be a substitute for value judgments. The person or group responsible for choosing a course of action can make a more informed decision when they have more light on what the results of each action are likely to be, but they still have to decide which results they prefer.

Sometimes a person or a group utilizes for this purpose statistical information already published or instruments already constructed by statistical methods. For example, a young person trying to choose a vocation is not likely to have the resources for gathering his own data on the income, the living conditions, the hours of work, or the demand for new entrants in several vocations, but there may be such data already in print. Suppose he learns from such data that there is great demand for new workers in vocation A — salaries are high, hours of work long — while in vocation B, salaries are lower, competition for jobs is more intense, and hours shorter and living conditions pleasanter. He must still choose which he prefers, but his choice is no longer blind.

Sometimes a statistical study is initiated to provide the basis for a specific, immediate decision. The field of market research provides a great many examples of this situation. A merchant employs interviewers to ask housewives whether they would use a certain product if it were put on the market, whether they prefer one type of product or another, etc., and uses the tabulated returns to make merchandising decisions. The sponsor of a program on radio or television analyzes data on program ratings to help him decide whether to continue a particular kind of advertising. Large manufacturing plants keep up a continuous statistical study of their products in order to detect flaws that might indicate the need to overhaul the machinery, in order to choose between alternate processes, and the like.

Sometimes a large investigation provides the basis for widespread, general decisions. This is the situation, for example, in most medical research. The immediate decision may be the choice between saying "yes" or saying, "The evidence is not convincing" to such a question as, "Do cigarette smokers have, in general, a shorter life-span than nonsmokers?" or "Does the Salk vaccine protect against polio?" But that decision may cause many individuals and groups to make other related decisions as to a course of action.

Action Suggested by Statistical Inquiry. A statistical investigation is not limited to providing a basis for choosing between alternatives which are known prior to the investigation. The purpose of the inquiry may be to suggest a new course of action. Some of the basic problems confronting our society, such as delinquency and alcoholism, do not yet have well-defined solutions even as possibilities. It is hoped that statistical studies underway on factors related to these problems will suggest remedial courses of action.

Basic Statistics. A large part of statistical enterprise concerns itself with compilation of statistical data — its summarization and presentation as a basis for a variety of decisions. In business, statistical data deal with such matters as items produced, labor used in production, sales, and profits or losses. In government, statistical data are concerned with such matters as size and composition of population, and wealth of the nation and its welfare.

The purposes to be served by the basic data are not always well defined at the time of compilation. Data obtained from a census may serve as a basis for revising congressional districts; they may help a chain store in establishing new branches; or they may point out the need for new facilities for higher education ten or fifteen years later.

In the presentation of basic statistics, consideration needs to be given to the uses to which they will be put in making decisions leading to action. A great deal of data, such as population or wealth of many localities, is presented in the form in which they were obtained. The users may then relate and summarize these data in ways which are most helpful to them.

Data for the nation as a whole, or for states, are often of sufficient interest so that governmental agencies present summaries of them in a variety of ways. As an illustration of such a summarization, consider the consumers' price index prepared by the United States Bureau of Labor Statistics. This is a weighted average of retail prices expressed as a percent. This index of prices is very important in interpreting wages and costs under the conditions of varying prices.   Other well-known summaries of this sort are indices of stock prices and of production.

Summary of Purposes.   Statistical investigations are justified by their usefulness in leading to improved courses of action.   Some investigations are directly related to a specific purpose and are planned accordingly.   Other investigations do not have clearly defined purposes, but it is expected that the information obtained in these investigations will serve a variety of purposes.

Issues Preliminary to Any Statistical Inquiry.   At this point the reader may be mistakenly assuming that by studying a text in statistics he will learn certain statistical computations and a kind of universal routine for attacking a statistical problem, and that he can then apply that routine and perform those operations in any situation he wishes to explore statistically.   This is a serious misapprehension of the way a statistical study should be approached.   Before any statistical enterprise is begun, whether it be on a large scale or a small scale, whether its pattern be simple or complex, certain general issues must be faced.   Decisions must be reached on the following points:

(1) What concrete questions is the study designed to answer? The ability to ask good questions is one of the marks of an effective, imaginative, creative research worker.   Help at this point must come primarily from the content field rather than from methodological consideration.

(2) To what class of individuals are the answers intended to apply?   To those individuals examined only or to some larger group?

(3) If the answers are to have some general import beyond the cases actually observed, how is the sample to be chosen?   How large should it be?   Are there any elements of bias in the proposed plan for selecting the sample of individuals to be examined?

(4) What observations or measurements are to be made on these individuals, and how?   Each content field has its own special methodology for making observations and measurements, and this methodology must be learned by the specialist in that field.   In this text only general matters related to a wide variety of fields can be mentioned.

(5) How shall data be assembled for analysis?   Some useful methods are described in Chapter 2.

(6) What summary measures shall be computed?   This is the main theme of the book.

(7) How shall results be presented?   Some aspects of this problem are discussed in Chapters 3 and 4.

2
Gathering and Recording Data

Once the purpose of a statistical investigation has been defined, the problem is to collect data which are relevant to that purpose, to analyze these data, and to present them in a meaningful manner. This chapter will deal somewhat sketchily with problems of gathering and recording data in order to facilitate their analysis and interpretation.

Subjects of the Investigation. Statistical data may be considered broadly as observations made on subjects. Subjects differ vastly from one inquiry to another. Sometimes subjects are individual persons, sometimes they are families or institutions or communities, sometimes they are physical objects such as buildings or machines or samples of a manufactured product. The variety of things which may be made the subjects of inquiry is practically endless.

Before the investigation begins, it is necessary to *define the units* about which investigations are to be made. For example, in planning a study of low rent public housing developments in a city, it would be necessary to decide whether observations are to be made on families, on persons, on dwelling units, or on some other type of individual. If the family is selected as unit, any of the following definitions might be selected, as well as many others: (a) a family moving into one of these developments during the period covered by the study; (b) a family living in one of these developments for any portion of the period covered by the study; (c) a family applying for entrance to the development during the period covered by the study. It would also be necessary to define "family." If single persons are accepted, does a single person constitute a "family" for the purpose of the inquiry? Do two or three single persons living in the same apartment constitute one family? If so, does that family have a "head" to be enumerated when the heads of families are classified? If the person who signs the lease has relatives other than wife and children living in the same apartment with him, is there one family or two? Using an apartment in one of the developments as unit would permit making observations on all the persons living in it during a designated period, thus securing information about turnover which could not be obtained from a study of family units. Almost every study presents similar perplexities of definition which must be resolved before the data are gathered. Each unit or subject is also called *an individual,* and sometimes *an element.* Obviously the term *individual* does not necessarily mean a person.

Variables. For each subject of an investigation, one or more characteristics are observed. These characteristics are selected in the light of the purposes of the investigation. For example, the observations made on a family might include the number of persons in the family, the number of children, the number of adults, the number of children of school age, the number of persons employed, the total family income, the occupation of each parent, the country of birth of each parent, the language customarily spoken in the home, the number of persons per room, the number of years of education for each adult in the family, and so on and on.

Observations on a characteristic of individuals permit those individuals to be grouped in different classes, or categories. All the individuals in one class are then said to have the same *value* of that characteristic. Thus, if applicants for a position are classified by sex, the characteristic sex is said to have the two values, male and female.

If a characteristic has the same value for all the individuals in an investigation, that characteristic is called *a constant.* If it has different values for different individuals, it is called *a variable.* Thus, for the children in a public elementary school, such characteristics as sex, age, intelligence quotient, or score on any standardized test would be variables. In a boys' school, sex would be a constant and the other characteristics variables.

A variable which has only two possible values is called a *dichotomy.* Dichotomies are very familiar — people are classified as male or female, as living or dead, as employed or not employed, as native born or foreign born, as literate or illiterate; answers are classified as correct or incorrect; schools are classified as public or private, as sectarian or nonsectarian; plants are classified as exogenous or endogenous; candidates for an office are classified as winners or losers; and so on and on.

Variables which can take three or more values can be classified with respect to *whether their possible values have a necessary order.* Thus automobiles might be classified according to such ordered variables as price, number of miles they have been driven, condition of the tires, and year of manufacture; or according to such unordered variables as make, state in which they are currently registered, and company with which they are insured. College students might be grouped in ordered classes on such variables as age, number of siblings, scores on a prognostic test, tuition paid, and popularity; or in unordered classes on such variables as place of birth, type of college attended, and department in which enrolled.

Ordered variables may be classified as to whether *their values have been placed on a numerical scale* or have only been described in a *series of ordered categories (or classes).* Of the variables mentioned in the previous paragraph, condition of the tires of an automobile might be described in such ordered but unscaled categories as: (a) beyond all usefulness, (b) badly worn, (c) slightly worn, (d) very good, (e) entirely new. Popularity of college students might be described in such ordered but unscaled classes as: (a) most popular, (b) popular, (c) not well liked, (d) greatly disliked. The other ordered variables named in the preceding paragraph are scaled variables.

Scaled variables may be classified as to *whether the scale is discrete or continuous.* Thus age and height are continuous variables because they can take any value — integer or fraction — along the scale, which is continuous, without a break. On the other hand, number of siblings is a discrete variable. The values of the variable must be integers and cannot take any of the fractional values between the integers.

Sample or Entire Population. The question as to whether observations are to be made on all the individuals with whom the study is concerned (i.e., the *population*) or only on some sample of those subjects must be decided in each situation on its own merits. An example of an inquiry in which the goal is to make observations on all individuals is the United States Census. On the other hand when norms are to be established for a mental test, it is obvious that it is neither necessary nor economical to attempt to measure all children of the appropriate age in the country. Even if that could be done, the test would be used for children born at a later time and so not included in the original study. Clearly, the group on which test norms are established must be considered a sample of a larger population.

The procedures of sampling in experiments and in surveys are treated in several excellent textbooks, and are beyond the scope of this book. However, an indication of the general logic of sampling will be given in Chapter 13.

Instruments for Making Observations. If observations are to be made on subjects, instruments for making these observations must be provided. In work with physical materials, or mechanical devices, the instruments are devices for measuring size, strength, chemical composition, electrical charge, and so on.

In the behavioral sciences — psychology, sociology, anthropology, education — the instrument might be a questionnaire, a rating scale, an interview, a galvanometer, a performance test, a pencil and paper test, an observation that certain behavior does or does not occur, etc.

Every book on a content field, whether intended for the administrator, the research worker, the practitioner, or the layman, is directly or indirectly concerned with the collection of data. Each field has its special lore which cannot be rehearsed here where we are dealing chiefly with problems common to many fields. The choice of instruments to be used in a particular investigation depends on the purpose and the subjects of that investigation. The construction of instruments must be made by persons well trained in the subject-matter field and its particular techniques of measurement. However, there are two important general requirements which must always be met if observations are to furnish dependable information.

The first requirement is that observations should be *reliable* — i.e., that repetition of the observation on the same subjects should produce approximately the same results. The second requirement is that observations should be *valid* — i.e., that they should provide a true measure of the characteristic they purport to measure.

Both reliability and validity are amenable to statistical investigation. Chapter 10 will describe such investigation and will discuss further these important characteristics of observations.

The manner in which an instrument is to be used is also an important consideration. Precise instructions must be prepared to assure that observations are made in a uniform manner. If the instrument is a mental test with limited time, the entire test, or its component parts, must be timed accurately and uniformly for all subjects. If the instrument is a form on which information is to be recorded by an interviewer, careful training must be given all interviewers so that practice will be uniform and records comparable.

Personnel of the Investigation. In some enterprises carried out by a small team and in many individual studies, the same person or persons determine the goals of the study, plan its design, and execute the details. However, in a governmental agency or in a large business enterprise, the purpose of the investigation is likely to be decided by higher administrative officials of the organization, and the conduct of the investigation is likely to be turned over to technicians who work in consultation with the administrative officials.

The planning of the investigation and the construction of instruments require skill of very high order. Specialists in one or more subject-matter fields and in statistics participate in this aspect of the investigation. The actual use of the instruments in making observations may often be left to personnel with more limited training. Such personnel may have a variety of titles, depending upon the area of work. In industry, they are often called inspectors. In census work, they are called enumerators.

The statistical analysis of the data is carried on under supervision of persons with advanced training in statistics. However, tabulations and computations may be performed by clerical workers and by operators of the various mechanical devices used in statistical work. The preparation of the final report is again likely to be an enterprise which is carried out by analysts of the highest skill.

Source of Observations. In many statistical undertakings the observations are made specifically for the purpose at hand; in fact, the instruments are devised for the sake of the investigation. However, many other investigations use observations which have been accumulated as operating records of a public agency or a commercial organization. The problem of devising instruments is then minimized or even eliminated, but the problems of sampling, organizing data, analyzing, and reporting still remain.

Original Records. For observations to be useful in a statistical investigation, it is necessary that they be recorded. Important considerations in the planning of forms for the original recording of data are:

> Accuracy of the record
> Simplicity of recording
> Identification of the subject
> Accuracy and ease of reading the record
> Simplicity of use in further analysis
> Completeness of record in respect to its later use

The time card in Figure 2–1 satisfies all the requirements here listed. Accuracy of the record is assured by an exact time mechanism which automatically stamps the time. The record is made simply by inserting the card into the mechanism. The pressure of the card operates the mechanism. The employee is clearly identified. Since the record shows the date, hour, and minute stamped in a preassigned position, it is easy to read. The tabular arrangement simplifies computing time for pay-roll purposes.

BROWN, JONES, SMITH & CO.

TIME CARD

Week beginning August 4, 1958

Roe, Richard

Packer

Shipping Department

	Time in	Time out	Time in	Time out
Mon.	8:30	12:00	12:55	5:00
Tues.	8:31	12:00	12:55	5:00
Wed.				
Thurs.				
Fri.				

Fig. 2–1   Time Card.

An IBM answer sheet for a test in multiple-choice form is shown in Figure 2–2. This answer sheet requires further processing. An electric scoring machine will give the number of correct answers either for the entire sheet or for a specified portion of it.

The examples which have been given provide a separate form for the original record of each individual, but often a single form is used for a group of individuals. The sheets used in census enumeration have 40 lines on each side, all the data for one person being placed on a single line of that sheet. One advantage of such recording is that if an enumerator in the field handles only a few large sheets, he is less likely to lose one than if he handles many small sheets.

The original record form may also provide for recording subsequent action on the basis of the information. Bills customarily have space for endorsement as having been paid. Applications for employment may also provide space for later evaluation, as approved or disapproved for employment.

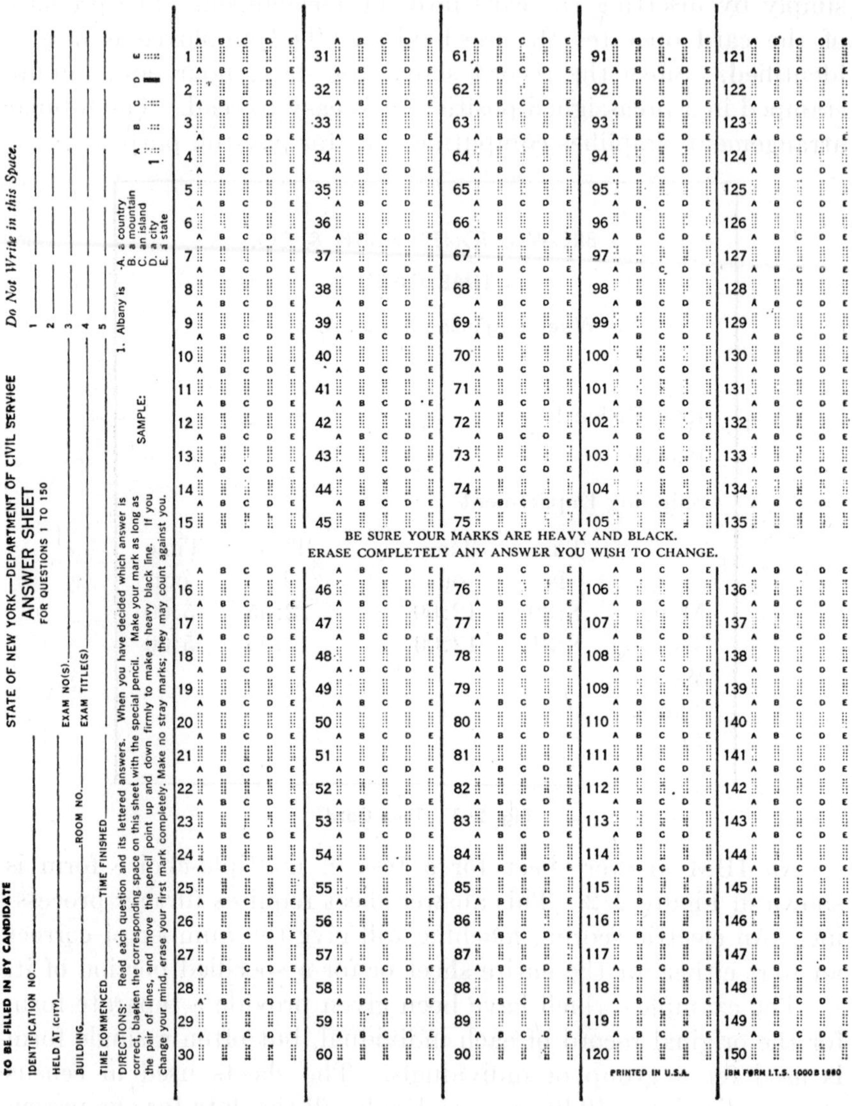
TO BE FILLED IN BY CANDIDATE

STATE OF NEW YORK—DEPARTMENT OF CIVIL SERVICE

ANSWER SHEET

FOR QUESTIONS 1 TO 150

Do Not Write in this Space.

IDENTIFICATION NO.

HELD AT (CITY)

EXAM NO(S).

BUILDING — ROOM NO. — EXAM TITLE(S)

TIME COMMENCED — TIME FINISHED

DIRECTIONS: Read each question and its lettered answers. When you have decided which answer is correct, blacken the corresponding space on this sheet with the special pencil. Make your mark as long as the pair of lines, and move the pencil point up and down firmly to make a heavy black line. If you change your mind, erase your first mark completely. Make no stray marks; they may count against you.

SAMPLE: 1. Albany is A. a country B. a mountain C. an island D. a city E. a state

BE SURE YOUR MARKS ARE HEAVY AND BLACK.

ERASE COMPLETELY ANY ANSWER YOU WISH TO CHANGE.

PRINTED IN U.S.A.

IBM FORM I.T.S. 1000 B 1080

Fig. 2–2 IBM Answer Sheet for Multiple-choice Test.

Summary Records. Frequently data on several variables for the same individual, gathered on separate original records, must be brought together on one single summary record. A familiar example of such a summary record is a teacher's record book, where one line is allocated to each pupil and various columns to the tests. The original test records from the answer sheets of the pupils are transcribed into the appropriate spaces in the class book. At the end of the school term the various test scores are averaged. The class book is also likely to have a space for a final grade.

In order to simplify further analysis it is often convenient to enter summary data on a separate form for each subject. The chief advantage of using such separate summary forms is the convenience in sorting under a variety of classifications. Three illustrations of summary forms in common use will be described.

The Punched Card for Electrically Operated Machines. Several firms have constructed electric machines which can be used for sorting, tabulating, and making computations from data which have been recorded by punching holes in cards. Figure 2–3 shows a punched card which was used in devising a battery of tests for selecting employees.

One card is prepared for each subject, or sometimes more than one card if there are a great many variables. In each column of this card any digit from 0 to 9 can be recorded by punching a hole in the space identified with that digit. For a number consisting of several digits, several columns will be needed — one column for each digit of the number. In designing the plan for punching the

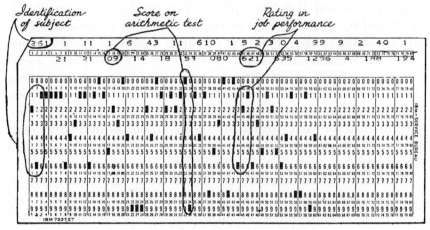

Fig. 2–3 Punched Card for IBM Machine.

cards, each variable is allotted as many columns as the maximum number of digits required for an entry on that variable. The set of columns assigned to a variable is called its *field*. A field is also allotted to identify the subject, usually by means of a code number. As each card contains 80 columns, 80 digits can be recorded. In the hands of an experienced person these 80 digits suffice for the record of a very large amount of information, and the novice will find it a great economy to submit his instruments to such an expert before he gathers his data. Without expert advice *in advance,* one may incur much avoidable expense in transcribing data from the original instruments to the punched cards. In some of the columns, letters of the alphabet can be recorded, but these are used in reporting results, not in analysis. This type of card is used in connection with equipment made by the International Business Machines Company (IBM).

The electric equipment can be used to sort cards into classes, to count cards, to list some or all the entries, and to make a variety of complex computations. Such equipment is expensive to rent or to buy and is customarily used only in an organization with a volume of work sufficiently great to warrant the expense. Card equipment which is much cheaper to buy will be described in the following paragraphs.

Edge Marking Cards. Even if the size of a study does not justify the use of electric equipment, it may still be convenient to record all the data for one individual on a single card and to sort these cards by hand into piles according to the classes for a particular variable. Even sheets of paper such as test blanks are sometimes sorted thus into piles. The mechanics of sorting is facilitated by placing easily recognized symbols in designated locations on the cards. Thus, for example, a red check mark in one corner of the card might indicate a boy and a blue check mark a girl.

The procedure of sorting can be further facilitated by making marks at designated positions at the very edge of the card. A code is drawn up showing exactly which of the numbered positions represent the field for each variable and a record on the individual card is made by drawing a line from a numbered position to the edge of the card.

Figure 2–4 shows the face of a Thurstone Edge Marking card. It is 5 by 8 inches, with 65 numbered positions on each side and space in the center for identifying data or written comment. There are many ways to fill out and use such a card. As a very simple illustration, suppose position 30 is to be used for recording the Yes-No answer to some question. For persons who say *Yes,* a black pencil could be used to continue the short line in position 30 to the edge of the card; for persons who say *No,* a red pencil could be used; for persons who fail to answer, the line could be left blank. If a variable can take more than two values, a more complicated scheme is required.

After each card has been marked, the cards are stacked with all edges precisely even. Then by carefully riffling the cards, the markings for any one variable can be exposed in such a way that the cards can be very easily sorted into piles according to the categories for that variable.[1]

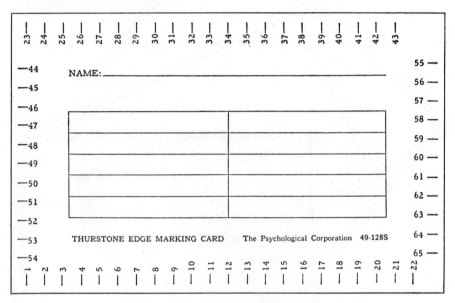

Fig. 2–4   Thurstone Edge Marking Card.

Edge Punched Cards. Such cards represent a mechanical improvement over the edge marking cards in that they can be more efficiently sorted. Cards with a row of little holes around the edge, or sometimes two rows, can be purchased in various standard sizes as illustrated in Figure 2–5. If a study is to involve a very large number of individuals, it may be economical to have a card specially printed by one of the commercial firms handling such materials.

Data are recorded by notching the card, from a hole to the edge. A special clip must be used for this, as it is important that the notch be made smoothly and accurately. If a variable has only two values, a single hole can be assigned to that variable; then a notch may represent one value and the absence of a notch,

---

[1] The Thurstone Edge Marking cards, together with a manual for their use, can be obtained from the Psychological Corporation, 522 Fifth Avenue, New York, N.Y. The content of this manual originally appeared as a paper by L. L. Thurstone in the *Journal of the American Statistical Association*, **43** (1948), 451–462. See also "The Edge-marking of Statistical Cards" by A. M. Lester, *Journal of the American Statistical Association*, **44** (1949), 293–294.

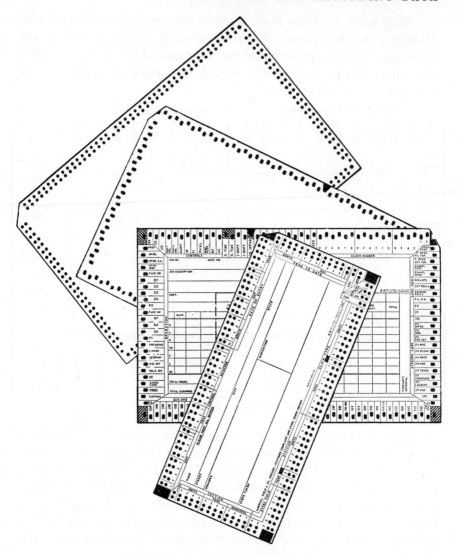

Fig. 2–5 Examples of Edge Punched Cards.

another. If a variable has more than two values, a field of several
holes may have to be assigned to the variable. When cards of
a certain category are to be selected, a needle is passed through
the appropriate holes of the entire batch of cards. As the needle
is lifted, the cards not classified in the category are drawn out with
the needle, the other cards which have been notched remaining
behind. More elaborate systems for complex classifications with
edge punched cards are described in the technical literature on this
subject.

Use of Recorded Data. Gathering and recording data are the first steps in a statistical investigation, as they are, in fact, in any scientific enterprise. To make the recorded data useful to the investigation, it is necessary to select pertinent sections of the data and to analyze them in a variety of ways. The decision as to which data are to be selected for further analysis depends on the special purposes of the study. The remaining chapters of this book will be concerned with methods of analysis of data which are common to many statistical investigations.

3

Construction and Use of Tables

One of the simplest and most revealing devices for summarizing data and presenting them in a meaningful fashion is the statistical table. The table may be only an intermediate step leading to further analysis, or it may be an end product of the entire statistical investigation.

A well-planned table is a unified, coherent, and, in a sense, complete story about some aspect of a set of data. Elements of the data are set up in rows and columns so as to indicate important relationships. The story is carried by the title and by suitable phrases which describe the actual numbers in the rows and columns. The elements of the table and their functions will be described and illustrated in the following pages.

The Table as a List. The simplest kind of table is a mere list of the subjects — usually in the vertical *column* at the left of the table — with certain facts about the subjects in the other columns of the table, all the facts for one subject appearing in the same horizontal line, or *row*. Such listings are illustrated in Tables VIII and IX in the Appendix. While in these tables the order in which the subjects are listed is of no particular importance, in many tables the subjects are placed in a meaningful order. Thus in a table giving data for the 48 states, the names of the states might be placed in alphabetical order for readers who wished to locate a particular state readily; in a historical study, the names might be placed in order of their admission to the Union; or, if the purpose of the table were to compare the states with respect to some characteristic such as density of population or per pupil expenditure for education, that characteristic might be placed in descending order. A list of candidates who have passed a civil service examination is usually arranged in the descending order of their examination scores because their relative position on this list — their rank in the group — determines their eligibility for appointment to a position.

If the data to be tabulated are on cards, with a separate card for each subject, these cards can be sorted in any desired order and then the data can be transcribed. If the original data already appear as a list, but a new list in some other order is desired, it may be helpful to prepare a set of cards, one for each subject, and then to sort these cards in the desired order prior to setting up the new list. A convenient feature of electric equipment for use with punched cards is that it makes possible an automatic listing, in tabular form, of the data on the punched cards.

Summary Tables. A list is often a preliminary table, providing a basis for other tables which summarize the information contained in the list and present it in a way which brings forward important facts and relationships contained in the data. The remainder of this chapter will be concerned with the methodology of constructing summary tables.

The Elements of a Table. Table 3.1 is a simple table which summarizes and makes evident information contained in the listing of Table VIII about the sizes of Sections I, II, and III. Although it is a simple table, it contains the elements which characterize tables generally. These include:

TABLE 3.1 Enrollment in Three Sections of a First Course in Statistical Methods

Teachers College, Columbia University, February, 1950

Section	Number of students
I	41
II	27
III	28
Not identified	2
Total	98

THE TABLE NUMBER	*Table 3.1.*
THE TITLE	*Enrollment in Three Sections of a First Course in Statistical Methods.* The title is a brief description of the contents of the table.
THE HEAD NOTE	*Teachers College, Columbia University, February, 1950.* The head note may be used to provide additional information about the centents of the table which would make the title undesirably long if included in it.

THE FIELD — The tabular entries, which in this table are the frequencies *41, 27, 28, 2* and *98*.

THE COLUMN HEADS — *Section* and *Number of students*. A column head describes the entries in a column.

THE STUB — The left hand column, which contains the major scheme of classification of the tabular entries. In Table 3.1 the stub consists of the entries *I, II, III, Not identified*, and *Total*.

LINE CAPTION — Each entry on a line of the stub. Thus *I, II, III, Not identified*, and *Total* are line captions.

STUB HEAD — A statement placed above the stub and used to describe the line captions in the stub. As the stub is a column, the stub head, *Section*, is also one of the column heads.

The significance of these structural elements is more clearly brought out in Table 3.2 which will be discussed in some detail with reference to its structure as a table, and from the point of view of procedures needed to obtain the entries.

TABLE 3.2 Number of Men and Women in Each Section of a First Course in Statistical Methods

Teachers College, Columbia University, February, 1950

Section	Number of students		
	Men	Women	Total
I	28	13	41
II	24	3	27
III	18	10	28
Not identified	1	1	2
Total	71	27	98

Table 3.2 tells in greater detail the same story as Table 3.1. Because it shows another variable — namely, the sex of the students — two more columns are needed. There are now three columns in the field, and each column requires an explanatory heading. Instead of saying in this heading "Number of Men," "Number of Women," the phrase "Number of Students" is placed as brace heading (also called a spanner head) over all three columns. Note the use of a horizontal ruling to indicate the relation of the spanner head to the column heads.

Tallying. The entries, or frequencies, in Table 3.2 could be obtained from the entries in the first two columns of Table VIII in the Appendix by counting all the entries for a given section which are unstarred in the first column, and then counting all the entries for the same section which are starred in the first column. This process could be repeated for all three sections. The results of these counts could then be checked against the complete counts for the sections made by ignoring the stars, as in Table 3.1, or by counts of all starred entries and all unstarred entries separately, ignoring sections. A check of some sort is absolutely essential for accuracy.

However, this method of obtaining the frequencies is laborious and likely to produce errors because it is so easy to lose count. It is better to obtain the frequencies by *tallying*.

First, we note the nature of the breakdown desired for the final table, which, in this case, must provide for one classification into two groups (men, women) and for a second classification into four groups (three sections and a group of those "not identified"). A diagram having 2 by 4 boxes or cells will be required and each cell must be large enough to hold all the tallies likely to be placed in it. Suitable headings should be placed on the rows and columns so that the person tabulating will not make a mistake by forgetting which is which.

Next, for each of the subjects in turn we enter in the appropriate box a short stroke called a tally (|). Thus for subject number 1, a tally is placed in the box which is in row III and the column "Men." The fifth tally in each set is drawn across the other four |||| to facilitate counting the tallies. Sometimes the line for each tenth tally is slanted at a different angle to facilitate counting by tens, thus: ||||| ||||| ||||| ||||| ||. The diagram and the tallies which have been inserted in it are shown in Fig. 3–1.

Accuracy of tallying is considerably increased and eyestrain decreased if one person can read from the raw data while a second person enters tallies in the diagram.

Fig. 3–1 Diagram Showing Tallies for Frequencies in Table 3.2.

Section	Men	Women
I	||||| ||||| ||||| ||||| ||||| |||	||||| ||||| |||
II	||||| ||||| ||||| ||||| ||||	|||
III	||||| ||||| ||||| |||	||||| |||||
Not identified					

Table Containing Percents. Table 3.2 would be more informative if the percents as well as the numbers of the men and women in the three sections were exhibited as in Table 3.3. Some distinc-

TABLE 3.3   Percent of Men and Women in Each Section of a First Course in Statistical Methods

Teachers College, Columbia University, February, 1950

Section	Men		Women		Both	
	Number	Percent	Number	Percent	Number	Percent
I	28	68.3%	13	31.7%	41	100.0%
II	24	88.9	3	11.1	27	100.0
III	18	64.3	10	35.7	28	100.0
Not identified	1	50.0	1	50.0	2	100.0
All sections	71	72.4%	27	27.6%	98	100.0%

tive structural features of this table merit consideration. The words "Men," "Women," and "Both" are used as *spanner heads* (or *brace heads*) and appropriate horizontal rules indicate the relation of each to the two column heads under it.

The use of more than one kind of unit (numbers and percents) makes it imperative that the unit be named at the head of each column. To aid the eye in distinguishing which figures represent numbers and which represent percents, it is customary to place the % sign after the first figure in a column of percents and after the summary, if there is one. A similar convention applies to the use of the dollar sign.

The introduction of percents requires identification of the base on which each percent is computed. The entries of 100.0% in the final column make it clear that each number in that column is the base of the percents in its row. Thus, $\frac{28}{41} = 68.3\%$, $\frac{13}{41} = 31.7\%$, $\frac{41}{41} = 100.0\%$, and we have as a check $68.3\% + 31.7\% = 100.0\%$. Some authors record percents without indicating the numbers on which the percents are based. This practice is unfortunate because it leaves the reader uncertain as to what significance to attach to the percents. Clearly 50 percent means something quite different when it is based on 200 cases than when it is based on 2 cases.

In the final row of Table 3.3, the entries in the columns headed "Number" were obtained by adding the other entries in those columns, but the entries in the columns headed "Percent" were not obtained by adding other entries but by computing a new percent. Thus, $71/98 = 72.4\%$ and $27/98 = 27.6\%$. Although the summaries for the columns headed "Number" could properly be termed totals, those for the columns headed "Percent" cannot be so designated. To provide a heading appropriate for all entries the summary row has been labeled "All sections."

EXERCISE 3.1

1. From the data of Table 3.2, construct a table with percents based on the totals of the sexes instead of on the totals of the classes, as in Table 3.2.
2. From the same data, construct a table with column heads as follows:

	Number			Percent		
Section	Men	Women	Both	Men	Women	Both

TABLE 3.4 Number of Students in Each Section above or below the Middle of the Entire Group on Each of Two Tests

A First Course in Statistical Methods, Teachers College, Columbia University, January, 1950

		Number of students scoring					
		On midterm test			On arithmetic test		
Section	Sex	Below 53	53 or higher	Total	Below 33	33 or higher	Total
I	Men	11	17	28	7	21	28
	Women	5	8	13	3	10	13
	Both	16	25	41	10	31	41
II	Men	11	13	24	14	10	24
	Women	3		3	2	1	3
	Both	14	13	27	16	11	27
III	Men	12	6	18	13	5	18
	Women	6	4	10	8	2	10
	Both	18	10	28	21	7	28
All Sections	Men	34	36	70	34	36	70
	Women	14	12	26	13	13	26
	Both	48	48	96	47	49	96

Two cases with section unidentified have been omitted

A Table Containing Two Sets of Data. Table 3.4 is more complex than the preceding tables since it not only classifies the subjects by section and by sex, but also presents two sets of data on the same subjects — one set based on scores in a midterm test on the content of the course, and one on scores in a prognostic test in arithmetic given before the start of the course. The two sets of data are presented in a single table because the second set helps to explain the first.

Column headings not only indicate the two separate parts of the table, they also manage to name the tabular entries in the table's field. The stub is divided into four distinct blocks each of which designates a complete table, so that actually Table 3.4 consists of 8 subtables related in such a way that it is more useful to present them together than separately.

Another feature of this table is that for the first time in this chapter use is made of continuous variables. These are the scores on the two tests. The choice of the two breaking points at 53 and 33, respectively (noted in the column heads), may at first glance seem arbitrary. However, the entries in the final row of the table show that these scores divide the entire group into equal subgroups for the midterm test and into nearly equal subgroups for the arithmetic test. A procedure for finding such dividing scores will be described in Chapter 6.

The frequencies in Table 3.4 were obtained by a simple sorting procedure which could be easily carried out by anyone concerned with similar data. For each individual, a small slip of paper was prepared and on that slip was recorded the individual's code number, section, sex, score on midterm test, and score on arithmetic test. Not all these data were used in the first tabulation but they were all recorded so as to be available for later tabulations. The slip used for Student 1 is indicated below

1	III	M	33	58

The 96 slips of paper were filled out and checked for accuracy. The slips were then sorted by midterm test score and arranged in descending score order. From this sort, it was ascertained that 48 students scored 53 or above and 48 scored below 53.

The high (53 and above) and the low (below 53) subgroups were separated. Each subgroup was then sorted into six piles, by section and by sex within section. Obtaining the entries for the left-hand half of Table 3.4 was then merely a matter of counting the numbers of slips of paper in the piles. The right-hand half of the table was constructed similarly, using the same 96 slips of paper.

The analysis of the frequency distribution forms a major part of this book, and in effect the procedure just described was an elementary study of a simple frequency distribution.

Although this chapter is concerned mainly with the structure of tables rather than with the content of any one of them, the content of Table 3.4 foreshadows so much of the reasoning in this book, and in the authors' more advanced book on *Statistical Inference*, that an analysis of this table seems desirable. An additional reason for the discussion which follows is that it gives an indication of how a table can be analyzed.

First, we may note that while the entire group is divided into equal subgroups by the score of 53 in the midterm test, the same is not true of the Sections separately. In Section I three fifths of the students scored 53 or higher, but in Section II fewer than half, and in Section III only a third scored 53 or higher.

It is natural for the reader to wish to account for the differences among the sections. A first speculation might be that instruction was most effective in Section I and least in Section III. However, before accepting this explanation, it is necessary to look at the data on the prognostic test of arithmetic. Interestingly enough here also there are differences between the sections which parallel the differences observed in the other half of the Table. In Section I three fourths were among the highest half of the entire group, but in Section II the corresponding fraction is two fifths, and in Section III it is only one fourth. It seems logical to assume that the observed differences in achievement of sections in the course may be partly or wholly accounted for by differences in mathematical ability of the students in these sections.

The relation between midterm score and arithmetic score for these 98 students, and the extent to which the former score can be predicted from the latter, will be taken up in Chapters 9 and 10.

In practice, data like those in Table 3.4 would be treated by more powerful statistical methods than those exhibited in the table. However, a tabulation like that appearing in this table has various uses. It is helpful to the investigator in showing him direction for more extensive research. It is also helpful in displaying to readers who are not technically trained the relationships discovered by technical means.

Summary of the Structural Elements of a Table. It seems desirable at this point to bring together in summary form a description of the structural elements of the table. These structural elements are illustrated in relation to Table 3.4 in Figures 3–2, 3–3, 3–4, and 3–5.

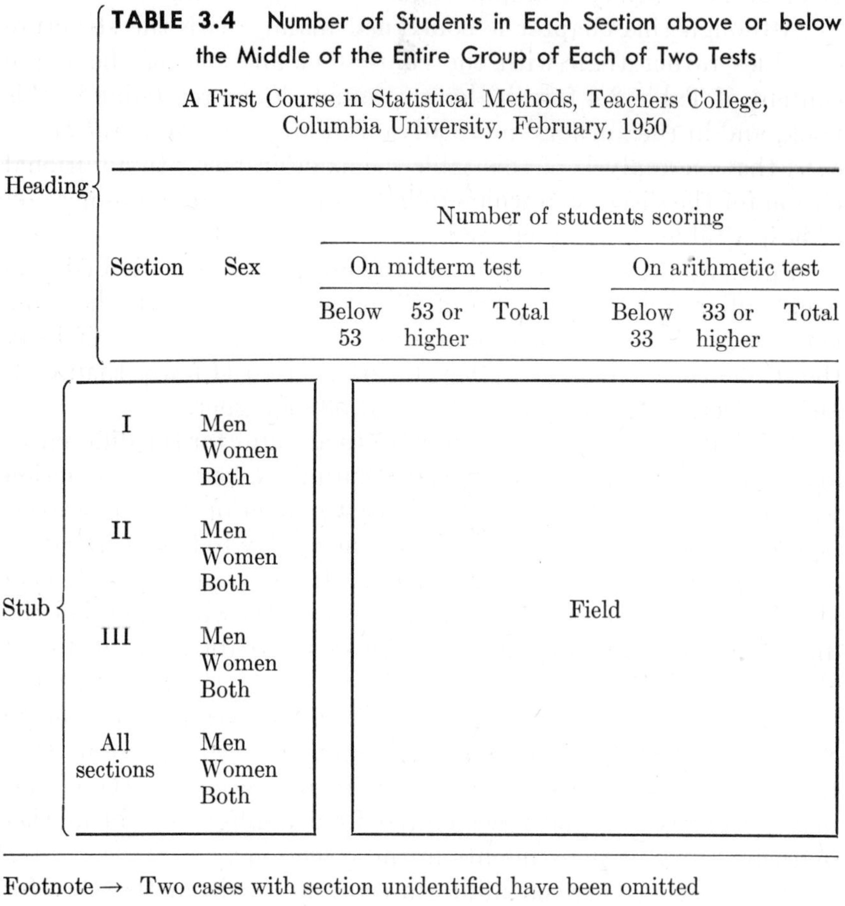

TABLE 3.4   Number of Students in Each Section above or below the Middle of the Entire Group of Each of Two Tests

A First Course in Statistical Methods, Teachers College,
Columbia University, February, 1950

Heading {

Section	Sex	Number of students scoring					
		On midterm test			On arithmetic test		
		Below 53	53 or higher	Total	Below 33	33 or higher	Total

Stub {

I	Men Women Both	Field
II	Men Women Both	
III	Men Women Both	
All sections	Men Women Both	

Footnote → Two cases with section unidentified have been omitted

Fig. 3–2   Major Parts of a Table.

Such elements are as follows:

1. *Heading*. The portion of the table which includes the table number, the title, the subtitle, if any, the headnote, if any, the column headings, and column spanners.

(a) *Table number*. If there are several tables in the same study, the tables should be numbered in sequence, either through the entire study or through each chapter. Reference to a table should usually be by its number. In referring to a table in the text, it is better to say "In Table 15—" than to say "In the following table —" or "In the preceding table —." In preparing a manuscript the writer cannot be sure what will be the exact position of a table in the final printed version — whether it will actually follow or precede the reference — but its number is clear and unambiguous.

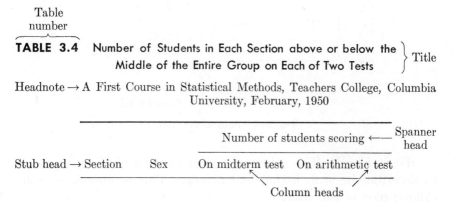

Fig. 3–3   Parts of the Heading.

(b) *Title.* A clear description of the content of the table in as concise form as possible. It should help the reader understand quickly what the table is about. To begin the title with unnecessary words, such as "Table showing —" or "A comparison of the numbers of —" blunts its effect.

(c) *Subtitle.* A second title used to supplement a briefer main title. Sometimes a table has a short display title and a longer, more explanatory, main title. Sometimes in a series of similar tables the titles might be so much alike as to be confusing. To distinguish them, each may be given a short main title calling attention to what is unique in the specific table and a subtitle which is similar for all tables in the series. The distinction between a subtitle and a headnote is not very important.

(d) *Headnote.* A statement or phrase below the title which serves to qualify the title or to provide information relating to the table as a whole. It may show units when all the units in the table are alike; it may show the source of the data. Not every table needs a headnote.

(e) *Column heading.* The descriptive title for all data in the column which it heads. Ideally, the column heading or the spanner heading should *name* the tabular entries in the column.

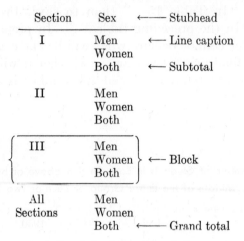

Fig. 3–4 Parts of the Stub.

(f) *Stubhead.* The column head or caption of the stub, used to describe the stub listing as a whole. This is sometimes considered part of the stub.

(g) *Spanner head.* A classifying or descriptive caption spreading across and above two or more column headings, and applying equally to all columns thus covered.

2. *The stub.* A description of the row classification appearing in the left-hand column. The stubhead is sometimes considered as part of the stub even though it is physically placed in the heading.

(a) *Line caption.* A descriptive title for the basic data appearing on a line. As a line is also called a row, the line caption is also called row caption.

(b) *Subhead.* A title which serves as a heading for several line captions.

(c) *Caption for summary line.* A description of the group to which the summary applies. When the summary is merely the sum of several preceding entries, this caption is usually "Total" as in Tables 3.1 and 3.2. When, for a combined group, the summary gives a percent or an average or similar measure *not* obtained by adding related measures for the component groups, as in Table 3.3, the term "Total" does not apply, but instead some such phrase as "Combined group," "All cities," "All ages," or the like is used.

(d) *Block.* A segment of the stub consisting of several related line captions and subheads.

3. *The field.* The part of the table extending downward from the heading to the bottom rule of the table, and to the right of the stub. It contains the tabulated data of the table.

(a) *Cell.* The space allotted for an entry. It lies at the intersection of a column and a row.

(b) *Tabular entry.* The information appearing in a cell of the table.

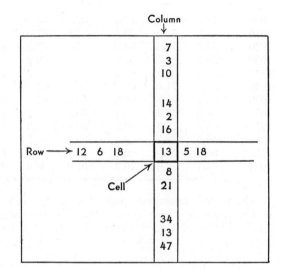

Fig. 3–5 Parts of the Field.

(c) *Line.* A horizontal array of cells with a common classification.

(d) *Column.* A vertical array of cells with a common classification.

4. *The footnote.* Information needed for interpreting a table which is placed in a note directly under the table. This may be information relating to the table as a whole, such as a statement concerning its source. A footnote may furnish an explanation of symbols used if their meaning is not obvious. When specific entries in a table are explained by footnotes, reference is usually made by means of such diacritical marks as *, **, ≠, or #, or by means of small letters, a, b, c, ... Numbers are not used for such reference because they might be mistaken for exponents. The tabular footnote does not become a part of the general system of footnotes used in the book or monograph. A footnote to a table is not placed at the bottom of the page but directly beneath its table.

Tables with Averages as Entries. Tables 3.5 and 3.6 are presented as examples of tables in which the entries are neither fre-

TABLE 3.5   Expectation of Life at Birth in the United States

	White			Nonwhite			All races		
Year	Male	Female	Both sexes	Male	Female	Both sexes	Male	Female	Both sexes
1900	46.6	48.7	47.6	32.5	33.5	33.0	46.3	48.3	47.3
1910	48.6	52.0	50.3	33.8	37.5	35.6	48.4	51.8	50.0
1920	54.4	55.6	54.9	45.5	45.2	45.3	53.6	54.6	54.1
1930	59.7	63.5	61.4	47.3	49.2	48.1	58.1	61.6	59.7
1940	62.1	66.6	64.2	51.5	54.9	53.1	60.8	65.2	62.9
1948	65.5	71.0	68.0	58.1	62.5	60.0	64.7	70.2	67.2
1949	66.2	71.9	68.8	58.9	62.7	60.6	65.4	71.0	68.0
1950	66.6	72.4	69.2	59.2	63.2	61.0	65.8	71.5	68.4
1951	66.5	72.4	69.2	59.1	63.3	61.0	65.8	71.5	68.4
1952	66.6	72.7	69.4	59.1	63.7	61.1	65.9	71.8	68.6
1953	66.8	72.9	69.6	59.7	64.4	61.7	66.1	72.1	68.8
1954	67.4	73.6	70.3	61.0	65.6	63.0	66.8	72.9	69.6

This table is taken from page 97 of the *1956 Life Insurance Fact Book*, Institute of Life Insurance, New York, 1956. The Institute obtained the data from the National Office of Vital Statistics, Department of Health, Education and Welfare.

TABLE 3.6   Expectation of Life at Various Ages in the United States 1954

	White		Nonwhite		
Age	Male	Female	Male	Female	All races
0	67.4	73.6	61.0	65.6	69.6
20	50.3	55.9	45.5	49.4	52.4
40	31.8	36.7	28.7	31.8	33.8
45	27.5	32.2	24.8	28.0	29.4
50	23.4	27.7	21.3	24.4	25.2
55	19.6	23.5	18.4	21.3	21.3
60	16.2	19.4	15.7	18.3	17.7
65	13.1	15.7	13.5	15.7	14.4
70	10.5	12.4	11.9	14.0	11.6

This table is taken from page 97 of the *1956 Life Insurance Fact Book*, Institute of Life Insurance, New York, 1956. The Institute obtained the data from the National Office of Vital Statistics, Department of Health, Education and Welfare.

quencies nor percents, but averages. Tables in which the tabular entries are standard deviations, percentiles, correlation coefficients, or other summary measures occur in many scientific journals and also in later chapters of this text.

The figures in Table 3.5 are predictions, based on evidence available in the year indicated, as to what would be the average number of years in the life span for persons in the category indicated. Thus in 1900, it was predicted that for all white males born that year in the United States the average age at death would be 46.6 years.

The figures in Table 3.6 are predictions, based on evidence available in 1951, as to how many more years, on the average, persons of a given age might be expected to live. Thus it is predicted that for all white males, aged 50, the average number of years before death would be 23.0 and, therefore, that for these men who have already survived to age 50 the average age at death would be 73.

EXERCISE 3.2

1. Locate and name the structural elements in Tables 3.5 and 3.6.

2. From Table 3.5 answer the following questions and indicate on what your answers are based:

(a) By how many years did the average life span increase for white males during the period 1900–1954? For nonwhite males? For white females? For nonwhite females? Has the increase been greater for males or for females? For whites or nonwhites?

(b) Was there any decade during this period in which the life expectation was greater for males than for females?

(c) Has the discrepancy between the average life span of males and that of females increased or decreased during this period? Does your answer hold good for both whites and nonwhites?

(d) Has the discrepancy between the average life span of whites and nonwhites increased or decreased during this period? Does your answer apply both to males and to females?

(e) Would it be correct to use the word *Total* as heading for the summary columns here called *Both sexes?* As spanner heading instead of the phrase *All Races?*

(f) Construct a new table in which the classifications by sex and by color are placed in the stub. Let the column headings be 1910, 1920, 1930, 1940, 1950. Over these columns place a spanner head reading "Increase in life expectation during the decade beginning." From the given data make the necessary computations to obtain the tabular entries for this new table.

    (1) In which decade occurred the greatest increase in life expecta-
tion for white men? White women? Nonwhite men? Non-
white women?

    (2) For all whites, which decade showed the greatest increase?
For all nonwhites?

  (g) Was the rate of increase less in the decade 1940–50 than in the
preceding decade? Is there some feature in Table 3.5 which might
invite a careless reader to make a mistake on this point?

3. Find in Table 3.6 data from which to answer the following questions:

  (a) What is the prediction as to the average age at death of all babies
born in the United States in 1954? Of all persons who are 20 years
old in 1954? Of all persons who are 70 years old in 1954?

  (b) Is there any age at which the life expectation of women is less than
that of men?

  (c) Is there any age at which the life expectation of white men is less
than that of nonwhite men? Any age at which the life expectation
of white women is less than that of nonwhite women?

4. On a small slip of paper write for each student listed in Table VIII his
number, his score in arithmetic, and his score on the midterm test.
Sort these slips of paper into four classes to provide entries for the
following tabulation:

		Arithmetic scores	
		below 33	33 and higher
Midterm test scores	53 and higher		
	below 53		

Construct a formal table using the tabulation just completed. Name
the structural parts of the table. Discuss the significance of the contents of the table.

4

Graphic Methods

The use of graphs to make relationships among statistical data vivid is so well known that this chapter needs no justification. Some of the more common statistical graphs will be discussed here. Essentially, a graph is a representation of numbers by geometric figures drawn to scale. The effectiveness of a graph depends on the ingenuity with which relations among the geometric figures can be used to represent relations existing among numbers.

The first consideration in drawing a graph, as in any undertaking, is its purpose. The most common purposes of graphs are representations of (a) numerical data, (b) partition of a total into component parts, (c) changes over time intervals, and (d) relationships among variables. Several purposes are often served by the same graph.

The second problem is the choice of geometric figures to represent the numbers. Then the scale must be chosen. Finally, the elements must be organized into the total graph. This organization involves arrangement of the geometric figures, indication of the scale, and formulation of a title. These problems will now be considered briefly.

The Title. The title of a graph is sometimes placed above the graph just as the title of a table is placed above the table, and is sometimes placed below the graph just as the title of a picture is customarily placed below the picture. The former practice is becoming common with newspapers and advertising agencies, the latter still holds in most technical books and periodicals. In reading either a table or a graph, one should look first at the title, then at such explanatory matter as the column headings of the table or the scales of the graph, and last at the tabular entries or the graph. In a table, the column heads are above the tabular entries; thus the title is most strategically placed above the table.

In a graph, the scales may be above the graph, below it, or both, and so there is no clear reason why the title is uniformly better in one position than in the other.

The Bar Graph. In this type of graph, numbers are represented by bars drawn to scale. When the bars are in vertical position, the bar graph is sometimes called a column graph. The simple bar graph in Figure 4–1 provides a visual picture of the data

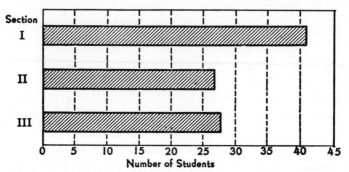

Fig. 4–1 Enrollment in Each Section of a First Course in Statistical Methods. Teachers College, Columbia University, February, 1950.

in Table 3.1 on page 21. The scale is shown here below the graph. When there are many bars, it may be helpful to show the scale at both the top and bottom of the graph. Vertical guide lines combine with the horizontal scale to form a *grid*. Identification of the section to which each bar relates is placed at the left and corresponds to the stub of a table.

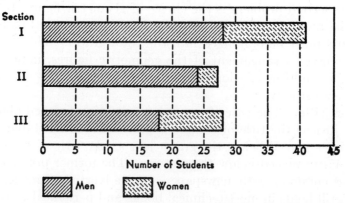

Fig. 4–2 Number of Men and Women in Each Section of a First Course in Statistical Methods. Teachers College, Columbia University, February, 1950.

In Figure 4–2 the bars as a whole are the same length as in Figure 4–1, but are subdivided to show the numbers of men and women. A limitation of this graph is that numbers of women are not easily compared across sections, since the crosshatched portions of the bars do not begin at the same scale value.

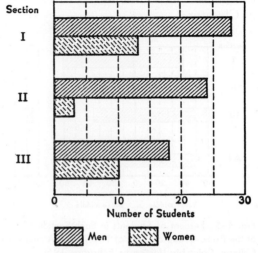

Fig. 4–3 Number of Men and Women in Each Section of a First Course in Statistical Methods. Teachers College, Columbia University, February, 1950.

This limitation is removed in Figure 4–3 where the bars for both sexes begin at a common zero point and all six bars can be compared. However, in this graph, total section enrollments cannot be easily compared.

If the purpose of the graph is to show only proportionate sex composition of the three sections, this purpose is better served by Figure 4–4 in which the sexes are represented by percent only.

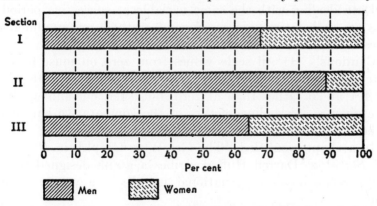

Fig 4–4 Percent of Men and Women in Each Section of a First Course in Statistical Methods. Teachers College, Columbia University, February, 1950.

A more elaborate bar graph is shown in Figure 4–5, which pictures the data in Table 3.4. To simplify the presentation, data for the sexes have been combined and percents rather than actual numbers are shown. The scales have been set up to indicate the percent of each subgroup in the upper or lower half of the entire group. This graph may be considered as a means of emphasizing the points made in the discussion which accompanies Table 3.4 in Chapter 3.

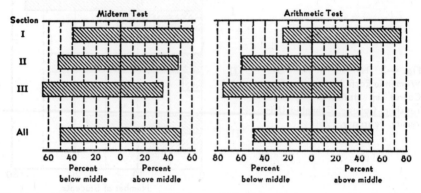

Fig. 4–5   Percent of Students in Each Section Who Scored above or below the Middle of the Entire Group on Each of Two Tests. A First Course in Statistical Methods. Teachers College, Columbia University, February, 1950.

A column chart used to represent similar data for different periods of time is shown in Figure 4–6. A group of three bars is shown for each year and two of these bars are divided. The original chart from which Figure 4–6 was copied used color most effectively, as many advertising media now do, but that color has not been reproduced here.

Data dealing with the same variable at successive periods of time are called *time series*. Several methods of graphing time series will be presented later in this chapter.

Cautions.   (1) All scale values from zero on must be represented. One might have been tempted to begin the scale of Figure 4–1 at 20 rather than at zero, but such curtailment would have given a misleading picture of the comparative enrollments of the sections.

In a chapter entitled "The Gee-Whiz Graph" in *How to Lie with Statistics*, Darrell Huff describes a graph designed to show a 10-percent increase in national income in a year. He comments:

Now that's clear enough. It shows what happened during the year and it shows it month by month. He who runs may see and understand, because the whole graph is in proportion, and there is a zero line at the bottom for comparison. Your 10 percent *looks* like 10 percent, an upward trend that is substantial but perhaps not overwhelming. That is very well if all you want to do is convey information. But suppose you wish

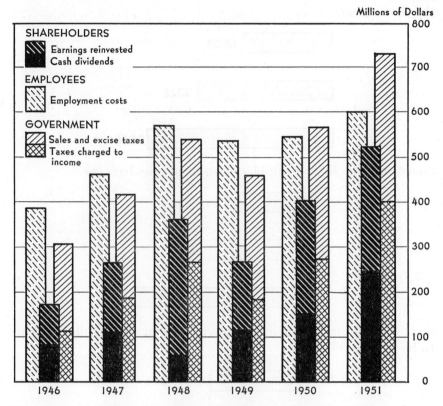

Millions of Dollars

SHAREHOLDERS
Earnings reinvested
Cash dividends

EMPLOYEES
Employment costs

GOVERNMENT
Sales and excise taxes
Taxes charged to income

Fig. 4-6 Amounts Gained by Shareholders, Employees, and Government. Source: Financial Statement of the Standard Oil Company of New Jersey for 1950.

to win an argument, shock a reader, move him into action, sell him something. For that this chart lacks schmaltz. Chop off the bottom. Now that's more like it . . . nothing has been falsified — except the impression that it gives. But what the hasty reader sees now is a national-income line that has climbed halfway up the paper in twelve months, all because most of the chart isn't there any more . . . a small rise has become visually a big one.

Valid exceptions to the requirement of beginning the scale at 0 are rare and should be allowed only after careful consideration. Some appropriate exceptions are described in the chapters on regression and correlation.

(2) Figures showing the numerical values represented by the bars should never be so placed as to distort the lengths of the bars. If such figures are placed outside the bars and close to their ends, they may mislead the eye by exaggerating the relative length of

the shorter bars, as in

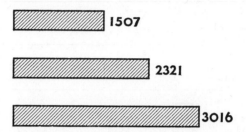

Sometimes the figures can be placed inside the bars, as

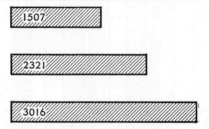

or at the left and sufficiently removed so that they do not appear to be part of the bar, as

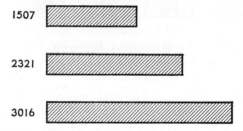

The Pie Chart. This type of chart is used to show the partitioning of a total into component parts. For example, Figure 4–7 shows the proportionate enrollment of three sections of a course in statistics. A very common use of the pie chart is to represent the division of a sum of money into its components. Thus the entire circle, or pie, may represent the budget of a family for a month, and the sections may represent portions of the budget allotted to rent, food, and so on.

The pie chart is so called because the entire graph looks like a pie, and the components resemble slices cut from the pie. To make the chart, a circle with arbitrary radius is drawn to represent the total. The size of the radius depends upon available space and other factors of presentation. The components are then apportioned according to angular measure. The ordinary protractor is based upon a scale in which the total circle is 360 degrees, but it is possible to purchase a protractor in which the entire circle is divided not into 360 but into 100 equal parts, so that the angle representing any desired percent can be read directly. Either protractor can be used to lay off the appropriate angles at the center of the circle, thereby setting up the components.

Ordinarily, the first radius is drawn vertically from the center. The components are then arranged in order in a clockwise direction. If there is no natural order among the components, they are usually arranged in decreasing order of size.

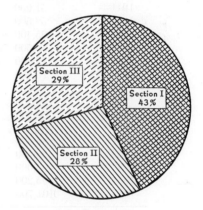

Fig. 4–7 Percent of Students in Three Sections of a First Course in Statistical Methods. Teachers College, Columbia University, February, 1950.

The Line Graph. In this section the line graph will be considered as a means of presenting corresponding numerical data at successive periods of time, or *time series*. Uses of the line graph to represent frequency distributions and relationships between variables other than time will be described in later chapters.

Several time series are shown in Table 4.1. The stub shows the time period, and each of the other columns shows a set of statistical data which has been changing over those time periods. Such data are called *time series*. In Figure 4–8 the horizontal scale shows the time periods from the stub of Table 4.1. Obviously, it is both unnecessary and impossible to show the zero point on this scale. The vertical scale shows number of workers expressed in units of 1,000,000. Here it is both possible and essential to show the zero point. Place a sheet of paper over the lower part of Figure 4–8 and see how its meaning appears to be changed. The grid consists of a network of vertical and horizontal lines so drawn as to facilitate construction and reading of the graph.

Readers who are not familiar with the process of plotting points on coordinate axes should pay very careful attention to the construction of this chart, comparing it with Table 4.1. For the

TABLE 4.1 Old-age and Survivors Insurance
(000 Omitted)

Year	Number of living persons with wage credits year-end	Number of workers with taxable earnings in year	Number of workers fully insured * year-end
1940	44,900	35,393	24,200
1941	51,000	40,976	25,800
1942	58,500	46,363	28,100
1943	65,400	47,656	29,900
1944	69,500	46,296	31,900
1945	72,400	46,392	33,400
1946	75,000	48,845	35,400
1947	77,100	48,908	37,300
1948	79,200	49,018	38,900
1949	80,600	46,796	40,100
1950	82,400	48,100	59,800
1951	87,700	58,000	62,600
1952	90,500	60,000	66,600
1953	93,000	60,000	69,200
1954	95,200	60,000	69,800
1955	101,700	68,000	69,600

* Fully insured workers have at least 1 quarter of coverage (earned at any time after 1936) for each 2 quarters elapsing after January 1, 1951 (or after reaching age 21, if that is later) and before death or age 65, with at least 6 but never more than 40 quarters required.

Adapted from the 1956 Life Insurance Fact Book, which acknowledges as original source, the Social Security Administration.

year 1940, Table 4.1 indicates that 24,200,000 workers were fully insured. The chart conveys the same information by a dot placed directly above the point 1940 on the horizontal axis and directly to the right of the point 24,200,000 on the vertical axis. (Actually, the vertical scale cannot be read with complete precision and the numbers may be rounded to two places.) The reader should identify each point on the graph which represents a pair of entries in the table.

When a line graph is to be drawn, the scales are laid out on axes at right angles to each other, and a grid is constructed or a ready-made grid is obtained by using cross-section paper. There is no necessary relation between the units of the horizontal scale and the units of the vertical scale, and these are usually adjusted in such a way as to produce a figure which fits the page on which it is

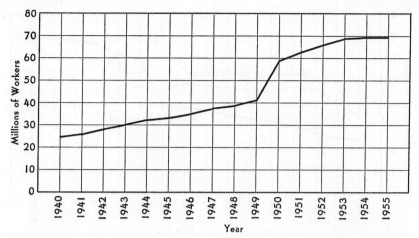

Fig. 4–8 Number of Workers Fully Insured at Year-end under Old Age and Survivors Insurance.

to be placed and which has dimensions that are esthetically pleasing. It must be noted, however, that the apparent story told by the graph can be altered by greatly changing one scale in relation to the other. After the grid is constructed, points are located in the manner described in the preceding paragraph and are connected by straight lines.

Figure 4–8 makes vivid to the eye the increase in the number of workers fully insured under old age and survivors insurance. That increase was fairly regular from 1940 to 1949, but between 1949 and 1950 there was a very rapid increase. Of course, the graph gives no indication of the reason for this sudden spurt, but the person looking at it may recall a change in the social security law which admitted many additional workers to old age and survivors insurance.

Placing two time series on the same graph facilitates comparison. In Figure 4–9 the number of workers fully insured can be compared with the number having taxable income. Figure 4–9 shows more vividly than the table does how until 1949 the number of workers fully insured was consistently less than the number with taxable income, but since 1950 the number of insured workers has been consistently greater. When several lines are drawn on one chart, they can be distinguished by using such varied forms as ...., or _____, or ....., as well as a solid line.

The Semilogarithmic Graph. Table 4.2 contains some very interesting figures about enrollments in the elementary school, the secondary school, and in institutions of higher education for 6

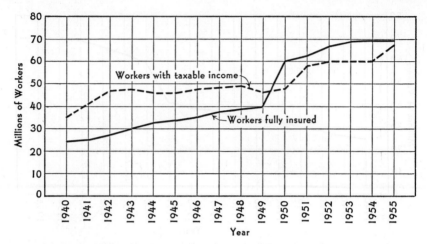

Fig. 4–9 Number of Workers with Taxable Income and Number Fully Insured at Year-end under Old Age and Survivors Insurance.

TABLE 4.2 Enrollment in the Elementary Schools, Secondary Schools, and Institutions of Higher Education and the Entire Population of the United States at the Census Years, 1900–1950

Year	Elementary school		Secondary school		Higher education		Entire population	
	$N*$	Percent change †	$N*$	Percent change †	$N*$	Percent change †	$N*$	Percent change †
1900	16,262		699		238		76,092	
1910	18,529	14%	1,115	60%	355	49%	92,407	21%
1920	20,964	13	2,500	124	598	68	106,466	15
1930	23,718	13	4,804	92	1,101	84	123,077	16
1940	21,107	−11	7,123	48	1,494	36	132,122	7
1950	22,202	5	6,427	−10	2,616	75	151,677	15

* In thousands
† Change between two consecutive census years divided by the figure for the earlier of the two years.

The figures were taken from various editions of the *Statistical Abstract of the United States.* There may be some minor inconsistencies because of changes in the manner of reporting. For example, the eighth-grade enrollments may sometimes be included in the figures for the elementary school and sometimes in the figures for the secondary school, depending on whether the organization is 8–4 or 6–3–3.

successive census years. Figure 4–10 shows the elementary school enrollments, secondary school enrollments, and the entire population of the United States by a line graph of the type previously described. It was not feasible to show enrollments in higher educa-

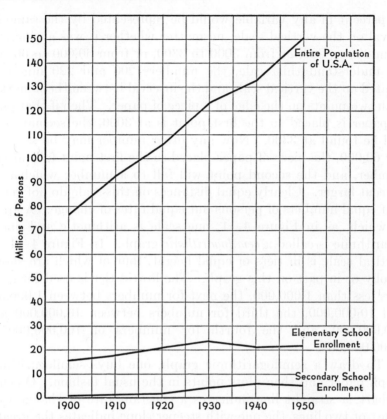

Fig. 4–10 Elementary and Secondary School Enrollments and Population Increase for the Years 1900–1950.

tion on this chart because they were so small in relation to the vertical scale that the line graph would be scarcely distinguishable from the horizontal axis. The chart creates a general impression that the total population has been increasing rapidly, while school enrollments have grown only slightly. In actual numbers such is the case, but certainly not in percents. Reference to Table 4.2 shows some very large percents of increase which are not reflected by Figure 4–10 in any satisfactory way.

In the scales discussed up to this point, equal intervals on the scale represent *equal amounts of change* in the variable. Such scales are termed *arithmetic scales*. We shall now make use of a scale in which equal intervals represent *equal percents of change* in the variable. Such scales are called *logarithmic* scales.

In Figure 4–11 the horizontal scale, representing time, is arithmetic, each 10-year period being represented by the same scale interval. The vertical scale is logarithmic, so that an increase of

10 percent in any variable would be represented by the same interval on the vertical scale, no matter whether it was an increase from 200 to 220, or from 3000 to 3300, or from 60,000 to 66,000. To understand this scale, the numbers 200 and 220 might be located on the vertical scale and the interval between them marked with two points on the edge of a piece of paper. Then if that piece of paper is placed so the first point is at 3000, the second point will be found at 3300. Now any other number may be selected, say 60,000, the piece of paper placed so the first point falls at this number, and the second point will fall to a number which is 10 percent larger. Clearly equal distances on this scale do not represent equal numbers of persons but equal rates of change. A graph in which, as in Figure 4–11, one scale is arithmetic and one is logarithmic is called a *semilogarithmic* graph. In Figure 4–11 the vertical scale is in tiers of equal height, four of which are shown wholly or in part on this graph. The lowest tier is used for numbers less than 1,000,000, the next for numbers between 1,000,000 and 10,000,000, the third for numbers between 10,000,000 and 100,000,000, and the fourth for numbers of 100,000,000 to 1,000,000,000.

To draw a semilogarithmic graph, one buys semilogarithmic graph paper and then plots points in the usual fashion. On such a chart, a straight line indicates a constant rate of change over time; of two lines, the one with steeper slope indicates the greater rate of change.

In Figure 4–11 the lines for elementary school enrollments and for the general population are nearly straight from 1900 to 1930 and are also nearly parallel. We draw the conclusion that they were increasing at about the same rate and that the rate of increase was relatively constant. Reference to Table 4.2 confirms that conclusion. Between 1940 and 1950 both were affected — the elementary school enrollments much more severely — by the drop in birthrate during the depression years.

The lines for enrollments in secondary school and higher education look roughly parallel from 1900 to 1930, but if you will measure the vertical increase for each between these two years, you will see that it was greater for the secondary school, indicating a greater percent of increase there. However, after 1930, increase proceeded more rapidly in higher education. Measure the vertical change for higher education over the 50-year period. You will see that the line has climbed more than the width of one complete tier, indicating that enrollments were more than ten times as great

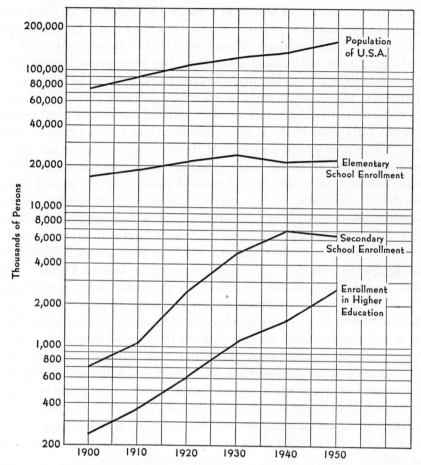

Fig. 4–11 Enrollments for Secondary School and Higher Education and the Population of the United States for the Years 1900–1950.

in 1950 as in 1900. Verify this conclusion by reference to the table.

Figure 4–11 shows vividly how much more rapid has been the rate of increase for enrollments in secondary and higher education than for elementary school enrollments or the general population of the country.

The Pictograph. In a pictograph, numbers are represented by rows of little pictures presumably symbolic of the variable in question. Thus the number of agricultural workers in a region might be represented by a row of men carrying rakes, the number of office workers by a row of men with brief cases, etc. Each figure would stand for a specified number of workers. Although pictographs have been in use for a long time, they enjoyed a period of great popularity in the 1930's under the influence of Otto von Neurath of Vienna who had the idea that they could be developed into a universal language of science. To the person not familiar with graphs or with statistical ideas, the pictograph is probably more interesting than the undecorated bar graph or the line graph. However, the modern trend is to create interest through the use of color and of background pictures and the number of good pictographs published today is much smaller than it was twenty years ago. The pictograph has several disadvantages over other types of graph: (1) Drawing little symbols takes some inventiveness; they must be very simple and must depend more on outline than on detail; different symbols used in the same chart must be easily distinguished. (2) The construction of a bar graph or a line graph is easier except for large agencies which can have a symbol reproduced by a rubber stamp. (3) The pictograph is inflexible and suitable only for very simple data; the data of Figures 4–8, 4–9, and 4–10 could not be effectively presented by a pictograph.

Role of Graphs in Presentation of Data. While this chapter has described a variety of methods for presenting data graphically, it is not the intention of the authors to suggest that all, or even nearly all, data should be so presented. The preparation of graphs consumes a great deal of time and effort. Graphs also occupy a great deal of space when included in a report. For these reasons, data should be presented graphically only when such a presentation makes an essential contribution beyond that which might be attained by reference to data in a paragraph or by presentation in a table.

Several of the earlier graphs shown in this chapter deal with data which do not justify graphic presentation, since the mere presentation of the frequencies involved makes the point with sufficient effectiveness. These graphs were constructed as a means of introducing the topic by use of simple materials. Figure 4–9 presents an illustration of a graph which performs an essential function by making relationships vivid in a situation in which tabular presentation would have been less successful.

In deciding whether or not data are to be presented graphically, or in making a choice between diverse ways of graphing data, account must be taken of the audience to which the presentation is directed and the circumstances under which the presentation is to be made. Data which are easily comprehended by one group, when presented in tabular form, may require presentation in graphic form to a less sophisticated group. Graphic presentation helps even a sophisticated group to see trends and relationships when the data are sufficiently complex. When it is expected that an audience will have little time to devote to the comprehension of statistical data, it is very helpful to devise graphic means for making the data readily comprehensible.

5

Data on a Scaled Variable
Tabulating and Graphing

This chapter and the three which follow it will be devoted to problems of summarizing and analyzing data on a scaled variable. The most elementary of those procedures, tabulating and graphing, will be the subjects of this chapter.

Several of the frequency distributions in Chapter 3 relate to data classified in unordered categories. Thus in Table 3.1, students are classified in three sections. True, these sections are labeled I, II, and III, but the numerals are merely names and the sections might as well have been called A, B, and C. In other tables in that chapter, students were classified according to sex as well as according to class section; these are unordered classes.

For a scaled variable, the values have a necessary order and numerical relation to each other.

Frequency Distribution on a Scaled Variable. A tabulation of data on the scaled variable age is shown in Table 5.1. The original records in the decennial census were for age at the last birthday but here, for convenience of presentation, the original data have been grouped in larger intervals. Each interval except the highest is an interval of 5 years. No upper limit is stated for the highest interval and so it is called an *open* interval. Every individual — or subject — in the study is allocated to one of these intervals which we call *class intervals*. Thus the 150,697,361 persons enumerated in the 1950 census have been classified in the age groups named. These classes are called *mutually exclusive* because it is impossible for any one subject to belong to more than one of them.

A set of mutually exclusive classes and the number of individuals belonging in each class constitute what is called a *frequency distribution*. The number of individuals in any one class is called a *frequency* and in this text will usually be indicated by the letter

TABLE 5.1 Population of the United States in 4 Census Years, Classified by Age

Age in years *	Number of persons † enumerated in the Census			
	1950	1940	1930	1920
Total, all ages	150,697	131,669	122,775	105,711
Under 5	16,164	10,542	11,444	11,573
5–9	13,200	10,685	12,608	11,398
10–14	11,119	11,746	12,005	10,641
15–19	10,617	12,334	11,552	9,431
20–24	11,482	11,588	10,870	9,277
25–29	12,242	11,097	9,834	9,086
30–34	11,517	10,242	9,120	8,071
35–39	11,246	9,545	9,209	7,775
40–44	10,204	8,788	7,990	6,346
45–49	9,070	8,255	7,042	5,764
50–54	8,272	7,257	5,976	4,735
55–59	7,235	5,844	4,646	3,549
60–64	6,059	4,728	3,751	2,983
65–69	5,003	3,807	2,771	2,068
70–74	3,412	2,570	1,950	1,395
75 and over	3,855	2,643	1,913	1,470
Not reported	——	——	94	149

Source: United States Census Report for 1950, Vol. II, Part I

* As of last birthday at time of census enumeration

† To the nearest thousand.   For example, the total for all ages in 1950 was 150,697,361, which is approximately 150,697 thousands.   Annexing 000 to each figure will give a good approximation to the original value.

f unless it is named in words, as it is in Table 5.1.   Table 5.1 presents four different frequency distributions all having the same set of classes.

In order to understand something of the contribution to statistical thought which a frequency distribution can make, it may be worthwhile to take a closer look at the entries in Table 5.1. Look first at the figures for 1920.   Letting the eye run down that column, it will be noticed that the entry for any 5-year period selected is smaller than the entry for the preceding 5-year period. In other words, the number of persons living at a given age decreases as age increases.   This phenomenon is a natural consequence of mortality.   Of course, the frequency for the open period "75 and over" is larger than the frequency for the previous period, but this is understandable since "75 and over" covers more than a 5-year period.

None of the three later censuses shows this same steady decrease down the entire column. In 1930 there are fewer children under 5 than in the age group 5–9, obviously reflecting a lowered birth rate in the late 1920's, but after that youngest group, the number of persons living decreases as age increases.

The 1940 figures have been affected also by a second decrease in birth rate during the depression in the 1930's, and so we have the remarkable phenomenon of the number of living persons actually increasing over the first four age groups. The sharp rise in birth rate at the close of World War II is reflected in the 1950 figures in the large frequencies for the two youngest age groups. The three groups between ages 10 and 25 are still showing the effect of the lower birth rate in the earlier decades.

Reading across the table, comparing frequencies in the same row, is also instructive. Although the total population of the country increased every decade, the number of children under 5 decreased from 1920 to 1940 not only in proportion to the population but in actual numbers. The entries in rows near the bottom of the table show striking evidence of our aging population. The number of persons aged 75 and over has increased much faster than the total population. The total population increased about 43 percent from 1920 to 1950: $\dfrac{150,697}{105,711} = 1.43$; while the number in this oldest age group increased about 162 percent: $\dfrac{3,855}{1,470} = 2.62$.

Construction of a Frequency Distribution. The frequency distributions in Table 5.1 were presented to us in completed form, and our role in regard to them has been more or less passive. But suppose we had the active task of constructing such a distribution, what problems would we face? It has already been said that a frequency distribution is the result of assigning each individual in the group studied to one of a set of mutually exclusive classes. Then, obviously, the problems are the selection of classes and the allocating of individuals to them.

The matter of allocating individuals to classes has already been discussed in Chapter 3 and need not be treated further here. For the census data we have been discussing, an IBM card was punched for each person and the cards were sorted and tabulated electrically, according to the age intervals or classes shown in Table 5.1. The number of cards in each age interval is the frequency in the interval.

We shall give some attention to the manner in which the intervals of a frequency distribution are set up. To accomplish this, it will be necessary to examine closely the nature of a scaled variable and the way in which it can be divided up to provide appropriate classes for a frequency distribution.

Discrete and Continuous Variables. Some scaled variables — such as the number of children in a family, the number of books loaned by a library in a week, the number of automobiles sold by a dealer in a specified period — can take values only at certain discrete points on a scale. Such variables have already been termed *discrete variables*.

Other scaled variables — such as age, weight, or temperature — are termed *continuous* because they can have values at every point on a continuous scale.

Obviously, not all the infinitely many actual values of a continuous variable can be reported. One of the first tasks confronting a person who is to gather data on such a variable is to decide in advance what values he will report. Thus in measuring weight he might decide to report no fractions of a pound, so that a child who weighed a little less than 52.5 lb would be reported as 52. In such a scheme 50, 51, 52, 53, 54, etc., would be reportable values, whereas 52.5 would, by prior decision, not be a reportable value. However, if it were agreed to report to the nearest half pound, such values as 51.5, 52.0, 52.5, 53.5, etc., would be reportable values, whereas 51.25 would not be.

For the analytic procedures which follow, it will be convenient to treat all scaled variables as continuous. Consequently, a rather detailed discussion of the scale of a continuous variable will be presented.

The Scale of a Continuous Variable. In order to graph the frequency distribution of a continuous variable or to make and report computations with scaled data, it is essential to understand the representation of scores on the scale of such a variable.

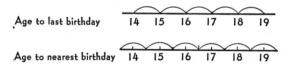

For the census data shown in Table 5.1, age was reported *to the last birthday*. Thus some of the persons reported as 16 years old have barely passed their sixteenth birthday while others are on the verge of their seventeenth. Age is a continuous variable but age reported by the census enumerator is a discrete variable, and only integers are reported. If an age scale is marked off in units of 1 year, for the census data or any data recorded as "age in years at last birthday," the single number 16 represents all ages in the interval from 16 to 17 with midpoint at 16.5. If age is reported "to the nearest birthday," the number 16 represents the interval from 15.5 to 16.5 with midpoint at 16.0. Many people would find great difficulty in deciding which is their nearest birthday and, therefore, many studies of age call for the last birthday. Because both methods of reporting are in use, there is considerable ambiguity in age data unless an author tells exactly what a unit means. A column head should never be simply "age" or even "age in years," unless somewhere in title or subhead or footnote there is an explanation of where the year begins.

A year is sometimes indicated by its end point, as when a small child says he is "going on four" or an old man says, "I will be 95 at my next birthday." Because we name centuries by their end points, the century in which we are now living is called the twentieth. If a questionnaire item reads, "How many years have you been in your present position? Include the present year," each answer would represent a year interval named by its end point. Thus an interval named 6 would extend from 5 to 6, with midpoint at 5.5. The foregoing discussion is intended to emphasize the importance of thinking carefully about the meaning of scale units and giving the reader adequate information for interpreting them correctly.

For most scaled variables other than age, it has become customary to name a unit by the value of its midpoint. The width of the unit in which measurement is made indicates the degree of precision of the measurement — the narrower the unit, the more precise the measurement. Thus in measuring lines to the nearest inch, the line OA will be reported as 3 inches long; in measuring to the nearest half inch, as 3; in measuring to the nearest quarter, as $2\frac{3}{4}$.

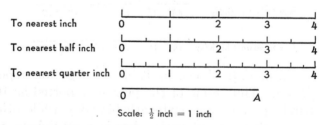

Scale: $\frac{1}{2}$ inch = 1 inch

In measuring to the nearest inch, the number 3 represents a unit 1 inch wide extending from $2\frac{1}{2}$ to $3\frac{1}{2}$, with midpoint at 3.

In measuring to the nearest half inch, the number 3 represents a unit one-half inch wide, extending from $2\frac{3}{4}$ to $3\frac{1}{4}$ with midpoint at 3.

In measuring to the nearest quarter inch, the number 3 represents a unit one quarter of an inch wide, extending from $2\frac{7}{8}$ to $3\frac{1}{8}$, with midpoint at 3.

EXERCISE 5.1

1. Suppose that in measuring a continuous variable the scores used in reporting measurements are as given below, each number being considered as representing the midpoint of a unit on the scale, exactly what portion of the scale is covered by the unit labeled 7? How wide is the unit?

   (a) 5, 6, 7, 8, 9, 10, 11, 12
   (b) 3, 5, 7, 9, 11, 13, 15, 17, 19
   (c) 5.5, 6.0, 6.5, 7.0, 7.5, 8.0
   (d) 4, 7, 10, 13, 16, 19, 22
   (e) 6.8, 6.9, 7.0, 7.1, 7.2, 7.3
   (f) $5\frac{3}{4}$, 6, $6\frac{1}{4}$, $6\frac{1}{2}$, $6\frac{3}{4}$, 7, $7\frac{1}{4}$, $7\frac{1}{2}$

2. Suppose a continuous variable is measured with the degree of precision shown below. Write five numbers representing five successive scale units, and let 20 be the second of the five numbers.

   (a) 0.5   Answer: 19.5, 20.0, 20.5, 21.0, 21.5
   (b) 0.1   .   20.0   .   .   .
   (c) 3.0   .   20.0   .   .   .
   (d) 0.01   .   20.0   .   .   .

Grouping Scores into Wider Intervals. In setting up Table 5.1, ages originally recorded in units of 1 year have been combined into 5-year intervals. Thus the ages originally recorded as 5, 6, 7, 8, or 9 have been combined into an interval labeled 5–9. From the original meaning of the year unit, it is clear that the interval 5–9 includes ages of children who have passed their fifth birthday but

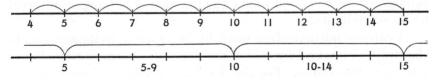

not their tenth and so on a linear scale it represents an interval of width 5 extending from 5 to 10 with midpoint at $7\frac{1}{2}$.

For almost any other type of scaled data, an interval 5–9 would represent an interval of width 5 extending from $4\frac{1}{2}$ to $9\frac{1}{2}$ with midpoint at 7.

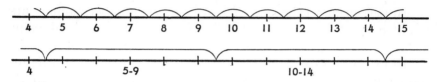

Examine the preceding sketch in which a scale unit is named by its midpoint, and look at the interval which includes the five units, 10, 11, 12, 13, and 14; it has been named 10–14 and these numbers are called its *score limits*. However, the interval actually extends from point 9.5 to point 14.5, and the interval limits 9.5–14.5 are called *true limits* or *real limits*. The midpoint of this interval is at 12, which is halfway between the real limits, $\frac{1}{2}(9.5 + 14.5) = 12$; and is also halfway between the score limits, $\frac{1}{2}(10 + 14) = 12$. This midpoint is the *class value*, or the *class index*, or the *class mark*. The *size of the class interval*, or the *width of the interval*, is the difference between the real limits, $14.5 - 9.5 = 5.0$, and shows the *degree of precision* of the measurement. It is commonly denoted by the letter i (for interval). The class interval is also called the *step interval* or the *class sort*. Study the relation of these various terms as illustrated for several successive intervals:

Scores included in the interval	Real limits	Score limits	Class index	i
20, 21, 22, 23, 24	19.5–24.5	20–24	22	5
15, 16, 17, 18, 19	14.5–19.5	15–19	17	5
10, 11, 12, 13, 14	9.5–14.5	10–14	12	5
5, 6, 7, 8, 9	4.5–9.5	5–9	7	5

Some authors prefer to name an interval by its real limits. However, that practice seems to invite mistakes in tabulation, as the person tabulating might place the number 14 in the interval marked 14.5–19.5 instead of in the one marked 9.5–14.5 where it belongs. This book will follow the practice of naming an interval by its score limits.

A careless mistake often made by beginners is to underestimate the width of interval by taking the difference between score limits instead of real limits. For the data we have been discussing, this mistake would result in saying $i = 14 - 10 = 4$, or $i = 9 - 5 = 4$. Look again at the sketch of the scale to see what parts of that scale $9 - 5 = 4$ and $14 - 10 = 4$ cover and to see exactly why i is not 4 but 5. The width of interval is, of course, also the difference between successive class indices which are 7, 12, 17, and 22.

EXERCISE 5.2

1. Draw a scale and mark on it the score points 6.0, 6.5, 7.0, 7.5, 8.0, 8.5, 9.0, 9.5

    (a) Draw a brace to represent the interval which includes scores 6.5, 7.0, and 7.5.

    (b) Fill in the blanks below:

Scores in interval	Real limits	Score limits	Class index	i
9.5, 10.0, 10.5	——	——	——	——
8.0, 8.5, 9.0	——	——	——	——
6.5, 7.0, 7.5	——	——	——	——

2. If each score is an integer, and real limits are as indicated, fill in the blanks:

    (a)

Score limits	Scores in interval	Real limits	Class index	i
17–19	——	——	——	——
14–16	——	——	——	——

    (b)

Score limits	Real limits	Class index	i
30–39	——	——	——
20–29	——	——	——
10–19	——	——	——

    (c)

Score limits	Real limits	Class index
70–76	——	——
63–69	——	——
56–62	——	——

3. If the score limits of two consecutive intervals are 29–31 and 32–34, what are the score limits of the next two higher intervals, what is the value of i?

Choice of Class Interval. The choice of interval depends partly on the unit in which the original observations were made and partly on the purpose for which the distribution is to be used. Inasmuch as the census data on age were recorded by the census enumerators in units of 1 year, no subsequent tabulation could possibly be made with intervals of, say, 1 month, or 3 months, or 18 months. It behooves any research worker to consider, before he gathers data, the use to which the data will be put and the degree of precision which will be desirable in later tabulations.

If considerable precision is required in analysis or computation, nothing is gained by reclassifying subjects into intervals larger than the units in which observations were first recorded. If great precision is not required, the use of larger intervals may simplify computation and clarify analysis. The presentation of a frequency distribution in a report is more effective if it can be so planned that the number of intervals is not too great and not too small. When the number of cases is small and the number of intervals is large, the distribution is likely to be irregular or ragged. By grouping cases in larger intervals or by obtaining a larger number of cases, the form of the distribution may be presented more vividly. However, the intervals can be made so wide that much of the available information is lost. If the number of intervals were reduced to the absurd extreme of having only one interval, we would lose all information about the form of the frequency distribution. In general, for purposes of effective presentation of data, it is a good plan to use between 10 and 20 intervals.

Combination of an odd number of units into an interval has the slight advantage of making the midpoint of the interval fall on one of the scores, whereas combining an even number makes the midpoint fall halfway between two scores. However, an interval of 10 units is generally preferred to one of 9 or 11 partly because tabulation by tens seems easy and natural. Intervals of 3, 5, or 10 units are most often used in reports.

The Cumulative Distribution. An important aid to interpreting a frequency distribution is the cumulative distribution which will now be illustrated from the 1950 and the 1920 data of Table 5.1. In Table 5.2 the two columns labeled *frequency* are identical with the corresponding columns in Table 5.1 except for the omission of the row for "all ages" and the omission of the frequency for which age was not reported in 1920. Let us concentrate attention on the 1950 data. An entry in the frequency column shows the number of persons in the United States of the ages indicated in the given interval; an entry in the cumulative frequency shows the number of persons of those ages or younger. The entries in the cumulative-frequency column are obtained by the successive addition of the entries in the frequency column, beginning with the frequency in the lowest interval on the scale of age. Thus the cumulative frequency in the interval 5–9 is $16,164 + 13,200 = 29,364$ and means that the number of persons who are 9 or younger — that is, persons who have not passed their tenth birthday — is approximately 29,364,000, to the nearest 1000. The next cumulative frequency is $29,364 + 11,119 = 40,483$, and so on.

Entries in the cumulative-percent column are obtained by ex-

TABLE 5.2 Cumulative Distribution of the Population of the United States in 1920 and 1950, Classified by Age

Age * in years	1950 Census			1920 Census		
	Fre- quency †	Cumula- tive fre- quency	Cumula- tive percent	Fre- quency †	Cumula- tive ‡ fre- quency	Cumula- tive percent
Under 5	16,164	16,164	10.7%	11,573	11,573	11.0%
5–9	13,200	29,364	19.5	11,398	22,971	21.8
10–14	11,119	40,483	26.9	10,641	33,612	31.8
15–19	10,617	51,100	33.9	9,431	43,043	40.8
20–24	11,482	62,582	41.5	9,277	52,320	49.6
25–29	12,242	74,824	49.7	9,086	61,406	58.2
30–34	11,517	86,341	57.3	8,071	69,477	65.8
35–39	11,246	97,587	64.8	7,775	77,252	73.2
40–44	10,204	107,791	71.5	6,346	83,598	79.2
45–49	9,070	116,861	77.5	5,764	89,362	84.7
50–54	8,272	125,133	83.0	4,735	94,097	89.1
55–59	7,235	132,368	87.8	3,549	97,646	92.5
60–64	6,059	138,427	91.9	2,983	100,629	95.3
65–69	5,003	143,430	95.2	2,068	102,697	97.3
70–74	3,412	146,842	97.4	1,395	104,092	98.6
75 and over	3,855	150,697	100.0	1,470	105,562	100.0

Source: United States Census Report for 1950, Vol. II, Part I
* To the last birthday
† Rounded to the nearest 1000
‡ Not including those for whom age was not reported

pressing the corresponding cumulative frequencies as percents of the total. Thus for the interval 20–24, we have for the 1950 census $\frac{62,582}{150,697} = .415$, indicating that in 1950, 41.5 percent of the population were 24 years old or younger. The corresponding figure for the 1920 census is $\frac{52,320}{105,562} = .496$.

The cumulative columns facilitate comparison of the 1920 and 1950 populations but, because the totals are different, this comparison can be most easily and meaningfully made after the cumulative frequencies have been reduced to percents. Let your eye travel between the two cumulative-percent columns, comparing the two figures for the same interval. The percent is always considerably larger for the year 1920, showing that regardless of what age we choose, the percent of persons younger than that age was greater in 1920 than in 1950.

The figures in Table 5.2 have been cumulated upward, beginning with the lowest interval on the scale — that is, the interval for the lowest age. It may be equally interesting to cumulate downward, beginning with the interval in which age is highest. According to census custom, the "lowest" interval in this sense is at the top of the page. Thus in the two upper intervals for 1950, the sum of the frequencies (in thousands) is $3,855 + 3,412 = 7,267$; in the three upper intervals, it is $7,267 + 5,003 = 12,270$, etc. From such a cumulation we could learn that in 1920 the percent of the population 60 years or older was 7.5 and in 1950 that percent had risen to 12.

Graphs of the Frequency Distribution. While there are many different ways of picturing a frequency distribution, certain devices contribute especially to the general understanding of the statistical measures which will be discussed in later chapters. These devices are the histogram, the frequency polygon, the cumulative-frequency graph, and the cumulative-percent graph.

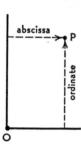

It will be convenient in discussing frequency graphs to use the conventional mathematical terms *ordinate* and *abscissa*. When a point P is located in reference to two axes at right angles to each other, the vertical distance from the horizontal axis to the point is called the *ordinate* of that point, and the horizontal distance from the vertical axis to the point is called its *abscissa*. Together the ordinate and abscissa are called the *coordinates* of the point. The term abscissa originated in medieval surveying manuals written in Latin, in which that portion of a horizontal distance cut off by the shadow of a vertical staff was called the *pars abscissa* or the "part cut off."

1. *The Histogram.* Table 5.3 has been prepared from the data presented in Appendix Table IX. To prepare a histogram from the frequencies in Table 5.3, lay off the scale of scores on a horizontal axis, the scale increasing from left to right. This scale must be marked in

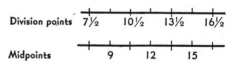

such a way that the division points between intervals can be identified. With infinitely many points on the scale to select from, a few must be chosen to mark for identification. The most common methods of marking the scale are to show the values of the division points between intervals or the values of the midpoints of intervals as in sketch above.

TABLE 5.3 Scores on Modern School Achievement Test of Reading Speed Made by 109 Fourth-Grade Children

Score	f	Cumulative f	Cumulative percent
50–52	2	109	100%
47–49	2	107	98
44–46	7	105	96
41–43	7	98	90
38–40	6	91	83
35–37	4	85	78
32–34	5	81	74
29–31	14	76	70
26–28	18	62	57
23–25	16	44	40
20–22	7	28	26
17–19	5	21	19
14–16	7	16	15
11–13	3	9	8
8–10	5	6	6
5–7	1	1	1
Total	109		

It is most important to label the scale of scores properly.

At right angles to the scale of scores, erect a scale of ordinates. *The zero point must be shown on the ordinate scale,* but not necessarily, or even usually, on the scale of scores. Now represent each of the 109 individuals in Table 5.3 by a small rectangle with horizontal length equal to one class interval on the scale of scores and vertical height equal to one unit on the scale of ordinates. This rectangle is an area unit which represents one frequency unit. In Figure 5–1 the 109 rectangles are shown but ordinarily only the column outlines need be drawn. Often even the vertical lines between columns are omitted.

In Figure 5–1 the frequency in an interval appears to be satisfactorily represented either by the area of a bar or by its height. However, in later sections we shall encounter situations (the frequency polygon in this chapter, the normal distribution in Chapter 11) where frequency cannot be represented by the height of an ordinate but only by the area between two ordinates. It is wise to form the habit of thinking of frequency as represented by area.

2. *The Frequency Polygon.* If we should try to compare two distributions by presenting two histograms on the same grid, the result would probably be a confusing mass of vertical lines difficult

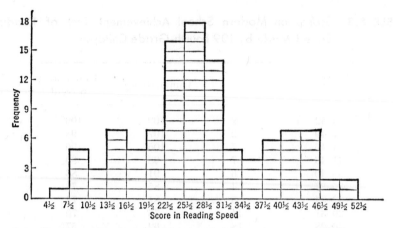

Fig. 5–1 Histogram: Distribution of Scores of 109 Fourth-grade Children of City X on Modern School Achievement Test of Reading Speed. (Based on frequency distribution of Table 5.3.)

to identify. The picture is much easier to interpret if frequency polygons are used instead of histograms.

For a frequency polygon, the horizontal and vertical scales are laid off exactly as for a histogram. For each interval, a point is located directly above the middle of the interval so that its vertical distance represents the frequency in that interval measured on the frequency scale. In other words, the abscissa of the point is the score at the middle of an interval and its ordinate is the frequency in that interval. Note that if an interval has zero frequency, the point representing that frequency will lie on the horizontal axis, and also that there is always such a point at each end of the dis-

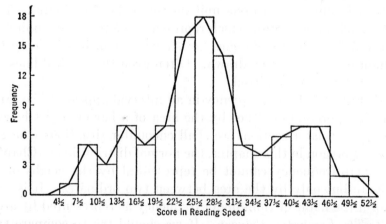

Fig. 5–2 Frequency Polygon Superimposed on Histogram. (From data of Table 5.3. Compare with Fig. 5–1.)

tribution. The points thus located are connected by straight lines to form a frequency polygon.

The relation between the histogram and the frequency polygon can be seen in Figure 5–2 where they have been graphed on the same axes. Examination of this figure shows that the areas of the two figures are exactly equal, because every triangle which is in the histogram but not in the frequency polygon is exactly matched by one which is in the polygon but not in the histogram. The fact that both figures represent frequency and that they have equal areas but not uniformly equal ordinates suggests that frequency is more satisfactorily represented by area than by ordinate in these two figures. Because the ordinate of a frequency polygon is related to frequency but does not actually measure frequency, the ordinate is often called the *frequency density* and the vertical scale is called the *density scale*.

3. *The Cumulative Graph.* To draw a cumulative chart, the horizontal scale is laid off in score intervals as before and a vertical scale is drawn to show cumulative frequency (or cumulative percent). Points are plotted very much as for the frequency polygon except that (a) it is cumulative frequency or percent instead of interval frequency that is plotted on the vertical scale, and (b) the points are not placed above the middle of an interval but above its upper real limit. The third and fourth columns of Table 5.3 show cumulative-frequency and cumulative-percent distributions and Figure 5–3 shows the graph of the cumulative-percent distribution.

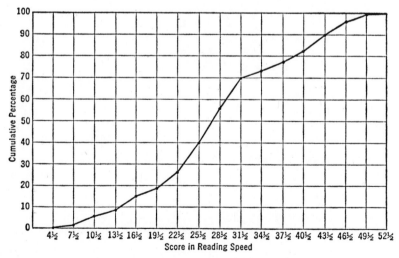

Fig. 5–3 Cumulative-percent Curve: Percent of Children with Reading Speed Score Less than a Given Score. (From data of Table 5.3.)

The graph of a cumulative curve is usually a reflex curve, with the center of curvature lying to the right in one portion of the curve and to the left in another portion. In architecture, an ogive arch (also called ogee) is one which has a reflex curve. Because cumulative-frequency or percent graphs are usually reflex, Francis Galton named them *ogives* and the name is still used for this type of presentation even when the graph is not reflex.

EXERCISE 5.3

1. Make a graph for the cumulative-percent columns of Table 5.2, placing the data for 1920 and 1950 on the same axes. You will notice that these cumulative graphs do not have the usual ogive form.

2. Construct a table showing the frequency distributions of the artificial language scores for the three sections from the data of Table VIII in the Appendix. First, select an appropriate interval. As the highest score is 60 and the lowest is 14, an interval of 3 units would give 16 or 17 intervals, while one of 5 would give 10 or 11 depending upon where the interval starts.

3. From the above table, construct three frequency polygons on the same base line. It might be noted in passing, how confusing it would be to try to present three histograms on the same base line.

4. From the table called for in Question 2, construct and graph the three cumulative-frequency distributions.

6

Percentiles

Here and in the following chapter we shall consider methods of describing and comparing distributions in terms of certain typical scores and of describing the relative positions of individuals in those distributions. The methods considered in this chapter are based on the *order*, or the *ranking*, of scores in the distribution of scores.

Some very simple data will illustrate the basic ideas. A count has been made of the number of times a monkey changes his activity during a 20-minute period, with results as shown in Table 6.1 for three monkeys each observed over five periods. It would

TABLE 6.1 The Number of Times Each of Three Monkeys Changed His Activity During a 20-minute Period, Recorded for Each of Five Periods

Monkey	Number of changes of activity in period					Median	Range
	1	2	3	4	5		
A	95	72	80	66	103	80	103 − 66 = 37
B	77	56	0	61	101	61	101 − 0 = 101
C	125	13	29	107	98	98	125 − 13 = 112

be convenient to have a single number to characterize each monkey, and this might be obtained by arranging the numbers for each monkey in ascending order and taking the middle one. Thus for *A*, the rearrangement is 66–72–80–95–103. The middle number, 80, describes the characteristic pattern of activity for monkey *A* and is called his *median* number. We can easily see that for these five periods *C* had the largest median, 98, and *B* the smallest, 61. We might also be interested in the consistency of the monkeys from period to period, as indicated by the range or the difference between their largest and smallest numbers. This range was only 37 for monkey A, indicating that he did not fluctuate much from one period to another and so the median gives a fairly good idea of his score in any selected period. For B and C, however, the numbers differ widely from one period to another, the ranges being, respectively, 101 and 112. If a sixth observation was to be made on each monkey, we could make a much better guess as to how A would come out than as to B or C. Thus each monkey has been characterized in terms of a typical score, the median, and the spread or variability of his scores, as indicated by the range of his scores.

If the number of records had been even, say, six instead of five, how would we define the median? Let us suppose that A's record in a sixth period was 69, so that his rearranged scores are 66–69–72–80–95–103. There is now no midscore, and any value between 72 and 80 will have half the values smaller and half larger than itself. Actually, any number between 72 and 80 will satisfy the definition of a median, as given below. However, in such a case it is customary to take an average and call $\frac{1}{2}(72 + 80) = 76$ the median.

The Median. The three sections of a class in elementary statistical method, raw data for which are presented in Table VIII of the Appendix, have already received some attention. Table 3.4 on page 25 shows in a general way that Section I had the most and Section III the fewest members making high scores in the midterm test and also in the arithmetic test. Now we shall make more explicit comparison of the three sections in terms of their midterm test scores.

From Table 3.4, we note that exactly half of the combined group of 96 students had scores of 53 or more, and half had scores of less than 53. The lower limit of the interval in which 53 stands — that is, 52.5 — is, therefore, a point on the scale of scores having unique interest. It serves to describe this distribution by the fact that half the cases fall below and half fall above it. The score corresponding to this point is called *the median*, or the *fiftieth percentile*.

The median of a distribution is a value such that half of the scores in the distribution are larger and half are smaller than that value.

The medians of the three sections cannot be obtained from Table 3.4. To obtain them we must have the frequency distribution of each section, as shown in Table 6.2 without grouping, or in Table 6.3 with scores grouped in intervals of 5. We shall first compute the section medians from the ungrouped scores of Table

TABLE 6.2 Distribution by Sections of Midterm Scores from Appendix
Table VIII

Ungrouped frequencies

	Number of cases					Number of cases			
Score	I	II	III	Total	Score	I	II	III	Total
71	1	1		2	48				
70					47	4	1	4	9
69					46	1	1		2
68	1			1	45				
67					44	1	2	1	4
66					43	1	2		3
65	1			1	42				
64	2	1		3	41	1			1
63					40		1	1	2
62	5	3	1	9	39				
61	4	2	2	8	38			1	1
60					37			3	3
59	2	2		4	36				
58	5	1	3	9	35				
57					34				
56	1		2	3	33				
55	1	1	1	3	32				
54					31				
53	2	2	1	5	30	1	1		2
52	3	4	1	8	29				
51					28				
50	2	2	1	5	27			1	1
49	2		4	6	26				
					25			1	1
					Total	41	27	28	96

6.2 and then make more general computations from the grouped
scores of Table 6.3.

Let us first examine the distribution for Section III. Since
$N = 28$ and $\frac{1}{2}N = 14$, the median is a score such that 14 scores
are smaller and 14 larger. Counting up from the lower end of the
distribution, we discover that there are 12 cases below the point
48.5 and 16 cases below 49.5. The median, therefore, is between
48.5 and 49.5. We may think of the 4 cases for which $X = 49$ as
having scores not precisely identical but distributed evenly
throughout the score interval. It turns out very neatly that 2
of the 4 may be considered as below and 2 above the midpoint,
which is 49.0. Thus 49.0 is a point on the scale of scores such that
$12 + 2 = 14$ scores are below it and $2 + 12 = 14$ are above it. The
median of Section III is 49.

For Section I, $\frac{1}{2} N = \frac{41}{2} = 20.5$. Counting up from the lower end, we find that 20 cases have scores of 56 or less, and 25 have scores of 58 or less. The point we seek is in the interval from 57.5 to 58.5, where there are 5 cases. If the 5 cases are evenly distributed over that interval, we may picture them as in the sketch.

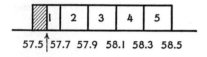

57.5 | 57.7 57.9 58.1 58.3 58.5

There are 20 cases below the beginning point of this interval; we are looking for a point below which 20.5 cases fall. Thus we want to divide the interval by a point such that $20.5 - 20.0 = 0.5$ case may be represented as below (that is to the left of) that point and the other $5 - 0.5 = 4.5$ cases above — that is to the right. The point marked with an arrow in the adjacent sketch meets these requirements and its score value is readily seen to be 57.6.

In similar fashion, the median of Section II is computed as 52.375, or 52.4. For a small group it is usually not important to carry the computation of the median to more than the first decimal place.

Go back now to Table 6.2 and place an asterisk in each column to show the location of the median for the section to which the column belongs. Clearly the larger the median of a group, the higher is the general placement along the scale of scores. The medians show a difference between Sections I and II which was not brought out by their ranges, inasmuch as in both sections the lowest score was 30 and the highest 71.

Computation of the Median from a Grouped Frequency Distribution. In many situations the original data are no longer avail-

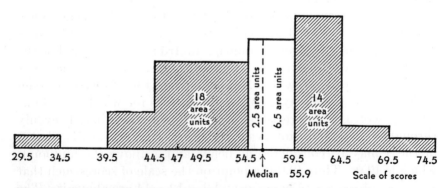

Fig. 6–1 Histogram Illustrating the Position of the Median of the Midterm Scores of Section I. (Data from Table 6.3.)

able and the statistician has to work from grouped frequencies. To illustrate this general procedure, Table 6.3 has been constructed by grouping the frequencies of Table 6.2 in intervals of 5. We shall now carry out in detail the computations for Section I and leave those for the other sections as an exercise for the reader.

Reference to the histogram in Figure 6–1 will make the general process clear. As before, we are looking for a point on the scale of scores below which 20.5 cases will fall. In the histogram, frequency is represented by area, so the 18 cases below 54.5 are represented by 18 area units. The point sought must fall somewhere in the interval marked in Table 6.3 as 55–59, which is actually the interval from 54.5 to 59.5. This interval includes 9 cases, of which $20.5 - 18 = 2.5$ are to be to the left of the median. From the adjacent sketch we see that $\dfrac{AB}{AC} = \dfrac{2.5}{9}$ and, therefore,

	2.5 area units	6.5 area units
A=54.5	B=?	C=59.5

$AB = \dfrac{2.5}{9}(AC)$. Since $AC = 59.5 - 54.5 = 5$, or the width of the interval, the length of AB is $\dfrac{2.5}{9}(5) = 1.4$. Thus the value attaching to the point B, which value is the median, is $54.5 + 1.4 = 55.9$. This result is not precisely identical with that obtained previously from the ungrouped scores, because we have here assumed that the 9 scores in the interval 54.5–59.5 are distributed evenly throughout the interval and such is not actually the case.

TABLE 6.3 Grouped Frequency Distribution, by Sections, of Midterm Scores from Table 6.2

Score	Number of cases			
	I	II	III	Total
70–74	1	1		2
65–69	2			2
60–64	11	6	3	20
55–59	9	4	6	19
50–54	7	8	3	18
45–49	7	2	8	17
40–44	3	5	2	10
35–39			4	4
30–34	1	1		2
25–29			2	2
Total	41	27	28	96

TABLE 6.4 Procedure for Computing the Median

Step	General statement	Application to Table 6.3
1	Find 50% of number of cases $= \frac{1}{2}N$	$\frac{1}{2}(41) = 20.5$
2	Find the interval which contains the median	Counting to 20.5 cases either from the top or the bottom brings us into the interval with limits 54.5 to 59.5
3	Find the number of cases below the true lower limit of the interval located in Step 2	Number of cases below 54.5 is 18
4	Subtract the number obtained in Step 3 from the number obtained in Step 1	$20.5 - 18 = 2.5$
5	Find the frequency in the interval which contains the median	$f = 9$
6	Find the ratio of the number in Step 4 to the number in Step 5	$\frac{2.5}{9}$
7	Find the width of the step interval	$i = 5$
8	Compute the median as follows: Lower limit of interval which contains the median plus the product of the ratio in Step 6 by the width of interval in Step 7	$\text{median} = 54.5 + \dfrac{2.5}{9}\,5 = 55.9$

The procedure for computing a median may be schematically expressed as follows:

$$\text{Median} = \begin{bmatrix} \text{lower limit} \\ \text{of interval} \\ \text{which contains} \\ \text{the median} \end{bmatrix} + \begin{bmatrix} \text{width} \\ \text{of} \\ \text{interval} \end{bmatrix} \left[\frac{\frac{1}{2}N - \begin{bmatrix} \text{frequency below lower} \\ \text{limit of interval which} \\ \text{contains the median} \end{bmatrix}}{\begin{array}{c}\text{frequency in interval} \\ \text{which contains the median}\end{array}} \right]$$

This procedure is displayed step by step in Table 6.4. It is an example of the general process of interpolation discussed in Chapter 14 of Walker, *Mathematics Essential for Elementary Statistics.*

Try your skill on the other distributions, computing their medians from the grouped frequency distribution of Table 6.3.

The results should be as follows:

	I	II	III	Total Group
Median from ungrouped frequencies	57.6	52.4	49.0	52.5
Median from grouped frequencies	55.9	52.9	48.2	53.1

It is interesting to note that sometimes the grouping has increased, sometimes decreased, the median. Such changes due to grouping are called "grouping errors."

Other Percentiles. The three sections have now been compared with respect to their central positions as measured by the median, but this tells only part of the story. The median alone gives no indication of the clustering or scatter of scores about this central value, and no basis for comparing distributions at points other than the central values.

Because 50 percent of the scores in a distribution are smaller than the median, the latter score is called the *fiftieth percentile*. By selecting other percents we can compute other percentiles. The only difference in the procedure is at the beginning. For example, to obtain, let us say, the 81st percentile, we start by finding, not $\frac{1}{2}N$, but 81 percent of N; to obtain the 13th percentile, we start by finding 13 percent of N. From that stage on, the procedure you have already learned for computing a median is followed exactly.

In this text we shall use the symbol $X_{.50}$ to denote the 50th percentile which is also the median, $X_{.81}$ to denote the 81st percentile, etc. There is no generally accepted symbol to represent a percentile, but these symbols are convenient and simple.

The 81st percentile of a distribution is defined as a *score such that 81 percent of the cases in that distribution have smaller scores.* In some situations this definition does not lead to a clear computational routine and so it will be modified as follows: *The 81st percentile is the score corresponding to a point on the scale of scores such that 81 percent of the area of the histogram lies below an ordinate at that point.* These definitions may be adapted to any other percentile by substituting the appropriate number for 81.

We shall now show the computation of several selected percentiles for Section I. When several percentiles are to be computed for the same distribution, it is convenient to set up a cumulative frequency distribution, as in Table 6.5. To understand the following computations, you should examine Table 6.5 to identify each number appearing in the computation.

TABLE 6.5 Cumulative Frequencies for the Midterm Scores of Section 1, Taken from Table 6.3

Score	f	Cumulative f	Cumulative percent
70–74	1	41	100.0%
65–69	2	40	97.6
60–64	11	38	92.7
55–59	9	27	65.9
50–54	7	18	43.9
45–49	7	11	26.8
40–44	3	4	9.8
35–39		1	2.4
30–34	1	1	2.4
	41		

What is the 25th percentile?

25% of $N = (0.25)(41) = 10.25$

$$X_{.25} = 44.5 + \left(\frac{10.25 - 4}{7}\right)(5) = 49.0$$

$X_{.25}$ is also called the *first quartile* or the *lower quartile* and may be denoted Q_1 or Q_L.

What is the 75th percentile?

$$75\% \text{ of } N = (0.75)(41) = 30.75$$

$$X_{.75} = 59.5 + \left(\frac{30.75 - 27}{11}\right)(5) = 61.2$$

$X_{.75}$ is also called the *third quartile* or the *upper quartile* and may be denoted Q_3 or Q_u.

What is the 12th percentile?

$$12\% \text{ of } 41 = 4.92$$

$$X_{.12} = 44.5 + \left(\frac{4.92 - 4.0}{7}\right)(5) = 45.2$$

In each of the three illustrative computations note the fraction enclosed in parentheses. Its denominator is the frequency in the interval in which lies the particular score we are seeking. (Verify this from Table 6.5.) Its numerator is the additional frequency we need in order that the frequency below the score point sought will be the correct proportion of N. Thus the fraction is the ratio of one frequency to another frequency and is a *pure* number. That ratio is always a multiplier of the width of the step interval, which is 5 for the data we are using. The product of this ratio and the step interval gives us the distance which we must move into the interval along the scale of scores. Thus we have:

$$\frac{\text{Lower limit}}{\text{of interval}} + \left(\text{ratio}\right)\left(\begin{array}{c}\text{width of}\\\text{interval}\end{array}\right) = \text{percentile sought}$$

In addition to the terms *median, quartile,* and *percentile,* with which you are now familiar, you are likely to meet the term *decile.* The nine percentile values $X_{.10}$, $X_{.20}$, $X_{.30}$, . . . and $X_{.90}$ are also called the first, second, third, . . . and ninth deciles. All these values belong to the same general family and all of them may be called *quantiles.* Many attempts have been made to drop the first syllable of the term *percentile* on the ground that *centile* would be more consistent with *decile* and *quartile.* This change would be a very sensible one, but somehow it never catches on. Most people who have put any thought on the matter express approval of the shorter term but go on using the longer one. Not only were the terms median, quartile, percentile, and decile invented by Francis Galton before 1885, but also certain other related terms such as octile, dodecile, and permille, which have long since passed out of the statistician's vocabulary. The generic term *quantile* is of recent origin.

Computation of Percentiles for a Small Number of Scattered Scores. Gaps in a small set of scattered scores sometimes produce a puzzling situation. For example, suppose a teacher has obtained scores for 20 students which when arranged in order are as follows:

6, 7, 9, 12, 12, 13, 15, 16, 16, 18, 19, 21, 22, 22, 24, 26, 27, 30, 32, 35

She wishes to know $X_{.75}$ so she computes 75 percent of 20 = 15 and looks for a score such that 15 cases have lower scores. Obviously, this condition is met by any value between 24.5 and 25.5. Some arbitrary decision must be made, and the one which seems most reasonable is to select a value 75 percent of the way from 24.5 to 25.5, namely, 25.25. In a similar manner, $X_{.15}$ would be computed as lying 15 percent of the way between 9.5 and 11.5, or as 9.8.

Variability. It is often as important to know something about the variability of a group as to know a measure of central position such as the median. Neither the median nor any single percentile can give any clue as to whether the scores in a distribution scatter widely or cluster closely about a typical value. Measures of variability are also called measures of *dispersion,* of *scatter,* of *spread,* or of *variation.*

The following examples show the importance of studying variability: The Chamber of Commerce of a community, which shall be nameless, advertised that the median annual temperature there was 70° (a true statement) and claimed that this implied a Bermuda-like climate. They failed to mention that sometimes the temperature rose to 110° in summer and fell to − 20° in winter and that the number of days was small on which it actually hovered in the neighborhood of 70°. The median temperature would be considerably less important than the range for a person planning to move into the community.

Two classes in college physics contain the same number of students and have the same median score on a prognostic test, but the range of scores in one is three times as great as the range in the other. The problems of teaching these classes will be very different.

The people who live in village A and those who live in village B have almost the same median annual income. However, A is a very homogeneous community in which the difference between the highest income and the lowest income is small. In B, on the other hand, although there are a few middle income families, the population consists largely of two extreme groups, one composed of high salaried business and professional people and the other composed of domestic servants and unskilled workers. To describe these communities, it is clear that information about median income needs to be accompanied by some measure of income dispersion.

The Range. As a measure of the scattering, or dispersion, of the scores in a distribution, the range comes first to mind. The range is simply the difference between the highest score and the lowest. From Table 6.2, we see that the range for each section and for the total of all sections is

$$
\begin{aligned}
&\text{For Section I,} && 71 - 30 = 41 \\
&\text{For Section II,} && 71 - 30 = 41 \\
&\text{For Section III,} && 62 - 25 = 37 \\
&\text{For all sections,} && 71 - 25 = 46
\end{aligned}
$$

The range is meaningful but notoriously unstable, subject to the accidental presence or absence of extreme cases in the group studied. Note for yourself how the range for Sections I or II would have been affected if the person scoring 71, or the person scoring 30, or both, had dropped out of the course or changed to another section.

Interpercentile Range. To obtain a measure of dispersion which is more reliable than the total range, it is common practice to report the difference between two symmetrically placed percentiles, such as $X_{.90} - X_{.10}$, which gives the range of scores of the middle 80 percent of the cases, or $X_{.95} - X_{.05}$, which gives the range of the middle 90 percent. Most widely used of all such

TABLE 6.6   Selected Quantiles Computed from the Data of Table 6.4

Quantile	Value of the quantile			
	I	II	III	All sections
$X_{.95}$	66.9	64.2	62.2	64.2
$X_{.90}$	64.0	63.1	59.8	63.1
$X_{.80}$	62.1	60.8	57.4	60.7
$X_{.75}$	61.2	59.7	56.2	59.5
$X_{.70}$	60.3	58.1	55.0	58.2
$X_{.60}$	58.2	54.8	50.8	55.7
$X_{.50}$	55.9	52.9	48.2	53.1
$X_{.40}$	53.4	51.2	46.5	50.4
$X_{.30}$	50.4	49.6	44.8	47.7
$X_{.25}$	49.0	46.4	42.0	46.3
$X_{.20}$	47.5	43.9	39.0	44.9
$X_{.10}$	44.6	41.2	35.5	40.3
$X_{.05}$	41.2	39.8	28.0	35.5
Range of				
middle 50%	12.2	13.3	14.2	13.2
middle 60%	14.6	16.9	18.4	15.8
middle 80%	19.4	21.9	24.3	22.8
middle 90%	25.7	24.4	34.2	28.7
entire group *	45.0	45.0	40.0	50.0

* Upper limit of top interval minus lower limit of bottom interval.

interpercentile ranges is the difference between the first and third quartiles, called the *interquartile range*. For Section I, $Q_3 - Q_1 = 61.2 - 49.0 = 12.2$. Interquartile ranges for the other sections will be found in Table 6.6, and it is interesting to see how similar the three sections are in regard to this measure of variability.

Relation of Quantiles to the Cumulative-percent Curve. In Chapter 5, we became acquainted with the cumulative-frequency curve and the cumulative-percent curve. Now we shall put the latter to new uses, first for determining the quantiles graphically and later for comparing groups.

The relation between the first and last columns of Table 6.5 is displayed graphically in Figure 6–2. Such a graph, in which the

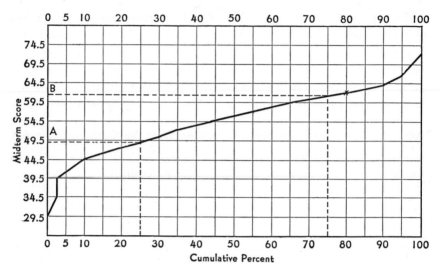

Fig. 6–2 Cumulative-percent Curve for the Midterm Scores of Section I. (Data from Table 6.5.)

scale of scores is shown on one axis and the cumulative percent of the frequency below a given score is shown on the other axis, is called an *ogive*. The scale of scores may be placed on either axis. However, when two or more groups are to be shown together (as in Figure 6–3) and the scale of scores is placed on the horizontal axis, the group with higher scores is represented by the lower line; that effect tends to confuse a person not thoroughly familiar with graphs. Therefore, when showing such a graph to persons to

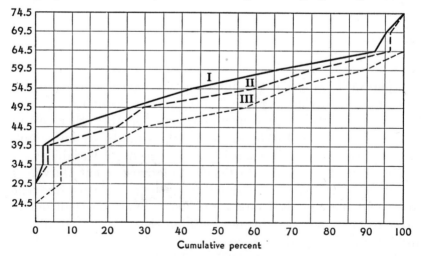

Fig. 6–3 Cumulative-percent Curves for Midterm Scores for Three Sections. (Data from Table 6.3.)

whom this type of presentation is new — as perhaps to a school board or a parents' organization — less explanation will be required if the scores are placed on the vertical rather than the horizontal axis.

As this graph was constructed, the scale of scores is on the vertical axis; plotted points lie on horizontal lines through those score points which mark the boundaries between consecutive intervals. Now let us plot on the same grid the percentile data for Section I shown in Table 6.6. The subscript for one of the percentiles will indicate a point on the horizontal axis and the value of that percentile will indicate a point on the vertical axis. Consider, for example, $X_{.80} = 62.1$. This pair of values is represented by a small cross which falls exactly on the ogive previously drawn. In a similar fashion, plot the points $X_{.10}$, $X_{.40}$, $X_{.90}$. Each of the plotted points should lie exactly on the ogive. In drawing the graph, points were located by finding the cumulative percent corresponding to given score points. Points are now being located by finding scores (i.e., percentiles) corresponding to given cumulative percents. Points located in either way fall on the same line of relation.

Now use Figure 6–2 to determine graphically some of the other entries in Table 6.6. For example, to find Q_1 locate the 25-percent point on the base line, draw a vertical line from it to the curve, then a horizontal line which meets the scale of scores at the point A. The scale value of A is Q_1. Verify that the point B represents Q_3. Then the segment AB represents the range of the middle 50 percent, or the interquartile range. Estimate the length of AB as accurately as possible and compare that estimate with the computed value shown in Table 6.6.

Use of Ogives for Comparing Groups. The ogive for each of the three sections is shown in Figure 6–3, drawn in the same way in which the ogive for Section I was drawn in Figure 6–2. It will be noticed that the percentile values for the three Sections found in any one row of Table 6.6 can be read in this figure on a vertical line through the appropriate cumulative-percent point. It will also be noticed that the graph immediately conveys the correct impression — that Section I has the highest scores, and III the lowest. If the axes were reversed, this relation would not be so immediately obvious.

We have already seen in Table 6.6 on page 75 that the median of the combined group was 53.1. Find this point on the scale of scores and draw through it a horizontal line cutting each of the three section curves. On the horizontal scale, read the values of the corresponding percents. These appear to warrant the statement, "The percent of cases with scores below the median of the combined group is 39 for Section I, 51 for Section II, and 65 for Section III." If computed from the ungrouped data of Table 6.2, the exact percents are $\frac{16}{41} = 39$ percent for Section I, $\frac{14}{27} = 51.8$ percent for Section II, and $\frac{18}{28} = 64.3$ percent for Section III.

EXERCISE 6.1

1. By computing from the data of Table 6.3, verify enough of the entries in Table 6.6 to assure yourself that you have no difficulty in computing percentiles.

2. The combined group has a greater total range than any of the sections. (a) Could it possibly have a smaller range than one of the sections? (b) In terms of the other four measures of spread, does the total group appear to be more variable than any one of the three sections?

3. Could the values for the total group be found exactly by adding the corresponding values for the sections and dividing by 3? Are the values for the total group exactly equal to the median of the three corresponding values for the sections?

4. Which section appears least variable if you base your opinion on the total range? Which if you base it on the interquartile range? On the value of $X_{.80} - X_{.20}$? On the value of $X_{.90} - X_{.10}$? On the value of $X_{.95} - X_{.05}$?

5. What is the 9th decile for the total group? Is the 9th decile a score or a portion of the frequency? Then, would you say that a particular person has a score *above* the 9th decile or *in* the 9th decile?

6. In Section I, does the median lie nearer to Q_1 or to Q_3, or is it exactly halfway between them? In Section II? In Section III? In the combined sections?

7. In Figure 6–2, locate $X_{.90}$ and $X_{.10}$ on the vertical scale and mark the line segment which represents the range of the middle 80 percent of the frequency.

8. Make a graph for either Section II, or Section III, or the combined group, similar in plan to Figure 6–2.

9. The medians of four groups are respectively: Group A, 38.6; Group B, 49.2; Group C, 24.7; Group D, 41.3. Arrange the four letters in the order in which the groups appear to stand on the scale of scores, placing first the group with highest standing.

10. The percents of individuals with scores below 85 in five groups are as follows: Group A, 23 percent; Group B, 36 percent; Group C, 18 percent; Group D, 76 percent; Group E, 53 percent. Arrange the

five letters in the order in which the groups appear to stand on the scale of scores, placing first the group with highest standing.

11. If 28 percent of Group A have scores below the median of Group B, which group appears to stand higher on the scale of scores?

12. In the sketch below, one tenth of the area of the histogram lies to the left of the line BN and one tenth to the right of the line GI. The

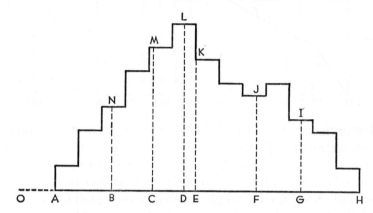

line EK divides the area in half. One fourth of the area is to the left of CM and one fourth to the right of FJ. The point D is at the middle of the interval having the greatest frequency. Answer each of the following questions by naming some part of the sketch. If the part is a line segment, name it by the letters on the ends, as "Line AB." If it is an area, you can name it by several letters, as "Area $BCMN$" or by such a phrase as "Area between BN and CM." If the part is a point, name it by a single letter. You may assume that the zero point of the scale is at 0.

What represents:

(a) The median
(b) The mode (= midpoint of interval having greatest frequency)
(c) Q_3
(d) Q_1
(e) The interquartile range
(f) The middle half of the cases
(g) The upper 10 percent of the cases
(h) The 10th percentile
(i) $X_{.90} - X_{.10}$

13. From the sketch on page 80, answer the following questions:

(a) On which axis are percentile values measured?
(b) What name would you give to the score of point A? Of B?
(c) How many different names can you think of for point C?
(d) What does the segment AE represent? The segment BD?
(e) What does the segment FH represent? The segment OG?

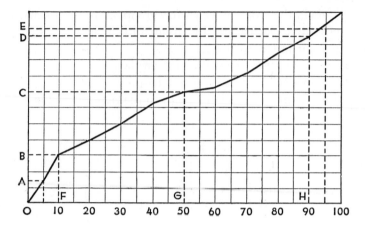

Comparisons among Individuals within a Group. Suppose a very important position is to be filled and the committee responsible for the appointment has narrowed its choice to five persons each of whom has different strengths and weaknesses. The committee finds itself unable to give *scores* to the candidates but after long deliberation places the names in an order of preference. In other words, it *ranks* the candidates.

There are many such situations in which it is not feasible to *measure* subjects but very feasible to *rank* them. For this purpose it is not necessary to know by how much one subject exceeds another but only to know that he does exceed him. There are other situations in which, although it is possible to obtain scaled measures, it is preferable to use ranks.[1] It is common practice to assign rank one to the subject standing highest in the characteristic under consideration and to assign succeeding ranks in descending order. That practice will be followed in this text. However, the reader should be warned that several recent writers on mathematical statistics reverse the order, using one for the lowest rank and that this practice was followed by Lincoln Moses, who wrote Chapter 18 of Walker and Lev's *Statistical Inference.*

Changing Scores to Ranks. To transform scores to ranks presents no difficulty unless there are ties — that is, two or more individuals with the same score. For example, suppose we have six individuals with scores as indicated:

Subject:	A	B	C	D	E	F
Score:	12	9	8	11	9	10

[1] Most of the reasons why ranks would be used in preference to scaled scores cannot be clearly explained at this stage. The reader is referred to Chapters 16 and 18 of Walker and Lev, *Statistical Inference,* and the sources quoted there.

We assign rank 1 to A, because he has the highest score; rank 2 to D, rank 3 to F. Now B and E are tied and must receive the same rank, but, if we give them both rank 4 and then give C rank 5, the group of individuals will have no one ranking sixth. If it had been possible to distinguish between B and E, one of them would have had rank 4 and one rank 5. Therefore, it is proper to give each of them rank $\frac{1}{2}(4 + 5) = 4.5$, and to give the individual following them rank 6.

When N individuals are ranked, the sum of their ranks is always

(6.1) $$\frac{N(N + 1)}{2}$$

and this fact may be used as one check on the correctness of the ranks which have been assigned. Thus, for 6 individuals, the sum of the ranks should be $\frac{6(7)}{2} = 21$. Add the ranks indicated below to see that their sum is 21.

Subject:	A	B	C	D	E	F
Score:	12	9	8	11	9	10
Rank	1	$4\frac{1}{2}$	6	2	$4\frac{1}{2}$	3

EXERCISE 6.2

For each of these sets of scores, change the scores to ranks and check the sum of the ranks by formula (6.1):

1.

Subject:	A	B	C	D	E	F	G
Score:	25	21	18	24	20	21	21

2.

Subject:	A	B	C	D	E	F	G	H	I
Score:	6	9	13	6	14	8	12	5	2

3.

Subject:	A	B	C	D	E	F	G	H	I	J	K	L
Score:	12	8	7	10	6	7	9	7	13	8	14	5

4.

Subject:	A	B	C	D	E	F	G	H	I	J	K	L	M	N
Score:	5	4	7	9	8	5	3	5	9	12	8	2	13	6

Ambiguities in Ranks. Suppose your neighbor tells you that his son has written home that he stands tenth in his Freshman class in college; should you congratulate or commiserate? The meaning of this rank of 10 depends on the size and the nature of the group with which he is being compared. The boy may be near the top of a class of several hundred students or near the bottom of a very small class. The college in which he is enrolled may have very strict or very loose admission requirements.

A measure of relative position must always derive part of its meaning from the nature of the group with which the individual is compared. A child of 10 may feel very tall and very mature in a group of younger children but, if transferred to a group in which he is the youngest, he may feel very small and inexperienced. He has not changed, but the standard of comparison has changed. A measure of an individual's position relative to his group has obvious meaning for understanding persons and group behavior. Especially in the field of education and psychological testing are scores completely without meaning unless they can be referred to some standard, some bench mark. What does it mean to say merely that a student scored 29 on a test? Nothing at all. This may be a phenomenally high score or a phenomenally low one, or it may be the average for students of comparable age and training.

Now consider the ambiguity in ranks due to size of the group. Suppose John, whose height is 52 inches, ranks third as to height in a group of boys. Can we express his position in terms of the percent of boys who are shorter than he?

If there are 10 boys in the group, one might at first thought say that 7 boys, or 70 percent, are shorter while 2 boys, or 20 percent, are taller. This statement accounts for only 70 percent + 20 percent = 90 percent of the group, John himself constituting the other 10 percent.

If there are 50 boys in the group and John is third, one might, on the same basis, say that 47 boys, or 94 percent, of the group are shorter and 2 boys, or 4 percent, are taller. This statement accounts for 94 percent + 4 percent = 98 percent of the group, John himself constituting the other 2 percent.

These two statements are much more meaningful than the mere statement that John has rank 3. The statements can be further improved if we think of histograms for the two distributions of ranked scores. In the histogram for 10 scores, John's rank is at the 75th percentile of the distribution. In the histogram for 50 scores, John's score is at the 95th percentile. We can rephrase these statements conveniently by saying that John's score has a *percentile rank* of 75 in the first distribution and a *percentile rank* of 95 in the second.

Percentile Score and Percentile Rank. If John is 52 inches tall and his height has third rank among 10 boys, the following statements may be made:

(a) 75 percent of the group have height less than John.

(b) 75 percent of the group have height less than 52 inches.

(c) The 75th percentile of height for this group is 52 inches.

(d) John's height is the 75th percentile.

(e) John has percentile rank 75 in height.

(f) The height 52 inches has percentile rank 75.

Study these statements carefully noting that they all express the same relationship but with different emphases, just as the two sentences "John is Mary's brother" and "Mary is John's sister" express the same relationship with different emphases. Note that statements (c) and (d) employ the term *percentile* while statements (e) and (f) employ the new term *percentile rank*. Compare each of these with statements (a) and (b), noting that 52 inches, which is a score, is called the percentile, while 75 percent, which is a relative frequency, furnishes the percentile rank.

EXERCISE 6.3

Give two translations of each of these statements, by filling blanks in the two sentences which follow the statement.

1. Exactly 57 percent of the teachers in a given school system receive salaries less than $5840.
   —— is the —— percentile of the distribution of salaries.
   —— is the percentile rank of ——.

2. Of the deaths recorded from a given disease for a given year in a given community, 87 percent were of persons under 12 years old.
   —— is the —— percentile of the age of persons dying from this disease.
   —— is the percentile rank of age ——.

3. Exactly one half of the scores in a given distribution are less than 72.0.
   The —— percentile is ——.
   The percentile rank of —— is ——.

4. Exactly 5 percent of all persons consulted had annual incomes larger than $6850.
   The —— percentile is ——.
   The percentile rank of —— is ——.

Determining Percentile Rank from a Frequency Distribution and from a Graph. What is the percentile rank in Section I of a student who scored 47? Since we have already available the ogive of Figure 6–2, the easiest way to answer this question is to read the required percentile rank there. We locate 47 in the scale of scores, which is the vertical scale, and draw a horizontal line through that point to the curve. Then on the horizontal scale we read the corresponding cumulative percent. That cumulative percent is the percentile rank. In Section I the percentile rank of 47 is approximately 18. Note that in Figure 6–2 *percentiles (which are scores)* *are measured along the vertical scale while percentile ranks (which are cumulative percents) are measured along the horizontal scale.*

The same result could, with a little more work, be obtained from Figure 6–1 or Table 6.3 if the ogive were not already drawn. Note the position of score point 47 on the scale of scores in the interval 45–49. We need to know what proportion of the frequency (that is, the area of the histogram) would lie to the left of an ordinate at this point. Either from the histogram or the table we can see that the number of cases below this point is $1 + 3 +$ part of the 7 cases in the interval 45–49. To decide how many of the 7 cases in the interval 45–49 should be considered as below 47, we may examine the adjacent sketch. If x represents the num-

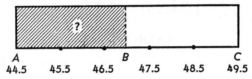

ber of cases in the given interval below the point B, then

$$\frac{x}{7} = \frac{AB}{AC}, \quad \text{or} \quad \frac{x}{7} = \frac{47 - 44.5}{49.5 - 44.5} \quad \text{and} \quad x = 7\left(\frac{2.5}{5}\right) = 3.5$$

The number of cases below the point 47 is, therefore,

$$1 + 3 + \left(\frac{2.5}{5}\right)7 = 7.5$$

and the percent of cases below that point is $\dfrac{7.5}{41} = 18.3$ percent.

The score 47, therefore, has percentile rank of 18 in Section I.

Another way to think of this computation is to note in Table 6.3 that 4 cases fall below the score point 44.5 and 11 below 49.5, and to interpolate to find the missing number:

Score point	Number of cases below score point
49.5	11
47	?
44.5	4

What would the percentile rank of score 47 be in Section II?

$$1 + 5 + \left(\frac{2.5}{5}\right)2 = 7$$

$$\text{and } \frac{7}{27} = 25.9 \text{ percent}$$

Its percentile rank would be 26.

What would its percentile rank be in Section III?

$$2 + 4 + 2 + \left(\frac{2.5}{5}\right)8 = 12$$

$$\frac{12}{28} = 42.9 \text{ percent}$$

Its percentile rank would be 43.

Note that the fraction enclosed in parentheses in each of these computations has for its denominator the width of the step interval and for its numerator the distance from the beginning of that interval up to the score point in question. The ratio of these two linear values is a *pure* number such that, when it is multiplied by the frequency in the interval, it gives us the portion of that frequency falling below the score point in which we are interested.

TABLE 6.7 Procedure for Computing the Percentile Rank of a Given Score

Step	General statement	Application to score 47 for Section I in Table 6.3
1	Find the interval in which the given score is located	Score 47 is in the interval with true limits 44.5 to 49.5
2	From the given score, subtract the lower limit of the interval in which it is located	$47 - 44.5 = 2.5$
3	Find the width of the interval	$i = 49.5 - 44.5 = 5.0$
4	Find the ratio of the number in Step 2 to the number in Step 3	$\dfrac{2.5}{5.0}$
5	Find the number of cases below the true lower limit of the interval located in Step 1	$1 + 3 = 4$
6	Find the frequency in the interval located in Step 1	$f = 7$
7	Compute the following: Value of Step 5 plus the product of the ratio in Step 4 by the frequency in Step 6	$4 + \left(\dfrac{2.5}{5.0}\right)(7) = 7.5$
8	Compute the percentile rank as the ratio of the value obtained in Step 7 to the total number of cases, expressed as a percent	$\dfrac{7.5}{41} = 18.3\%$

$$\begin{matrix} \text{Frequency} \\ \text{below} \\ \text{ordinate} \\ \text{at score point} \end{matrix} = \begin{matrix} \text{sum of} \\ \text{frequencies} \\ \text{in all lower} \\ \text{intervals} \end{matrix} + \begin{bmatrix} \dfrac{\text{score minus beginning}}{\text{point of interval}} \\ \text{width of interval} \end{bmatrix} \begin{bmatrix} \text{frequency} \\ \text{in} \\ \text{interval} \end{bmatrix}$$

The procedure is set out step by step in Table 6.7.

EXERCISE 6.4

The following tabulation shows the percentile rank, for each section and for the combined group, of four scores. Verify these by computation based on Table 6.3 and by reference to Figure 6–3.

Score	Percentile Rank			Total group
	I	II	III	
41	5	9	23	11
54	42	56	67	53
62	79	85	95	85
66	94	96	100	96

7

Mean and Standard Deviation

Chapter 6 was devoted to three problems: (a) how a frequency distribution can be characterized by a measure of position and a measure of variability; (b) how two or more distributions can be compared; and (c) how the relative position of individuals within a distribution can be described. This chapter will deal with the same three problems, the difference being that the measures used in Chapter 6 belong to the family of measures known as quantiles, all of which are based on some aspect of order or ranking, whereas in this chapter we shall use the mean as a measure of position and the standard deviation as a measure of variability. In Chapter 8, the two types of measures will be compared and criteria suggested for choice between them.

The Mean. Suppose five undernourished children are placed on an enriched diet, and during a given period of time make gains, measured in pounds, as follows:

John, 8; Sam, 2; Max, 3; Bob, 5; George, 12

What *average* gain might be reported? By the methods of the previous chapter, the median gain is immediately seen to be 5 lb and this is one type of average. Most people are also familiar with another type of average obtained by adding the scores of all the individuals and dividing by the number of individuals. This type of average is called the *arithmetic mean* (pronounced arithme′tic) or, usually, just *the mean*. The sum of the gains of these 5 boys is 30 and so the mean gain is $\frac{30}{5} = 6$.

Symbols. To reduce the burden of writing long sentences, we shall employ a few convenient symbols. As before, we shall let the letter X represent "any score." "The sum of" is customarily denoted by the capital Greek letter sigma, Σ, comparable to the capital S in our alphabet. Then ΣX means "the sum of all measures represented by the letter X." N will be used throughout this text to indicate the number of individuals under consideration. The mean will be denoted $\overline{X}$ and this symbol can be read either "mean of X" or "X bar" or "bar X." Note how vivid the definition of a mean becomes when translated into these symbols:

The mean	can be obtained by	finding the sum of all the scores	and dividing it by	the number of scores
$\overline{X}$	$=$	ΣX	$\div$	N

(7.1)   or better $\overline{X} = \dfrac{\Sigma X}{N}$

This formula constitutes a definition of the mean.

EXERCISE 7.1

Find the mean and the median of each of these sets of scores:

1. 3, 2, 7, 12, 9, 6, 4, 5, 7, 2
2. 19, 12, 18, 8, 23, 13, 19
3. 415, 402, 401, 405, 409, 410, 416, 412, 414, 406

A Measure of Variability. When the median is used as a measure of central position, variability can be measured by some interpercentile range such as $Q_3 - Q_1$ or $X_{.95} - X_{.05}$. However, when central position is measured by the mean, variability should be measured by a statistic based on deviations from the mean.

For each of the 5 boys mentioned at the beginning of this chapter, we might find the deviation of his score from the mean score, which is 6, $X - \overline{X} = X - 6$ and perform the following computations:

Boy	X	$X - \overline{X}$	$|X - \overline{X}|$	$(X - \overline{X})^2$
John	8	2	2	4
Sam	2	−4	4	16
Max	3	−3	3	9
Bob	5	−1	1	1
George	12	6	6	36
	30	0	16	66

The sum of the deviations from the mean is always identically zero no matter how great or how small the variability,

(7.2) $\Sigma(X - \overline{X}) = 0$

because positive and negative deviations from the mean exactly balance each other. Therefore, that sum provides no useful indication of variability.

We should like to have a statistic which will be zero only when there is no variability — that is, when all individuals have exactly the same score — and which becomes larger and larger as the spread among individuals is increased. To obtain such a statistic we have to get rid of the minus signs. Two methods of banishing them probably occur to you.

One method is simply to ignore the signs treating all deviations as absolute values. The customary symbol for the *absolute or unsigned value* of a number a is $|\,a\,|$. Thus $|-3| = |+3| = 3$. For the 5 individuals under consideration, the sum of the absolute values of the deviations from the mean is 16 and the mean of the unsigned deviations is $16/5 = 3.2$. This value is known as the *mean deviation from the mean.*

$$(7.3) \qquad \text{Mean deviation from the mean} = \frac{\Sigma\,|\,X - \overline{X}\,|}{N}$$

It tells us how much on the average the individuals in a group deviate from the mean. It is not easy to compute when the mean is not an integer or an easy fraction and when N is large. It has some other theoretical disadvantages and so is used only for very small samples, such as are sometimes drawn in industrial plants. We shall not consider it further in this text.

The other method of removing minus signs is to square each deviation and take the sum of the squared deviations. For our data, $\Sigma(X - \overline{X})^2 = 66$. However, this number reflects not only the variability of the group but also its size, and so we divide it by $N - 1$. The result is a measure of variability known as *the variance.*

$$(7.4) \qquad\qquad \text{Variance} = \frac{\Sigma(X - \overline{X})^2}{N - 1}$$

For our data, the variance is $\frac{66}{4} = 16.5$.

The computation of the variance for these five scores was particularly simple because the mean was an integer and values of the deviations $X - \overline{X}$ could be expressed exactly. This pleasant situation usually will not obtain and the method of computation we have used will involve large rounding errors unless deviations are carried to many decimal places. A formula equivalent to (7.4) but in most cases requiring less arithmetic work is

(7.5) $$\text{Variance} = \frac{N\Sigma X^2 - (\Sigma X)^2}{N(N-1)}$$

For our data, $\Sigma X^2 = 2^2 + 3^2 + 5^2 + 8^2 + 12^2 = 246$

Hence, the variance $= \dfrac{5(246) - 30^2}{5(4)} = \dfrac{330}{20} = 16.5$ as before.

Graphic Representation.   The variance is a measure of spread for which no graphic representation can be made.   Do not try to form a visual image of it.   Its square root, however, can be represented as a distance measured along the scale of scores.   That square root is called the *standard deviation*.   Later in this chapter, it will be used as a *standard* for measuring the *deviations* of individuals from the group mean, a use which appears to be responsible for its name.   At present, however, we are considering its use as a measure of the variability of a group.   The symbol [1] we shall use for the standard deviation is s.

(7.6) $$s = \sqrt{\text{variance}} = \sqrt{\frac{\Sigma(X - \overline{X})^2}{N-1}}$$

In Figure 7–1 each of the five scores we have been discussing is represented by a point on the scale of scores.   Each score has a frequency of 1, and these frequencies are represented by the shaded areas.   The mean is at the point 6.   The standard deviation is the line segment 4.1 scale units long, which is marked s.

The standard deviation and the variance will be used in most of the statistical problems you are likely to find of interest.   The

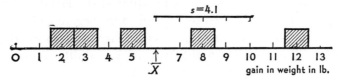

Fig. 7–1   Gain in Weight in Pounds Made by Five Boys. $\overline{X} = 6, s = 4.1$

[1] When the term *standard deviation* was coined by Karl Pearson in 1894, he used the small Greek letter sigma (σ) and defined it as

$$\sigma = \sqrt{\frac{\Sigma(X - \overline{X})^2}{N}}$$

Today, some writers use N and some use $N - 1$ in the denominator.   The use of N gives a biased estimate and the use of $N - 1$ an unbiased estimate of the variance in the population from which the sample was drawn.   Today many writers prefer, so far as possible, to use English letters as symbols for statistics computed from a sample and the corresponding Greek letters for theoretical rather than observed values.   Following this practice we shall use s to denote a standard deviation computed from observations but in the chapter on the normal curve we shall use σ for the standard deviation of that theoretical distribution.   In Chapters 13 to 16, both symbols will be used.

feeling of strangeness which you now entertain in relation to them will soon wear off as you meet them in a variety of situations. The rest of this chapter and much of the following chapter will serve to give you experience with the standard deviation, but before you can use this statistic in an actual situation you need to be able to compute it from a frequency distribution.

Computation When There Are Duplicate Scores. Now let us suppose that instead of 5 children there had been 25 and that several had the same score, as in Table 7.1. Here, there are 3 children with score 11 and so 11 must enter 3 times into ΣX. An easy way to achieve this is to multiply 11 by 3 and similarly to multiply every other score by its frequency before adding. The

TABLE 7.1 Computation of the Mean and Standard Deviation of the Gain in Weight for 25 Children During a Specified Period (Artificial Data)*

X Gain in lb	f	fX	fX^2
12	1	12	144
11	3	33	363
10	4	40	400
9	1	9	81
8	5	40	320
7	2	14	98
6	4	24	144
5	3	15	75
4	2	8	32
	25	195	1657

$$\overline{X} = \frac{195}{25} = 7.8$$

$$\text{Variance} = \frac{25(1657) - 195^2}{25(24)} = \frac{3400}{600} = 5.67$$

$$s = \sqrt{5.67} = 2.4$$

* Note that the purpose of this table is not to display data but to illustrate a computational method, and for that reason a title has been used which would be inappropriate in a treatise emphasizing content.

resultant sum may be appropriately labeled ΣfX. In the same manner, the 3 scores of 11 must contribute $11^2 + 11^2 + 11^2 = 3(121) = 363$ to ΣX^2. An easy way to accomplish this is to set up a final column headed fX^2, and to obtain each entry in this column by multiplying an entry in the fX column by its corresponding X.

Thus for $X = 11$, we have $11(33) = 363$ which is, of course, equal to $3(11^2)$.

Then for a distribution having duplication of scores, it is appropriate to insert an f in formulas (7.1), and (7.5), making them read

$$(7.7) \qquad\qquad \overline{X} = \frac{\Sigma f X}{N}$$

$$(7.8) \qquad\qquad \text{Variance} = \frac{N\Sigma f X^2 - (\Sigma f X)^2}{N(N-1)}$$

Even when the f is not written in the formula, it is always understood.

EXERCISE 7.2

1. Make a graph of the histogram for the distribution of Table 7.1. On the scale of scores mark the position of $\overline{X} = 7.8$, $\overline{X} - s = 5.4$, $\overline{X} - 2s = 3.0$, $\overline{X} + s = 10.2$, $\overline{X} + 2s = 12.6$. Draw a line segment of length $s = 2.4$.
2. Compute the percentile rank of score point $\overline{X} + s = 10.2$
3. Compute the percentile rank of score point $\overline{X} - s = 5.4$
4. Compute $X_{.50}$. For these data it happens that $\overline{X}$ and $X_{.50}$ are identical.
5. For these data, the range is equal to how many standard deviations?
6. Compute the median, mean, variance, and standard deviation of each of the following sets of scores:
   (a) 7, 15, 10, 9, 4, 3, 7, 10, 10, 8, 16
   (b) 24, 27, 22, 28, 26
   (c) 1, 2, 5, 6, 10, 11, 12, 14, 15, 15
   (d) 1, 9, 0, 1, 5, 1, 0, 11
   (e) 2, −3, 7, −9, +8
   (f) 9, −7, 0, −4, −6, 3, −9
7. For each of the distributions in the preceding question, what is the ratio of the range to the standard deviation?
8. From the values of $\overline{X}$ and s obtained in questions 6(d), 6(e), and 6(f), would you say it is possible for s to be larger than $\overline{X}$?

Computation from an Arbitrary Origin. Suppose it is necessary to find the mean of the 5 numbers, 27309, 27321, 27305, 27299, and 27296. No doubt many people would compute $\Sigma X = 136530$ and $\overline{X} = \dfrac{136530}{5} = 27306$. However, some of you who are more inventive may say to yourselves, "Now, obviously, the mean cannot be very far from 27300. I will just add together the amounts by which the various numbers differ from 27300 to see how much the mean differs from 27300. That gives me $9 + 21 + 5 - 1 - 4 = 30$. If all 5 cases produce an excess of 30, the mean excess must be 30/5 or 6. So I think the mean is $27300 + 6 = 27306$."

Now let us generalize this process, which is certainly much easier than adding the original numbers as required by the definition of Formula 7.1. The number 27300 may be called an *arbitrary origin* and designated as A. Then,

The mean	is equal to	the arbitrary origin	increased by	the mean of the deviations from that origin
$\overline{X}$	$=$	A	$+$	$\dfrac{\Sigma(X - A)}{N}$

(7.9)
$$\overline{X} = A + \frac{\Sigma(X - A)}{N}$$

Again suppose you were asked to compute the standard deviation of these numbers. Because the mean has already been found to be 27306 we have

X	$X - \overline{X}$	$(X - \overline{X})^2$
27309	3	9
27321	15	225
27305	−1	1
27299	−7	49
27296	−10	100
	0	384

By formula (7.4), variance $= \frac{384}{4} = 96$ and $s = \sqrt{96} = 9.8$. If $\overline{X}$ had not been an integer, it would not be economical to use formula (7.4) and we might have computed $\Sigma X = 136{,}530$, $\Sigma X^2 = 3{,}728{,}088{,}564$. Then by formula (7.5)

$$\text{variance} = \frac{5(3{,}728{,}088{,}564) - (136{,}530)^2}{5(4)} = \frac{1920}{20} = 96$$

as before. This procedure is correct but unnecessarily laborious. To shorten the process we shall again take an arbitrary origin at the convenient point $A = 27300$. Then

$$\Sigma(X - A) = 30$$
$$\Sigma(X - A)^2 = 9^2 + 21^2 + 5^2 + (-1)^2 + (-4)^2 = 564$$

and variance $= \dfrac{5(564) - 30^2}{5(4)} = \dfrac{1920}{20} = 96$ as before.

The procedure is symbolized by formula

$$(7.10) \qquad \text{variance} = \frac{N\Sigma(X - A)^2 - [\Sigma(X - A)]^2}{N(N - 1)}$$

and this can be seen to differ from formula (7.5) only in that the X of (7.5) has become $(X - A)$ of (7.10).

The original values (here denoted X) measured from an origin at zero are called *raw scores* or *gross scores*. When each score is reduced by some arbitrary value, the results (here denoted $X - A$) are called *deviations from an origin at A*. When gross scores are large, computation by such gross score formulas as (7.1), (7.5), (7.7), and (7.8) may be very laborious by hand computation though quite convenient if a machine is available. An arbitrary origin can be used to reduce the size of the numbers involved and thus to reduce the labor of computation.

To assure yourself that the choice of A is really arbitrary, compute the mean and variance of the numbers 23, 29, 21, 35, 31, and 36, using first one origin and than another, as for example:

A	$\Sigma(X - A)$	$\Sigma(X - A)^2$	$\overline{X}$	Variance
0	175	5293	$\dfrac{175}{6} = 29.17$	$\dfrac{6(5293) - (175)^2}{30} = \dfrac{1133}{30}$
20	55	693	$20 + \dfrac{55}{6} = 29.17$	$\dfrac{6(693) - (55)^2}{30} = \dfrac{1133}{30}$
30	−5	193	$30 - \dfrac{5}{6} = 29.17$	$\dfrac{6(193) - (5)^2}{30} = \dfrac{1133}{30}$
32	−17	237	$32 - \dfrac{17}{6} = 29.17$	$\dfrac{6(237) - (17)^2}{30} = \dfrac{1133}{30}$
25.5	22	269.5	$25.5 + \dfrac{22}{6} = 29.17$	$\dfrac{6(269.5) - (22)^2}{30} = \dfrac{1133}{30}$

The outcome will be exactly the same no matter what value is given to A, so the computer has free choice. However, in order to keep down the labor of computation it is wise to let A be an integer (20 or 26 would be better than 25.5), which is easy to subtract (20 would be better than 19 or 26), and which is small enough so that all deviations are positive (20 would be a better choice than 26).

Computation When Scores Are Grouped in Intervals. Until we could take up the situation in which scores are grouped in intervals, it has seemed wise to restrict attention to distributions with small N and narrow range. Mastering the type of problem discussed in this section, however, will make it possible to work with any distribution.

Even though you may be heartily tired of the midterm scores of the three sections of a statistics class, it will be instructive to go back to them again in order to see the relation of mean and standard deviation to the measures computed in Chapter 6.

TABLE 7.2 Three Computations of the Mean and Standard Deviation for the Midterm Scores of Section I Taken from Table 6.3

Score	f	I			II			III		
		X	fX	fX^2	$X-32$	$f(X-32)$	$f(X-32)^2$	x'	fx'	$f(x')^2$
70–74	1	72	72	5184	40	40	1600	8	8	64
65–69	2	67	134	8978	35	70	2450	7	14	98
60–64	11	62	682	42284	30	330	9900	6	66	396
55–59	9	57	513	29241	25	225	5625	5	45	225
50–54	7	52	364	18928	20	140	2800	4	28	112
45–49	7	47	329	15463	15	105	1575	3	21	63
40–44	3	42	126	5292	10	30	300	2	6	12
35–39		37			5			1		
30–34	1	32	32	1024	0	0	0	0	0	0
Sum	41		2252	126394		940	24250		188	970

Mean	$\dfrac{2252}{41} = 54.93$	$32 + \dfrac{940}{41} = 54.93$	$32 + \left(\dfrac{188}{41}\right)5 = 54.93$
Variance	$\dfrac{41(126394) - (2252)^2}{41(40)}$	$\dfrac{41(24250) - (940)^2}{41(40)}$	$25\left(\dfrac{41(970) - (188)^2}{41(40)}\right)$
	$= \dfrac{110650}{1640} = 67.47$	$= \dfrac{110650}{1640} = 67.47$	$= 25\left(\dfrac{4426}{1640}\right) = 67.47$
Standard deviation	$\sqrt{67.47} = 8.21$	$\sqrt{67.47} = 8.21$	$\sqrt{67.47} = 8.21$

In Table 7.2 three computations have been made from the same set of scores. Computation I makes use of gross scores, treating each score in the distribution as if it were situated at the midpoint of its interval, and using formulas (7.7) and (7.8) to complete the computation. Do not feel obliged to carry out the arithmetic, but examine the table to make sure you know what has been done. The numbers are large enough to seem rather formidable in hand computation and you will doubtless prefer Methods II and III.

Method II is exactly like Method I except that an arbitrary

origin has been taken at the midpoint of the interval 30–34, and so each value of X has been reduced by 32, thus making the numbers considerably smaller. Note that the final values of mean and variance are identical with those of Method I.

Method III makes use of what are called *coded* scores. Note that each value in column x' is exactly one fifth as large as the corresponding value in column $X - 32$ of Method II, and so $\Sigma x'$ is one fifth as large as $\Sigma(X - 32)$ and must be multiplied by 5 to give the same result in computing $\overline{X}$. Now 5 is the step interval, and we shall designate the width of the interval by i. Then,

$$(7.11) \qquad\qquad ix' = X - A$$

An x' is called a *coded score*. Such coded scores are obtained by writing 0 in the interval where the arbitrary origin is placed and labeling the intervals above that origin successively 1, 2, 3 . . . and the intervals below it −1, −2, −3 . . .. Thus the values of x' provide a new scale in which each step is one interval wide. To change this scale back to the scale of scores, we must multiply by i or i^2 as indicated in formulas (7.12) and (7.13).

$$(7.12) \qquad\qquad \overline{X} = A + i\left(\frac{\Sigma fx'}{N}\right)$$

$$(7.13) \qquad\qquad \text{variance} = i^2\left(\frac{N\Sigma f(x')^2 - (\Sigma fx')^2}{N(N-1)}\right)$$

Note that the only difference between formula (7.13) and the earlier (7.8) is that x' has taken the place of X and the whole has been multiplied by the square of the step interval. Note that the arbitrary origin is always taken at the midpoint of an interval.

In Method II, each value of X has been reduced by 32 but is still measured in score units. Therefore, $A = 32$ and $i = 1$.

Other Formulas Related to the Variance. The formulas given here for the variance, (7.5), (7.8), (7.10), and (7.13) have been selected out of many algebraically equivalent formulas because they present an economical computing routine. The student who reads widely in other books will probably discover some of the following formulas which are set down here only to reassure him that they are algebraically consistent with those presented in this chapter.

$$(7.14) \qquad \Sigma x^2 = \Sigma(X - \overline{X})^2 = \Sigma X^2 - \frac{(\Sigma X)^2}{N}$$

$$(7.15) \qquad \Sigma x^2 = i^2\left[\Sigma f(x')^2 - \frac{(\Sigma f x')^2}{N}\right]$$

$$(7.16) \qquad s^2 = \frac{\Sigma X^2 - \dfrac{(\Sigma X)^2}{N}}{N - 1}$$

$$(7.17) \qquad s^2 = i^2\left[\frac{\Sigma f(x')^2 - \dfrac{(\Sigma f x')^2}{N}}{N - 1}\right]$$

As formulas for the standard deviation are obtained from those for the variance merely by taking the square root, they need not be listed here.

As noted previously, many texts use N where this uses $N - 1$ as denominator for the variance.

Checking Results. Retracing the steps of a computation sel-dom catches mistakes. Check methods are needed to give a com-puter confidence in the results of his work, especially if he is com-puting without access to a machine.

If coded scores and an arbitrary origin are used, shifting the origin, recomputing $\Sigma x'$ and $\Sigma(x')^2$, and comparing these with the values under the first computation provides an easy check.

Raising the arbitrary origin by r intervals

$$(7.18) \qquad \text{changes } \Sigma x' \quad \text{to} \quad \Sigma x' - Nr$$
$$(7.19) \qquad \text{and changes } \Sigma(x')^2 \quad \text{to} \quad \Sigma(x')^2 - 2r\Sigma x' + Nr^2$$

Lowering the origin by r intervals

$$(7.20) \qquad \text{changes } \Sigma x' \quad \text{to} \quad \Sigma x' + Nr$$
$$(7.21) \qquad \text{and changes } \Sigma(x')^2 \quad \text{to} \quad \Sigma(x')^2 + 2r\Sigma x' + Nr^2$$

Now let us apply these principles to the computation by Method III in Table 7.2, where $i = 5$ and the origin was taken at the midpoint of the lowest interval in which any frequency occurs. This is a good place to take the origin because it keeps the values of x' small but positive. If we move it up, some values of x' will be negative which you will find is a nuisance when a computing machine is used. In the columns $\Sigma f x'$ and $\Sigma f(x')^2$ below are given the values you would obtain if you made a specified shift (r) in the value of A. Verify these from the data and then verify that they agree with the values in the check columns:

		$\Sigma fx'$		$\Sigma f(x')^2$	
A	r	from data	Check	from data	Check
37	1	147	$= 188 - 41(1)$	635	$= 970 - 2(1)(188) + 41(1)$
47	3	65	$= 188 - 41(3)$	211	$= 970 - 2(3)(188) + 41(9)$
22	−2	270	$= 188 + 41(2)$	1886	$= 970 + 2(2)(188) + 41(4)$

Relation of Standard Deviation to Range. Sometimes a large error — such, for example, as may result from misplacing a decimal point — can be detected by comparing the computed standard deviation with the range. The ratio of the range to s is almost never smaller than 2 or larger than 6; in fact, it is not often smaller than 2.5 or larger than 5.5. For example, the range estimated from the data of Table 7.2 is $74 - 30 = 44$ and $s = 8.21$, so the ratio of the range to the standard deviation is $44/8.2 = 5.4$. Suppose the decimal point had been misplaced in computing the variance, so the standard deviation was reported not as $\sqrt{67.47} = 8.2$ but as $\sqrt{6.747} = 2.6$. The presence of some serious error could have been surmised because $\dfrac{\text{range}}{s} = \dfrac{44}{2.6} = 17$, which is much too large to be reasonable. If the decimal point had been misplaced in the other direction so that s appeared to be $\sqrt{674.7} = 26$, the ratio of range to s would be $\frac{44}{26} = 1.7$ which is small enough to rouse suspicion. The comparison of the standard deviation to the range cannot prove the correctness of the computation of the standard deviation but it can sometimes reveal an error.

Comparison of Groups. The mean and the standard deviation have been developed to this point as summary measures useful in characterizing a distribution. The mean achieves this by identifying a point on the scale, usually near the center of the distribution; the standard deviation describes the spread of the distribution. One can also speak of this mean and standard deviation as characterizing the group on which the scores making up the distribution were computed. Thus we may speak of the mean IQ of a class being 100 and its standard deviation being 10.

The mean and the standard deviation can also be used to compare groups. Suppose, for example, that the mean IQ of one eighth-grade class is 103 and standard deviation 4.1, while the mean IQ of a second eighth-grade class of about the same size is 102 and standard deviation is 9.3. The means are approximately the same, but the spread of the second class is so much greater it will present different and more difficult teaching problems.

Both variance and standard deviation are expressed in the units of the original distribution. The standard deviation of the weights of a group of 12-year-old children from underprivileged homes might be compared with the standard deviation of the weights of a group from privileged homes because both standard deviations are in terms of weight units and the means are not very disparate. One could not, in the same way, ask whether a group of children are more variable in weight than in height, because one standard deviation is expressed in weight units and one in height units, and there is no basis for comparison. Nor would it be reasonable to say that adults are more variable in weight than babies merely because the standard deviation of adult weights is larger than that of infant weights. The means of the two groups would be so diverse that one feels inclined to inquire how large is the variability relative to the average. The ratio of the standard deviation to the mean, $\frac{s}{\bar{X}}$, is called the *coefficient of variation*.

Caution. At this stage there is a great temptation for the beginning student to run ahead of his information. He has, let us say, found that a group of 150 girls had a higher mean score and a larger variability than a group of 120 boys on a test of art appreciation. That is an observation, true for these particular cases. But the research worker is tempted to go further and to say, not that "these girls had a higher mean than these boys and were more variable" but that "girls have a higher mean and are more variable than boys," making a generalization from the particular cases observed to boys and girls at large. Such a generalization is known as a statistical inference, being an inference from an observed sample to the unknown population from which that sample is drawn. The more extended analysis on which such inferences must be based will be introduced in Chapter 13 of this text. For the present, the student would be well advised not to generalize on his data, and to report his conclusions in the past tense so that his readers will understand that they apply specifically to the groups studied.

EXERCISE 7.3

1. The basic data for computing the mean, variance, and standard deviation for the midterm scores of each section and the combined sections are given on page 100. Complete the computations and write your results on the blank lines.

	I	II	III	Combined group
From the ungrouped data of Table 6.2 on page 67				
ΣfX	2257	1425	1349	5031
ΣfX^2	126,979	77,291	67,569	271,839
$\overline{X}$	—	—	—	—
s^2	—	—	—	—
s	—	—	—	—
$\Sigma f(X - 50)$	207	75	−51	231
$\Sigma f(X - 50)^2$	3779	2291	2669	8739
$\overline{X}$	—	—	—	—
s^2	—	—	—	—
s	—	—	—	—
From grouped scores of Table 6.3 with $A = 52$ and $i = 5$				
$\Sigma fx'$	24	4	−22	6
$\Sigma f(x')^2$	122	82	120	324
$\overline{X}$	—	—	—	—
s^2	—	—	—	—
s	—	—	—	—

2. You will notice that there is very close agreement between the results obtained from the grouped and the ungrouped data. Why is the agreement not perfect?

3. Do the three sections stand in the same order with respect to the mean as they do with respect to the median?

4. For each Section find the value of $\overline{X} - X_{.50}$

Section   I   ————   Does there seem to be
    "   II   ————   fairly close agreement
    "   III   ————   between the mean and the
Combined group ————   median? Are they identical?

5. In terms of the standard deviation, place the three groups in order of variability, from most variable to least variable. Do the same in terms of the interquartile range. Is the order the same?

6. Compute the ratio of the range to the standard deviation for each section and for the combined group, working (a) with the ungrouped data and (b) with the grouped data.

7. Suppose you were reviewing the work of someone else and you found the statement that $\Sigma X = 920$, $N = 30$, and $\overline{X} = 3.06$, it would be clear that a mistake had been made because these three numbers are inconsistent. If you found the statment that $\overline{X} = 23.4$ and $X_{.50} = 16.9$, you would not be able to say that the results were correct but you would certainly have no evidence that they were not. For each of the following sets of data in which there is an inconsistency indicating that a *mistake* has certainly or probably been made, write M on the blank line. If there is no evidence of inconsistency and the data are quite *possibly* correct, write P on the line.

—— (a) $X_{.20} = 32$; $X_{.50} = 61$; $X_{.40} = 63$

—— (b) $\overline{X} = 1$; $s = 7.2$

—— (c) $N = 30$; if $A = 6$, $\Sigma x' = 23$; if $A = 5$, $\Sigma x' = 18$

—— (d) $N = 37$; $\overline{X} = 12$; $\Sigma(X - 12) = 26$

—— (e) $N = 60$; $\overline{X} = 7$; $\Sigma X = 420$

—— (f) The extreme scores in a distribution are 3 and 69; $\overline{X} = 31$, $s = 7.4$

—— (g) The extreme scores in a distribution are 5 and 36; $\overline{X} = 29$; $s = 7.9$

—— (h) $N = 60$; $\Sigma(X - 8) = 33$; $\Sigma(X - 9) = -27$

—— (i) $N = 80$; $\Sigma(X - 12) = -15$; $\Sigma(X - 11) = -95$

—— (j) $N = 100$; $\overline{X} = 31$; $\Sigma(X - 31)^2 = 502$

—— (k) $N = 100$; $\overline{X} = 31$; $\Sigma(X - 31)^2 = 502$; $\Sigma(X - 35)^2 = 421$

—— (l) $N = 30$; $\Sigma(X - 25) = 120$; $\overline{X} = 25 + \frac{120}{30} = 29$

—— (m) $X_{.25} = 52$; $X_{.50} = 60$; $X_{.75} = 73$

Mean and Standard Deviation of Combined Group from Those of Its Subgroups.

Sometimes the values of N, $\overline{X}$, and s are available for several subgroups and there is need to obtain the corresponding values for the combined group. This situation might arise when one is working over published data without access to the original scores. Even if original scores are available, going back to them and reconstructing a frequency distribution for the combined group may be unnecessarily laborious. Formulas (7.22) to (7.25) show an easy numerical procedure by which the statistics of the combined group (indicated by the subscript c) may be obtained from those of the various subgroups. The letter k is used to indicate the number of subgroups.

$$(7.22) \quad N_c = N_1 + N_2 + \cdots + N_k$$

$$(7.23) \quad \overline{X}_c = \frac{1}{N_c}\,(N_1\overline{X}_1 + N_2\overline{X}_2 + \cdots + N_k\overline{X}_k)$$

(7.24) $d_i = \overline{X}_i - \overline{X}_c$, or in words, d_i represents the amount by which the mean of the ith subgroup differs from the mean of the combined group

$$(7.25) \quad (N_c - 1)s_c^2 = (N_1 - 1)s_1^2 + (N_2 - 1)s_2^2 + \cdots + (N_k - 1)s_k^2$$
$$+ N_1 d_1^2 + N_2 d_2^2 + \cdots + N_k d_k^2$$

TABLE 7.3 Routine for Obtaining $\overline{X}_c$ and s_c for a Composite Group

Subgroup	N	$\overline{X}$	s	$N\overline{X}$	d	$(N-1)s^2$	Nd^2
I	41	55.05	8.27	2257	2.64	2736	286
II	27	52.78	8.95	1425	.37	2083	4
III	28	48.18	9.77	1349	-4.23	2576	501
	96			5031		7395	791

$$\overline{X}_c = \frac{5031}{96} = 52.406$$

$$95\,s_c^2 = 7395 + 791 = 8186$$

$$s_c = \sqrt{\frac{8186}{95}} = \sqrt{86.17} = 9.28$$

The use of these formulas will now be illustrated by application to the data of Table 6.3 on page 69. There, of course, the original scores are available, and direct computation from them produces the values $\overline{X}_c = 52.40$ and $s_c = \sqrt{86.14} = 9.28$. We shall now apply the formulas just as if all the information at hand were what is provided in Table 7.3 in the columns headed N, $\overline{X}$, and s.

The sum of the column N gives us 96 as the value of N_c according to formula (7.22).

The sum of the column $N\overline{X}$ divided by 96 gives us $\overline{X}_c = 52.41$ according to formula (7.23).

The values in column d are obtained by subtracting $\overline{X}_c$ from each value of $\overline{X}$.

The values in columns $(N-1)s^2$ and Nd^2 are filled in. The sums of these columns are added to provide the value on the right of the equality sign in formula (7.25). This number is 8186.

The computation of s_c is completed by finding $s_c^2 = \dfrac{8186}{95} = 86.17$ and $s_c = \sqrt{86.17} = 9.28$.

By direct computation from raw data, we had obtained $\overline{X}_c = 52.41$ and $s_c = 9.28$ and by application of the formulas we have the same values.

No similar procedure is possible for obtaining percentiles or percentile ranks of a combined group without recourse to the frequency distribution.

Standard Scores. In Table VIII we notice that the student with code number 3 has scores 38, 38, and 39, respectively, on the three tests of reading, artificial language, and arithmetic.

Can this be interpreted to mean that his standing in the group is about the same on the three tests? By the methods of the previous chapter we could compute his percentile rank in each test and we would thus discover that in reading he had percentile rank 62; in artificial language, 19; in arithmetic, 86. Obviously, the raw scores alone do not properly reflect his relative positions on the three tests.

To compute a percentile rank it is necessary to have the entire distribution of scores. Moreover percentile ranks can be used appropriately only when central position is measured by the median. If the mean is being used as measure of central position, relative standing should be indicated in terms of the mean and standard deviation and this can be done without reference to the distribution of original scores.

Comparing the scores of student Number 3 with the group means shown in Table 7.4, we see that he stood 2.3 points above the mean in reading; 8.4 below the mean in artificial language; and 7.6 above, in arithmetic. But can these differences be considered comparable when scores on the three tests were not equally variable? To allow for differences in the standard deviations of the three tests, his deviation from the mean of each test has been divided by the standard deviation of that test, producing the values $\left(\dfrac{X_3 - \overline{X}}{s}\right)$. These values might be called *standard scores*, inasmuch as they are expressed in terms of the standard deviation as unit. The three values in this column are directly comparable.

TABLE 7.4 Computation of Standard Scores on Three Tests for Student No. 3 of Appendix Table VIII

Test	X_3 Score of student 3	$\overline{X}$	$X_3 - \overline{X}$	s	$\dfrac{X_3 - \overline{X}}{s}$	$10\left(\dfrac{X_3 - \overline{X}}{s}\right) + 50$
Reading	38	35.7	2.3	7.7	.30	53
Artificial language	38	46.4	− 8.4	11.0	− .76	42
Arithmetic	39	31.4	7.6	7.3	1.04	60

To avoid the danger of overlooking a decimal point, it has generally been found convenient to multiply such standardized deviations by some number large enough to give a result from which we feel justified in dropping the final digit. The most convenient number to use for this purpose is 10. To eliminate the negative signs, we add some number large enough to make all results positive. The number 50 is ordinarily, but not necessarily, used for this purpose. (The transformed scores thus produced are also standard scores and to avoid confusion we shall refer to them as *transformed standard scores*) The transformed standard scores for student Number 3 in the final column of Table 7.4 agree with his percentile ranks in indicating that his standing was highest in arithmetic and lowest in artificial language.

When scores on several tests are to be averaged and it is desired to give them all the same weight in the average, they should be put in standard form before taking the average. If raw scores are averaged, the test with the largest standard deviation will exercise the greatest weight in the composite.

In the previous example, the three standard deviations (7.7, 11.0, and 7.3) were not very diverse, and so the advantage of transforming scores to standard form before averaging — if scores were to be averaged — is not very great. Suppose, however, that a teacher wants to average scores on three class tests in which the means and standard deviations are

$$\overline{X}_1 = 9 \qquad s_1 = 3$$
$$\overline{X}_2 = 41 \qquad s_2 = 7$$
$$\overline{X}_3 = 63 \qquad s_3 = 2$$

Consider the four students listed in Table 7.5 and note that, if raw scores are averaged, the students all seem to have the same standing but that, if scores are transformed to standard form before being averaged, it is clear that student D excels the others by a considerable amount. The individual scores and the standard deviations here were chosen deliberately to produce an effect somewhat more striking that you are likely to encounter in practice.

TABLE 7.5 Raw Scores and Standard Scores for Four Students on Three Tests (Artificial Data)

Test	$\overline{X}$	s	Raw score for student				Standard score for student			
			A	B	C	D	A	B	C	D
I	9	3	15	7	2	15	70	43	27	70
II	41	7	41	50	57	33	50	63	73	39
III	63	2	61	60	58	69	40	35	25	80
Sum			117	117	117	117	160	141	125	189
Mean			39	39	39	39	53	47	42	63

EXERCISE 7.4

1. For the midterm grades listed in Table VIII, the mean and standard deviation were approximately $\overline{X} = 52.5$ and $s = 9.3$. By inspection of the table, count to see how many students had scores in the range indicated, and then change these numbers to percents.

Range in symbol form	Range in scores	Number of students	Percent of students
Below $\overline{X} - s$	Below 43.2	——	——
Between $\overline{X} - s$ and $\overline{X}$	Between 43.2 and 52.5	——	——
Between $\overline{X}$ and $\overline{X} + s$	Between 52.5 and 61.8	——	——
Above $\overline{X} + s$	Above 61.8	——	——
Below $\overline{X} - 2s$	Below 33.9	——	——
Between $\overline{X} - 2s$ and $\overline{X}$	Between 33.9 and 52.5	——	——
Between $\overline{X}$ and $\overline{X} + 2s$	Between 52.5 and 81.1	——	——
Above $\overline{X} + 2s$	Above 81.1	——	——

2. Suppose marks on four class tests with means and standard deviations as shown are to be averaged. Convert the marks of the pupils named to standard scores and average those standard scores.

Test	$\overline{X}$	s	Mark for Jones	Mark for Smith	Mark for Brown
A	80.3	5.6	89	82	75
B	25.4	8.4	27	24	28
C	37.3	12.1	38	46	40
D	65.2	4.3	72	68	63

3. Below are given John's score, the mean, and the standard deviation on each of three tests. On which did he stand highest in relation to the group for which $\overline{X}$ and s were computed? On which lowest?

Test	$\overline{X}$	s	John's score
English usage	73.2	12.6	72
Algebra	58.6	4.2	61
U.S. History	41.3	6.8	50

8

The Frequency Distribution — A Summary

In a sense most of the material presented up to this point has dealt with the frequency distribution — tabulation, graphing, scaled variables, measures of central position, measures of variability. Certainly all of Chapters 5, 6, and 7, and considerable portions of 3 and 4 dealt with aspects of the frequency distribution. Nor will the rest of the book turn away from this extremely important topic. Before taking up problems of correlation and regression which involve two variables, it will be wise to summarize, amplify, and consolidate what has been said about the frequency distribution of a single variable. The discussion in the present chapter relates chiefly to the distribution of a scaled variable.

Summary Measures. In the two preceding chapters we have learned to describe frequency distributions by certain summary measures such as the mean, median, various percentiles, the difference between two percentiles, and the standard deviation. Other additional summary measures will be described in this chapter.

With so many measures at hand, the reader may well wonder what selection of them he should make for adequate description of a frequency distribution. Some guides will be presented in the following paragraphs. It may be pointed out at once that, if a distribution is fairly symmetrical (a matter which is discussed later in this chapter) and has its largest frequencies near the middle of the distribution, nearly as much information can be conveyed by giving a measure of central position and a measure of variability as by presenting the entire distribution. The question still remains as to which measure of central position and which measure of variability are to be chosen.

Measures of Position. The mean, median, and the percentiles all refer to points or positions on the scale of the frequency distribution, so that they may all be called measures of position or location.   The mean and median in particular commonly occupy a central position in the distribution so that they are called measures of central position.   These two measures are also called averages because they convey the meaning usually associated with the concept of the average of a group of numbers.

Another summary measure, which is usually associated with the mean and median as both a measure of central position and as an average, is the mode.   It should be noted, however, that the mode does not necessarily have to be either central or even unique, and that it can be computed when there is no scale.   It is that value which occurs most frequently in a distribution, just as the style of dress or hat or coat which occurs most frequently in a given season is called the mode.   In a grouped frequency distribution, the mode is considered to be at the midpoint of the interval in which the largest frequency occurs.   If two or more adjacent intervals have the same frequency, and it is larger than the frequency in other intervals, the mode is considered to be at the midpoint of the entire range covered by such intervals.   In a smooth frequency curve, the mode is the abscissa corresponding to the highest point on the curve.   Two kinds of mode should be distinguished.   The *mathematical mode* is a concept of considerable interest in theoretical work and is far more useful than the *crude mode*.   However, the mathematical mode is difficult to obtain; it can, in fact, be obtained only if the equation of a theoretical frequency curve is known, so that its maximum point can be found.   This is almost always a task calling for some mathematical erudition.   Therefore, the mathematical mode is not discussed in elementary treatises, and the term "mode" is ordinarily applied to what is more properly called the crude mode.

The crude mode is the measure described in the first three sentences of the preceding paragraph.   It is extremely easy to obtain, requiring no computation but merely inspection of the distribution.

Two other averages may be mentioned in passing.   Problems concerning time, rate, and distance — or time, rate, and work — often require the use of what is called the *harmonic mean*.   Problems that relate to a variable which is changing over a period of time at a fairly constant rate (not constant amount) often require the use of the *geometric mean*.   Rate of growth of an organism or a population is such a variable.   Further description of these means or presentation of their formulas is outside the scope of this book.   These means are seldom needed, but when they are needed there is no alternative. Any person who has a problem in averaging rates would do well to consult a text in which the geometric and harmonic means are discussed.

The Choice of a Measure of Central Position. Let us begin by looking at certain situations in which there really is no choice because not all three measures — mean, median, and mode — can be computed:

1. If the variable is expressed in unordered categories only, the mode is the only average which can be found. Suppose a panel of judges is deciding which of four exhibits shall receive a prize and they vote as follows:

Exhibit	A	B	C	D
Number of votes:	2	13	1	4

It is quite correct to say that *B* is the mode of this distribution. There is no mean and no median.

2. If the variable is not scaled but consists of a set of ordered categories, there is no mean but a rough median can usually be found, and a mode.

3. If the variable is scaled but has one or both ends open, there is a mean but it cannot be computed. The median and the mode can usually be obtained. An example of an open-ended distribution would be one in which the highest interval is designated as "75 years and over," or "more than $10,000," or the like; or the lowest as "less than 5 years," or the like.

Certain qualities which are desirable in an average are possessed by both mean and median and so do not furnish criteria for choice between them:

1. An average should be easy to comprehend and interpret. The mean, median, and mode meet this requirement.

2. It is desirable that an average be easy to compute. None of the three is difficult to compute. However, it might be noted that to obtain either the mode or the median it is necessary first to organize the scores into a frequency distribution (which is easy enough to do on an IBM sorter even if the number of cases is very large), but this step is not necessary for obtaining the mean.

3. It is desirable that the average should not be greatly affected by the process of grouping scores into intervals. Such grouping has very little effect on either mean or median unless the number of cases is quite small. However, it often affects the mode greatly. For an illustration, look at Table 6.2 on page 67. Here the frequencies are so scattered that the modes are not clearly defined.

Group I has two modes at 58 and 62, while the distribution for the combined sections has three modes at 47, 58, and 62. When the frequencies are grouped in intervals of 5, the position of the mode changes. In fact, as different beginning points are chosen for the interval, the mode shifts. To illustrate the instability of the mode as scores are grouped into intervals, the modes for the data of Table 6.2 under various conditions of grouping are shown here:

	I	II	III	All sections
Ungrouped frequencies	58, 62	52	47, 49	47, 58, 62
Highest interval 66–70	63	63	48	48
Highest interval 67–71	59	54	49	59
Highest interval 68–72	60	60	50, 60	60
Highest interval 69–73	61	51	51	51
Highest interval 70–74	62	52	47	62

4. It is desirable that the average fall in the middle of the distribution. The mean and median meet this condition but the mode sometimes stands at the very end of the distribution where it cannot serve satisfactorily as representative or type of that distribution.

Now having disposed of the less weighty issues we come to some really important considerations which relate to the choice among mean, median, and mode:

1. It is very important that an average have *sampling stability*. In general, the mean varies less from one sample to another than the median does, and this gives great advantage to the mean. Table 13.2 on page 216 presents the results of drawing 20 small samples from the same population and computing for each both the mean and the median. A glance at this table will reveal that the mean showed less variability from sample to sample than did the median.

However, in a distribution in which frequencies pile up at the ends instead of in the middle, the mean may vary more from sample to sample than the median. The presence of such extreme scores, even if they occur at both ends of the distribution, suggests the possibility that in another sample a few very high scores might occur without compensating low scores, or vice versa.

2. It is helpful to have an average obtained in such a way that it may be expressed by a formula based on *all* the scores in a distribution. Neither the mode nor the median possesses this

characteristic. Both of them depend only on scores in the interval in which they fall. Consider for example the eleven values in row *A*. If the values below 15 are made much smaller, as in row *B*, the mean is lowered but neither the median nor the mode reflects that change. If the scores above 15 are made larger, the mean is increased but not the median or the mode.

	$\overline{X}$	$X_{.50}$	Mode
A. 9, 10, 13, 14, 15, 15, 15, 16, 18, 19, 21	15	15	15
B. 2, 3, 6, 8, 15, 15, 15, 16, 17, 17, 18	12	15	15
C. 9, 10, 13, 14, 15, 15, 15, 19, 26, 35, 38	19	15	15

There are at least two distinct advantages which the mean possesses because it is an algebraic function of all the scores in the distribution. The first advantage is that it has been possible to develop a great deal more mathematical theory about the mean than about either of the other two averages. A second advantage is seen when several separate groups are to be combined into one single group. To obtain either the median or the mode of the combined group, it is necessary to construct its frequency distribution. The mean of the combined group can be obtained from the means and the N's of the component groups.

3. When extreme scores occur at one end of a frequency distribution, careful thinking about the meaning of the data is necessary in order not to use a measure of central position which will misrepresent. Consider Table 8.1. Here the mean, median, and mode for the two districts and for the combined group are as follows:

	District A	District B	Both districts
Mean	256.5	240.8	248.6
Median	201.0	201.6	201.4
Mode	175.0	175	175

Quoting only the mean would give a fantastically wrong impression, for in each group about three fourths of the families had incomes lower than the mean income. A few atypical families with relatively high incomes have affected the mean unduly. For these data both median and mode are of genuine interest and should be reported.

If a teacher wishes to compare the average of her class on a standardized test with published norms for the grade, it is better to have both norm and average expressed as medians because one or two atypical scores might influence the mean too greatly.

TABLE 8.1 Number of Families Having a Given Dollar Income in Two
Magisterial Districts

(Adapted from Mary B. Willeford, *Income and Health in Remote
Rural Areas* Teachers College, Columbia University, Bureau of Publications)

Income in dollars *	Number of families		
	District A	District B	Both districts
2975	1		1
1325		1	1
1275		1	1
1175		1	1
975	1		1
925		1	1
875	1	2	3
825			
775	3	2	5
725	2		2
675	3		3
625	2	1	3
575	4		4
525		2	2
475	2	2	4
425	7	1	8
375	2	7	9
325	10	5	15
275	15	14	29
225	48	62	110
175	57	67	124
125	30	24	54
75	5	3	8
25	7	4	11
Total	200	200	400

* Each entry represents the midpoint of an interval 50 units wide.

Describing a Distribution in Terms of Its Variability. Several
different measures of variability have been described — the total
range of scores, some interpercentile range, and the standard deviation. Each has its special usefulness. In general, the standard
deviation and the mean belong to the same family of measures and
are used together; an interpercentile range and the median belong
together; the total range may be used with either average.

Look again at Table 8.1 and note how the total range is in-
flated by the presence of one extreme case so that it grossly exag-

gerates the spread of the whole. Examine the figures for various measures of variability on which the data of Table 8.1 are based.

Measure computed from original ungrouped scores	District A		District B		Both districts	
Total range	2959–0	=2959	1311–0	=1311	2959–0	=2959
Range of middle 96%	754–34	= 720	890–50	= 840	870–43	= 827
Interquartile range	260–157=	103	242–164=	78	247–161=	86
Standard deviation	215		181		199	

When even 2 percent of the families are eliminated at each end of the distribution, the range for the combined districts drops from 2959 to 827, thus giving a fairer representation of the scattering in the group.

The relation between various measures of dispersion for four distributions of different form is seen in Figure 8–1. The dotted

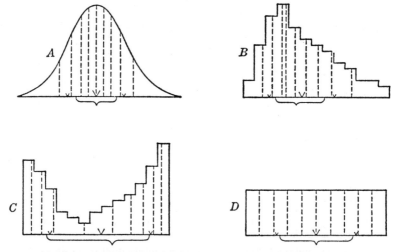

Fig. 8–1   Position of Decile Points in Frequency Distributions of Different Forms.
Dotted lines are erected at the decile points.
Brace extends from Q_L to Q_U with center at median.
Large arrow indicates mean.
Small arrows indicate points at distance of one standard deviation on either side of mean.

ordinates are erected at the decile points. The brace below each figure extends from $X_{.25}$ to $X_{.75}$ with its cusp at the median. The mean is indicated by a large V, the points one standard deviation from the mean by smaller v's.

Now take a card or piece of crisp paper and mark on its edge a distance equal to the standard deviation of Figure A. Lay this distance off along the base line to estimate the length of the range in standard deviation units. Do the same for each of the four figures. You will find that the ratio of the range to s is about $5\frac{1}{2}$ for A, about $4\frac{1}{2}$ for B, a little less than 3 for C, and about $3\frac{1}{2}$ for D. In general, you are unlikely to encounter a distribution in which the range is more than $6s$ or less than $3s$. It is impossible for it to be less than $2s$. In Figure A, the interquartile range is about $\frac{4}{3}s$; in B, about $\frac{3}{2}s$; in C, slightly more than $2s$; in D, slightly less than $2s$. Obviously, the relation of these measures of variability depends on the form of the distribution.

Describing a Distribution in Terms of Symmetry or Skewness. If the graph of a distribution can be folded along an ordinate at the median in such a way that the two halves of the figure coincide perfectly, that distribution is called *symmetrical*. In such a distribution the mean and median are identical. If there is a single mode, it is also identical with the mean and median. Of course, absolute symmetry is practically never encountered in real data, but the concept provides a convenient method of describing distributions in a general sort of way.

When $\overline{X} - X_{.50}$ is positive, a distribution is said to be *positively skewed* or to have *positive skewness*.

When $\overline{X} - X_{.50}$ is negative, a distribution is said to be *negatively skewed* or to have *negative skewness*.

The terms "skewed to the right" and "skewed to the left" are sometimes met but they are ambiguous and should be avoided. Writers who use these terms are not agreed on their meaning, some applying one term and some the other to the same type of distribution.

Various statistics are available for measuring skewness, but are not used often enough to justify describing them here.

Describing a Distribution in Terms of Its Peakedness. Figure 8–2 shows six histograms all of which are symmetrical, yet the six are obviously dissimilar. Their dissimilarity derives chiefly from the amount of peakedness they possess. The technical term for peakedness is *kurtosis*, or "arching." A moderately peaked distribution like A in Figure 8–1 or A in 8–3 is called *mesokurtic*. A distribution which goes up to a high, thin peak and has long tails, like A in Figure 8–2, is called *leptokurtic*. A squatty distribution, like D in Figure 8–2, or one which sinks down in the middle, like E and F, is called *platykurtic*. These terms are of no practical importance and need not be memorized. They are offered here for your amusement.

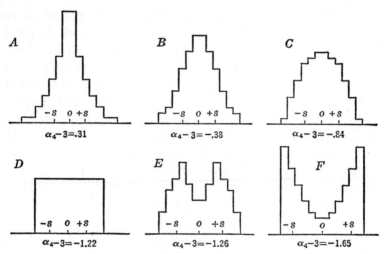

Fig. 8–2 Symmetrical Histograms Illustrating Different Degrees of Kurtosis.

Measures of kurtosis exist but are not needed often enough to warrant describing them here. Suffice it to say that the figure α_4 printed below the sketches in Figure 8–2 is such a measure; and that $\alpha_4 - 3$ is zero for a mesokurtic or moderately arched distribution; $\alpha_4 - 3$ is positive for a leptokurtic distribution and negative for a platykurtic distribution.

Figure 8–3 shows five distributions which differ both as to symmetry and as to skewness. The figure α_3 below them is a measure of skewness such that α_3 is positive for a distribution which is positively skewed; is negative for one which is negatively skewed; and is zero for one which is symmetrical.

U-shaped, I-shaped, J-shaped Distributions. These terms are vivid but not explicit. A distribution like *F* in Figure 8–2 or *C* in

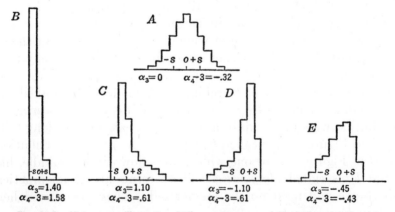

Fig. 8–3 Histograms Illustrating Different Degrees of Skewness and Kurtosis.

Figure 8–1, with a mode at each end of the distribution, is called U-shaped because it resembles the letter U.

A distribution which has a mode in the middle, no matter whether it is symmetrical or not, has some resemblance to a manuscript "i" and is called I-shaped. Sketches *A* and *B* in Figure 8–1, sketches *A*, *B*, and *C* in Figure 8–2 might be called I-shaped.

A skewed distribution with mode at one end only — at either end — is termed J-shaped. Examples are *B*, *C*, and *D* in Figure 8–3.

Bimodal Distributions. Distributions having two pronounced modes are unusual and, perhaps for that very reason, interesting.

Measuring the extent to which a child uses his right hand more skillfully than his left, Durost [1] computed for each of 1300 children a handedness ratio which is positive for right-handed persons. He obtained a distribution with two distinct modes, as shown in Figure 8–4. If an origin is taken at the point 0 which represents ambidexterity, one mode is as far to the left as the other to the right, but the mode at the right is much higher because of the predominance of right-handed children.

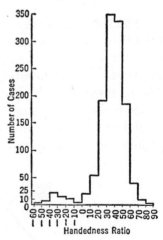

Fig. 8–4 Bimodal Frequency Distribution: Handedness Ratios. (From Durost, p. 302 *op. cit.*)

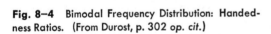

Table 8.2 shows a classical example of a bimodal frequency distribution in measures of cloudiness at the Greenwich Observatory during the month of July over a 15-year period. Relatively few days showed moderate cloudiness, most of the days were recorded as either very clear or very cloudy.

[1] W. N. Durost, "The development of a battery of objective group tests of manual laterality, with the results of their application to 1300 children," *Genetic Psychology Monographs*, **16** (October, 1934), 225–335.

TABLE 8.2   Degrees of Cloudiness as Observed at Greenwich during the Years 1890–1904 (Excluding 1901) for the Month of July*

Degree of cloudiness	Frequency
10	676
9	148
8	90
7	65
6	55
5	45
4	45
3	68
2	74
1	129
0	320
Total	1715

* From Gertrude E. Pearse, "On corrections for the moment-coefficients of frequency distributions when there are infinite ordinates at one or both of the terminals of the range." *Biometrika,* **20A** (1928), 336.

The Normal Curve. The "normal" curve is a theoretical distribution of great importance which will be treated more fully in Chapter 12. It is a smooth curve, not a histogram; it is symmetrical, and moderately peaked. It has an unlimited range. Mean, median, and mode are identical. The semi-interquartile range is about two thirds of the standard deviation. In this particular curve, the standard deviation is the abscissa of the point of inflection, as illustrated in Figure 8–5.

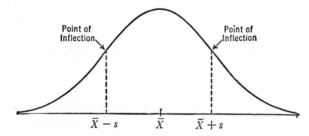

Fig. 8–5   Standard Deviation in a Normal Curve.

The Effect of Increasing Every Score in a Distribution by the Same Amount or of Multiplying Every Score by the Same Amount. On the following page is a list of nine scores and certain statistics computed from them.

	Scores								Mean	Median	Mode	Range	s^2	s
X	1	2	3	4	7	9	9	9	10	6	7	9	$10-1=9$	12.25	3.5
$X+4$	5	6	7	8	11	13	13	13	14	10	11	13	$14-5=9$	12.25	3.5
$2X$	2	4	6	8	14	18	18	18	20	12	14	18	$20-2=18$	49	7
$3X$	3	6	9	12	21	27	27	27	30	18	21	27	$30-3=27$	110.25	10.5

In the second line, $X + 4$, each of the original scores has been increased by 4. Examine the statistics computed for this row, compare them with the corresponding statistics in the first row, and formulate a general statement about the effect of adding a constant amount to every score in a distribution or subtracting a constant amount from every score.

In the third line, $2X$, each of the original scores has been doubled and in the fourth line, $3X$, tripled. Examine the statistics for these lines, compare them with the corresponding statistics in the first line, and formulate a general statement about the effect of multiplying (or dividing) every score in a distribution by the same amount.

Increasing (or decreasing) every score in a distribution by a given number will have no effect upon any measure of variability (range, interpercentile range, variance, or standard deviation) but will increase (or decrease) by that number every measure of position (mean, median, mode, or any percentile).

Multiplying (or dividing) every score in a distribution by a given number will have the effect of multiplying (or dividing) by that number every measure of variability except the variance and every measure of position. The variance will be multiplied by the square of the given number.

Geometric Representation of Various Statistics of a Frequency Distribution. Visualizing the position of a statistic on a histogram is an aid to understanding it. You will find it worth while to examine Figure 8–6 with some care. Remember that the scale of scores is the horizontal axis, and therefore the three averages, which are scores, are found on this horizontal scale. The median, $X_{.50}$, is almost always found between the mean, $\overline{X}$, and the mode. Note the position of these three values. The vertical line which divides the area into two equal parts serves to locate $X_{.50}$ on the base line. Its length does not represent any statistic. The vertical line at the midpoint of the interval with the largest frequencies serves to locate the mode on the base line, but the length of that vertical line is not the mode.

A measure of variability is represented by a line segment which is a portion of the horizontal axis. Note the segments representing

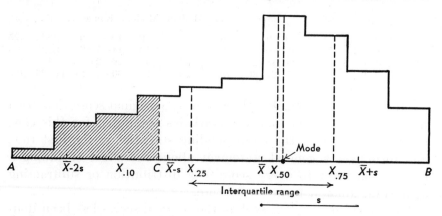

Fig. 8–6 Geometric Representation of Various Statistics. (Shaded area is percentile rank of Score **C.**)

the standard deviation *s* and the interquartile range. The segment *A B* represents the range.

Percentile rank of a score is represented by area to the left of an ordinate at the point on the base line which represents that score. Thus the shaded area represents the percentile rank of score *C*.

In Figure 8–6, $\overline{X}$ lies to the left of $X_{.50}$, indicating that the mean is smaller than the median, or $\overline{X} - X_{.50}$ is negative. Therefore, this distribution is *negatively skewed*.

9

Regression

The law of Regression tells heavily against the full hereditary transmission of any gift. Only a few out of many children would be likely to differ as widely as the more exceptional of the two Parents. The more bountifully the Parent is gifted by nature, the more rare will be his good fortune if he begets a son who is as richly endowed as himself, and still more so if he has a son who is endowed yet more largely. But the law is even-handed; it levies an equal succession tax on the transmission of badness as of goodness. If it discourages the extravagant hopes of a gifted parent that his children will inherit all his powers; it no less discountenances extravagant fears that they will inherit all his weakness and disease.

It must be clearly understood that there is nothing in these statements to invalidate the general doctrine that the children of a gifted pair are much more likely to be gifted than the children of a mediocre pair. They merely express the fact that the ablest of all the children of a few gifted pairs is not likely to be as gifted as the ablest of all the children of a very great many mediocre pairs.

— Francis Galton.

It is a commonplace of even the most elementary scientific as well as practical effort to use a score of an individual on one variable as a means of *determining*, or *estimating*, a score of the same individual on another variable. Sometimes the determination is exact, as in finding the cost of a piece of cloth from its cost per yard. At other times, the determination is inexact, as in estimating the performance of a student in a course in college mathematics from the knowledge of his score in a college entrance test in the same subject.

Estimation (or Prediction) of One Variable from Another. When two variables are of such nature that knowledge of a value of one provides information concerning the other, the variables are said to be *related*, or *associated*, and a *relationship* is said to exist between them. In such a matter as estimating a student's class performance from his score on a prognostic test, the test score comes first in point of time and so is said to be used to *predict* performance in the course. From such literal usage, the term *prediction* has spread to other situations in which, without any implication of futurity, a score on one variable is used to furnish information about another variable. Thus one may try to "predict" a child's weight from his height, or his mental age from his score on a test of paragraph meaning.

The purpose of this chapter is to consider inexact "prediction." However, the treatment of inexact prediction will be clearer if exact determination is discussed first.

The Exact Straight-line Relationship. Exact determination can be readily illustrated by the relationship between salary rate and annual earnings. Table 9.1 contains a listing of monthly salary rates and annual incomes for five employees. Once the salary rate for an employee is known, the annual income is fully determined, assuming, of course, that the employee works a full year at the same rate. These data are presented graphically in

TABLE 9.1 Monthly Salary Rate and Annual Income of Five Employees

Employee	Monthly salary rate	Annual income
A	$200	$2400
B	225	2700
C	250	3000
D	300	3600
E	400	4800

Figure 9–1, where each point represents the paired monthly salary rate and annual income for one employee. The graph provides a ready means for ascertaining the annual income of an employee whose monthly salary is some amount other than those given in Table 9.1.

To make a graph like that in Figure 9–1, horizontal and vertical scales for the two variables are drawn on coordinate paper. If no coordinate paper is at hand, a grid may be constructed by drawing horizontal and vertical lines at selected, usually equidistant, points on the two scales. Contrary to the advice given in Chapter

4, these scales do not need to begin at zero. A point for each individual is obtained in the way in which a point was located for a line graph in Chapter 4.

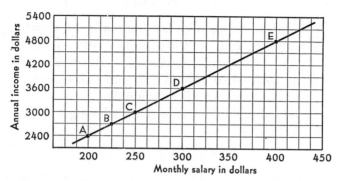

Fig. 9–1 Relation of Annual Income to Monthly Salary Rate for Five Employees, A, B, C, D, and E.

The Formula for an Exact Straight-line Relationship. The relationship of annual salary to monthly rate already shown by table and by graph can be succinctly stated in the word formula:

Annual salary = 12 times monthly rate

To reduce this word formula to an expression more compact, more vivid to the eye, and more easy to manipulate algebraically, we agree to let some letter (say Y) stand for "annual salary" and some other letter (say X) stand for "monthly rate," and write a symbolic formula as

$$Y = 12X$$

The reader may wish to substitute pairs of values from Table 9.1 in this formula. Thus for Employee C, $X = 250$, $Y = 3000$, and $3000 = 12(250)$. Now consider a sixth employee not included in Table 9.1. If $X = 275$, what is Y? $Y = 12(275) = 3300$.

The graph of $Y = 12X$ shown in Figure 9–1 is a straight line. When both variables are of the first degree, the graph of their relationship is a straight line and the relationship is called *linear* or sometimes *rectilinear*. (The terms X and Y are of first degree; X^2, Y^2, and XY are of second degree, X^3, X^2Y, XY^2, and Y^3 are of third degree.) Formulas showing the relationship between variables of degree other than the first will not be considered in this book. The graphs of such relationships are called nonlinear or curvilinear.

To introduce another form of the linear relationship, suppose that each of the five employees listed in Table 9.1 receives a year-end bonus of \$300 in addition to his monthly salary. The annual income Y then becomes

$$Y = 300 + 12X$$

It will be left as an exercise for the reader to develop a table and graph corresponding to the situation just described. This formula contains two variables, X and Y (quantities which may change from individual to individual), and two constants, 12 and 300, which are the same for all individuals.

The general expression for a formula whose graph is a straight line has the form

(9.1) $$Y = a + bX$$

where X and Y are variables changing from individual to individual, and where a and b represent numbers which are constant for any one set of data. Formula (9.1) is a general algebraic expression of the *linear* relationship between two variables.

Independent and Dependent Variables. The usefulness of such a relationship as is expressed in formula (9.1) becomes clear when for one or more individuals the variable Y is unknown and the formula is used to determine the unknown Y from the known X. In obtaining the formula it was necessary to know values of both variables for a group of subjects but, once the relationship has been obtained, it can be used to determine Y for other subjects for whom only the values of X are known. The variable whose values are known is called the *independent variable;* the one whose values are determined from the formula is called the *dependent variable.*

In most practical situations, the logic of the situation makes clear which variable is considered independent and which dependent. Thus the familiar formula $C = 2\pi r$ suggests that the radius of a circle is known or can be obtained by direct measurement, whereas the circumference is to be obtained not by direct measurement but by multiplication of the measured radius. Because $C = 2\pi r$ is an exact relationship, it may be algebraically transformed into the equivalent form $r = \dfrac{C}{2\pi}$. Here the independent and dependent variables have interchanged their roles. The new formula suggests that the circumference of a circle is known or can be readily obtained by direct measurement and the radius is to be ascertained from the circumference, as in obtaining the radius of a circular pipe or cylinder where only external measurement is possible. *When the relationship is inexact, the two variables cannot be thus interchanged algebraically* but a second and distinct relationship is required, as will be discussed in the next chapter.

Inexact Relationship. In statistical work the relationships between two variables are almost never exact. The kind of relationships which are obtained in statistical investigations are well illustrated in the relationship between scores on the arithmetic test and on the midterm test for the data in Table VIII. As in the discussion of exact relationships, the inexact relationship will be described by a table, a graph, and a formula.

The tabular statement of the relationship between scores on arithmetic and scores on the midterm test is provided by the two columns in Table VIII. A comparison of pairs of scores for the same students shows at once that no simple relationship exists between them. For example, students coded 1, 28, and 52 all have the same score on the arithmetic test (33) but have the scores 58, 47, and 62 on the midterm test. These differences may be accounted for by such considerations as that the score on the prognostic test may not reflect accurately the ability of a student, or that students with the same ability may be motivated differently in doing their course work.

The reader may be inclined to ask whether in the midst of such confusion any relationship at all can be found between these two variables. This question will be discussed in some detail.

Bivariate Frequency Distribution. To construct the bivariate frequency distribution shown in Figure 9–2 from the data of Appendix Table VIII, an appropriate step interval is selected for each of the two variables. The step intervals for the independent variable are laid off on a horizontal axis, those for the dependent variable on a vertical axis. A grid is obtained either by placing the axes on coordinate paper or by drawing in the network of horizontal and vertical lines.

Each of the 98 individuals in Table VIII is represented by one tally in Figure 9–2. Thus the student with code number 1 who has arithmetic score $X = 33$ and midterm test score $Y = 58$ is represented by a tally in the cell for which the interval on the horizontal scale is 30–34 and the interval on the vertical scale is 55–59. There are 7 tallies in this cell.

Transferring the data from such a table as VIII to the bivariate distribution is probably the most tedious part of all the procedures described in this and the following chapter, and mistakes in tabulation are easily made. The task is less boring and results are usually more accurate if one person reads while another tabulates. Cardboard guides can be used by both reader and recorder to reduce errors and prevent eyestrain. The reader needs some device to keep his eye from jumping to the wrong row or wrong column

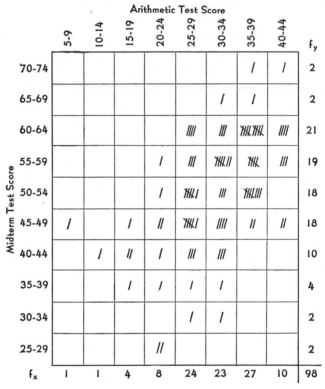

Fig. 9–2 Midterm Test Scores Shown in Relation to Arithmetic Test Scores (98 cases). (Data from Appendix Table VIII.)

on the data sheet, and to keep him from reading the same values twice or omitting others. The recorder will find it an advantage to prepare a strip of cardboard with an exact duplicate of the scale for the midterm test. As the arithmetic score is read, the recorder moves this strip so that the scale appears directly at the left of the appropriate column, with zero point properly aligned. It is a simple matter then to place a tally in the proper cell.

When a tally has been recorded for every individual, the marginal frequencies are obtained by adding across each row and down each column.

The tallies jointly make up a *bivariate frequency distribution*, also called a *scatter diagram* and a *correlation chart*. The set of marginal frequencies at the right of this figure, obtained by adding across the rows, is the frequency distribution for the midterm test scores; and as we are using the letter Y to denote these scores, these frequencies are labeled f_y. The set of frequencies at the bottom of the figure, obtained by adding down the columns, are the frequencies related to intervals of the X scale and so are labeled f_x. Frequencies in the interior of the figure represent the joint occurrence of a particular value of X and a particular value of Y and so could be called f_{xy}.

A cursory examination of the bivariate distribution shows that high scores in the arithmetic test tend to be associated with high scores in the midterm test, and low scores in the arithmetic test with low scores in the midterm. Because of this immediate evidence of relationship, one may speak of the two variables as being co-related or correlated. A measure of correlation will be described in the next chapter.

The Problem in Miniature. Before using the entire 98 cases in a study of the relationship between scores on the two tests, working out that relationship for a very small number of students may serve to clarify principles. Nine students have been chosen. Their code numbers and scores on the two tests have been recorded in the first three columns of Table 9.2. The remainder of that table shows computations based on these scores for the purpose of obtaining a formula to express the manner of estimating midterm test score from the arithmetic score. You should read the ensuing discussion before attempting to follow these computations.

In Figure 9–3 the nine pairs of scores have been plotted as a bivariate distribution. There appears to be a tendency for higher scores on one variable to accompany higher scores on the other, but the relationship is far from close and most people would have no clear conviction as to where to draw the line of relationship. It will be necessary in this case to obtain the formula first and to draw the line of relationship afterward as a graph of that formula.

This line is to be placed in a position which will best fit the nine points. But what is meant by "best fit"? Obviously, no matter where the line is drawn most, if not all, the points will deviate from it to some extent and there will be a discrepancy between the actual midterm score of an individual (which has been denoted Y), and the midterm score estimated by means of this line (which we shall denote $\tilde{Y}$, read variously as " Y tilde," "estimated Y," "predicted Y," or "regression Y"). If the relation

TABLE 9.2 Computation of Regression Equation to Predict Midterm Test Score from Arithmetic Test Score for Nine Cases from the Data in Table VIII

Code number of student	X Arithmetic score	Y Midterm score	X^2	Y^2	XY	$\tilde{Y}$	$Y-\tilde{Y}$	$(Y-\tilde{Y})^2$
10	37	44	1369	1936	1628	55.2	−11.2	125.44
20	17	37	289	1369	629	44.5	−7.5	56.25
30	25	52	625	2704	1300	48.8	3.2	10.24
40	32	58	1024	3364	1856	52.5	5.5	30.25
50	18	47	324	2209	846	45.0	2.0	4.00
60	25	52	625	2704	1300	48.8	3.2	10.24
70	27	50	729	2500	1350	49.9	0.1	.01
80	36	53	1296	2809	1908	54.7	−1.7	2.89
90	36	61	1296	3721	2196	54.7	6.3	39.69
Sum	253	454	7,577	23,316	13,013	454.1	− 0.1	279.01

$$\overline{X} = \frac{253}{9} = 28.1 \qquad b = \frac{9(13,013) - (253)(454)}{9(7,577) - (253)^2} = .539$$

$$\overline{Y} = \frac{454}{9} = 50.4 \qquad a = 50.4 - (.539)(28.1) = 35.3$$

$$\tilde{Y} = 35.3 + .539X$$

were perfect, every point would lie on the line and $Y - \tilde{Y}$ would be zero for every subject. In any reasonably good position of the line, some of these discrepancies will be positive and some negative, and so it is not enough to make the sum of all discrepancies zero. In fact, the sum of discrepancies from the horizontal line through the mean of the Y scale would be zero, yet that line does not represent the trend of the data at all well. The criterion commonly adopted for good fit is to make *the sum of the squares of the discrepancies* $(Y - \tilde{Y})$ *as small as possible*. This is the principle or the method called *least squares*. By it the numbers a and b in the formula

$$\tilde{Y} = a + bX$$

are computed. We are now writing $\tilde{Y}$ instead of Y because the relationship is between the known arithmetic score $(= X)$ and the best estimate which can be made of the midterm score $(= \tilde{Y})$, not the actual midterm score $(= Y)$. By calculus it can be proved that the values of b and a which give the best position of the line — that is, "best" by the criterion stated — can be computed by formulas (9.2) and (9.3).

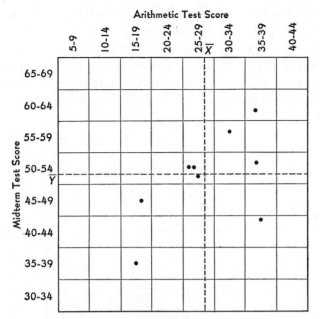

Fig. 9–3 Midterm Test Scores Shown in Relation to Arithmetic Test Scores (9 selected cases). (Dotted lines pass through means of the two variables.)

$$(9.2) \qquad b = \frac{N\Sigma XY - (\Sigma X)(\Sigma Y)}{N\Sigma X^2 - (\Sigma X)^2}$$

$$(9.3) \qquad a = \overline{Y} - b\overline{X}$$

In Table 9.2 the sums of the columns headed X, Y, X^2, and XY furnish the values which must be substituted in formulas (9.2) and (9.3). The result is the formula to predict Y from X:

$$\tilde{Y} = 35.3 + .54X$$

Let us now apply this formula to predict the Y score of the first subject listed in Table 9.2 from his X score. As that X score is 37, we have

$$\tilde{Y} = 35.3 + .54(37) = 55.2$$

The value of $\tilde{Y}$ has been computed for each of the nine subjects in this fashion and the results listed in the column headed $\tilde{Y}$. You should verify enough of these computations to be sure you understand the use of the regression equation.

If you should plot, for each of the nine students, the point representing his X and $\tilde{Y}$ scores, you would have nine points lying on one straight line, and that line would pass through the point whose paired values are $\overline{X}$ and $\overline{Y}$. Therefore, you could locate this line by plotting any two of these points.

Figure 9–4 shows the regression line superimposed on the scatter diagram of Figure 9–3, and also shows for each of the nine subjects the amount $(Y - \tilde{Y})$ by which the regression value was in error. The discrepancy $Y - \tilde{Y}$ is a deviation from the regression

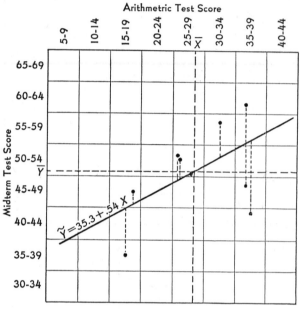

Fig. 9–4 Regression Line $\tilde{Y} = 35.3 + .54X$ and Errors of Estimate for the Nine Cases of Table 9.2.

line sometimes called an *error of estimate*, an *error of prediction*, and sometimes *a residual error*. The reader should check some of these discrepancies and compare them with the corresponding vertical lines in Figure 9–4.

For historical reasons which will be explained on page 137, the line drawn on Figure 9–4 is called a *regression line* and the value of b in the equation is called the *regression coefficient*.

Before leaving Table 9.2 we should take notice of certain relations among its figures:

(a) The sum of predicted values of Y should equal the sum of actual values except for rounding errors. Here we have $\Sigma Y = 454$ and $\Sigma \tilde{Y} = 454.1$.

(b) Because of the relationship just stated, the sum of the errors of estimate should approximate zero. Here we have $\Sigma(Y - \tilde{Y}) = -0.1$.

A General Routine of Computation for the Regression Formula.
The procedures illustrated for the 9 cases will now be applied to
all 98 cases of Table VIII. It is unnecessary to copy down the
scores as in Table 9.2, but sums can be obtained directly on a computing machine. With a wide carriage Monroe, all the sums needed
for the formula can be obtained in a single operation.[1] A method
of getting these same sums from a scatter diagram with or without
a computing machine will be described in the next chapter.

The sums obtained from the raw data of Table VIII have been
entered as Step 1 in Table 9.3. In subsequent steps in that table
the computations are shown in convenient form. The reader
will find it helpful to check these computations.

For the entire set of 98 cases, the regression equation is now
found to be

$$\tilde{Y} = 31.6 + .66X$$

whereas for the 9 selected cases it was

$$\tilde{Y} = 35.3 + .54X$$

The regression coefficient for the 98 scores is .66 and for the 9
selected scores is .54. If the reader should now take another small
sample and carry out the same computations, he will probably
get an equation with constants still different from these. If, for
example, he should use the first nine cases in Table VIII, he would
find $\Sigma X = 316$, $\Sigma Y = 504$, $\Sigma X^2 = 11390$, $\Sigma XY = 17762$, and $\tilde{Y} =
48.1 + .22X$. These differences in the values of the coefficients
of the regression formula illustrate the variation which results
from using different samples. Some aspects of the problem of
sampling variability will be discussed in Chapters 13 through 16.

Checks on Computation. Even when a computing machine is
used, a check on the accuracy of the sums entering into the regression formula is essential. (In the next chapter you will see
that these same sums are used in computing a correlation coefficient.) Recomputing is tedious and not very satisfactory because
a computer may make the same mistake twice. In Table 9.4 there
is illustrated one way of obtaining a foolproof verification of the
correctness of these sums. After $X + Y$ and $X - Y$ are written
down for each individual, the sums and sums of squares can be
readily obtained on a machine. The method would be laborious
for hand work.

---

[1] See Pease, Katharine. *Machine Computation of Elementary Statistics.* New York;
Chartwell House, Inc., 1949.

TABLE 9.3 Steps in the Computation of the Regression Formula with Application to the Data of Table VIII in the Appendix

X = Arithmetic Score, Y = Midterm Test Score, $N = 98$

Step	X	Y	XY
1.	$\Sigma X = 3{,}075$ $\Sigma X^2 = 101{,}581$	$\Sigma Y = 5{,}141$ $\Sigma Y^2 = 278{,}051$	$\Sigma XY = 164{,}694$
2.	$\overline{X} = \dfrac{3{,}075}{98} = 31.38$	$\overline{Y} = \dfrac{5{,}141}{98} = 52.46$	
3.	$N\Sigma X^2 - (\Sigma X)^2$ $= 98(101{,}581) - (3{,}075)^2$ $= 499{,}313$	$N\Sigma Y^2 - (\Sigma Y)^2$ $= 98(278{,}051) - (5{,}141)^2$ $= 819{,}117$	$N\Sigma XY - (\Sigma X)(\Sigma Y)$ $= 98(164{,}694) -$ $(3{,}075)(5{,}141)$ $= 331{,}437$
4.	$s_x^2 = \dfrac{499{,}313}{98(97)}$ $= 52.52$	$s_y^2 = \dfrac{819{,}117}{98(97)}$ $= 86.12$	
5.	$s_x = \sqrt{52.52} = 7.2$	$s_y = \sqrt{86.12} = 9.3$	

6. $$b = \frac{N\Sigma XY - (\Sigma X)(\Sigma Y)}{N\Sigma X^2 - (\Sigma X)^2} = \frac{331{,}437}{499{,}313} = 0.664$$

7. $$a = \overline{Y} - b\overline{X} = 52.46 - 0.64(31.38) = 31.63$$

8. $$\tilde{Y} = 31.63 + 0.664X$$

9. $$\Sigma(Y - \tilde{Y})^2 = \frac{1}{N}\left\{ N\Sigma Y^2 - (\Sigma Y)^2 - \frac{[N\Sigma XY - (\Sigma X)(\Sigma Y)]^2}{N\Sigma X^2 - (\Sigma X)^2} \right\}$$

$$= \frac{1}{98}\left\{ 819{,}117 - \frac{(331{,}437)^2}{499{,}313} \right\} = 6113.4$$

10. $$s_{y.x}^2 = \frac{\Sigma(Y - \tilde{Y})^2}{N - 2} = \frac{6113.4}{96} = 63.68$$

11. $$s_{y.x} = \sqrt{63.68} = 7.977 \quad \text{or} \quad 8$$

The Conditional Distribution of Y for a Given X. In Figure 9–5, the graph of the regression equation has been drawn on the bivariate frequency distribution for the 98 cases, a step which could not be taken until the computations of Table 9.3 were made. Each vertical column contains a frequency distribution of the midterm scores, Y, of a group of students who had arithmetic scores, X, so similar that they fall in the same X interval. For each of

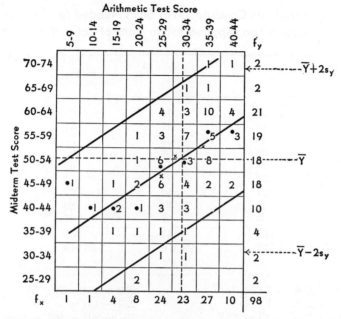

Fig. 9–5 Line of Regression of Midterm Test Score on Arithmetic Score with Parallel Lines at Distance $2s_{y.x}$ Above and Below the Regression Line (98 cases).

• Dots indicate position of column means.

x Crosses indicate means of three sections.

these Y distributions the mean has been marked by a small circle. As you can see, these circles are near the regression line, but some of the vertical columns contain so few cases that one must expect considerable irregularity.

Now try to imagine a chart in which the frequencies are much larger. There will still be a different Y distribution for each value of X, and this is the distribution of Y *on condition* that X has a particular value, or the *conditional distribution* of Y. If N could be made very large, we might expect that the mean of this conditional distribution would come close to $\tilde{Y}$, so that in one sense the regression line tends to overcome irregularities in the column means of a small sample. Therefore, we say that for each given X, $\tilde{Y}$ is the mean of the conditional distribution of Y.

In a great many kinds of data, when N is large, the standard deviations of the various Y distributions are surprisingly similar. Consequently, it seems reasonable to assume that all the Y distributions would have the same standard deviation in a very large sample and to compute this from all the scores in the entire distribution. The common standard deviation thus obtained belongs

TABLE 9.4 Checks on Computation of Sums Needed for Regression and Correlation, Applied to the Data of Table 9.2

Code number	X	Y	$X + Y$	$X - Y$
10	37	44	81	-7
20	17	37	54	-20
30	25	52	77	-27
40	32	58	90	-26
50	18	47	65	-29
60	25	52	77	-27
70	27	50	77	-23
80	36	53	89	-17
90	36	61	97	-25
Sum	253	454	707	-201
Sum of squares	7,577	23,316	56,919	4,867

$\Sigma X + \Sigma Y = \Sigma(X + Y)$	$253 + 454 = 707$
$\Sigma X - \Sigma Y = \Sigma(X - Y)$	$253 - 454 = -201$
$\Sigma(X + Y) + \Sigma(X - Y) = 2\Sigma X$	$707 - 201 = 506 = 2(253)$
$\Sigma(X + Y) - \Sigma(X - Y) = 2\Sigma Y$	$707 + 201 = 908 = 2(454)$
$\Sigma(X + Y)^2 + \Sigma(X - Y)^2 = 2(\Sigma X^2 + \Sigma Y^2)$	$56,919 + 4,867 = 61,786$ and $2(7,577 + 23,316) = 61,786$
$\Sigma(X + Y)^2 - \Sigma(X - Y)^2 = 4\Sigma XY$	$56,919 - 4,867 = 52,052$ $4(13,013) = 52,052$
$\Sigma(X + Y)^2 = \Sigma X^2 + 2\Sigma XY + \Sigma Y^2$	$56,919 = 7,577 + 23,316 + 2(13,013)$

equally to the Y distribution for each separate X, is the standard deviation of the conditional distribution of Y, and is equal to

$$(9.4) \qquad s_{y.x} = \sqrt{\frac{\Sigma(Y - \tilde{Y})^2}{N - 2}}$$

The symbol $s_{y.x}$ is read "s sub y point x" or "s y point x." This value could be obtained by computing $\tilde{Y}$ for each case in the distribution and subtracting it from Y but is much more easily obtained by first computing

$$(9.5) \quad \Sigma(Y - \tilde{Y})^2 = \frac{1}{N}\left\{ N\Sigma Y^2 - (\Sigma Y)^2 - \frac{[N\Sigma XY - (\Sigma X)(\Sigma Y)]^2}{N\Sigma X^2 - (\Sigma X)^2} \right\}$$

and substituting the result in (9.4).

Because $s_{y.x}$ measures the extent to which actual scores depart from the regression line, this standard deviation is a measure of the errors one would make in estimating or predicting the score of an individual by use of $\tilde{Y}$. For this reason $s_{y \cdot x}$ is called the *standard error of estimate*, or the *standard error of prediction*.

On Figure 9–5, two lines have been drawn parallel to the regression line, one at a distance of $2s_{y \cdot x}$ above it and one at a distance of $2s_{y \cdot x}$ below it. Note that these lines mark out a band within which nearly all the cases are contained.

Variation about the Regression Line. Computations near the end of Table 9.3 show the standard error of estimate to be $s_{y \cdot x} = 8.0$, while the standard deviation of Y had already been found as $s_y = 9.3$. Common sense suggests that because the regression line describes the trend of the Y scores more closely than the mean does, the variation of scores around the regression line should be less than the variation of those same scores about the general mean of the table. In fact, the sum of the squares of the deviations of scores from the mean, $\Sigma(Y - \overline{Y})^2$ is made up of two parts, one of which is the sum of the squares of the deviations of scores from the regression line, $\Sigma(Y - \tilde{Y})^2$ and the other is the sum of the squares of the deviations of regression values from the mean, $\Sigma(\tilde{Y} - \overline{Y})^2$. In symbols,

(9.6) $$\Sigma(Y - \overline{Y})^2 = \Sigma(Y - \tilde{Y})^2 + \Sigma(\tilde{Y} - \overline{Y})^2$$

To verify this relation, return now to Table 9.2. Compute $\Sigma(Y - \overline{Y})^2 = \Sigma Y^2 - \dfrac{(\Sigma Y)^2}{N} = 414.2$. Compute $\Sigma(\tilde{Y} - \overline{Y})^2$ by subtracting $\overline{Y} = 50.4$ from each of the 9 values of $\tilde{Y}$, squaring the remainders and summing. The result is 134.8. We have already found that $\Sigma(Y - \overline{Y})^2 = 414.2$ and $\Sigma(Y - \tilde{Y})^2 = 279.0$. Hence we have $134.8 + 279.0 = 413.8$ which is very close to 414.2. Rounding errors will usually prevent the verification from being perfect.

By formula (9.6), $\Sigma(Y - \overline{Y})^2$ can never be *less than* $\Sigma(Y - \tilde{Y})^2$.

Gain of Information about Y from Knowledge of X. In order to ascertain what information about Y scores of individuals is provided by information about their X scores, consider first the situation when knowledge of X scores is not available. In this situation, we find from Table 9.3 that the mean of the Y distribution is 52.46 and the standard deviation is 9.3. Hence, the point two standard deviations below the mean is 33.86 and the point two standard deviations above the mean is 71.06.

Let us consider now certain of the conditional distributions — that is, the distributions in the columns. For $X = 10$, $\tilde{Y}$ is 38.2 and $s_{y \cdot x}$ is 8.0. Hence $\tilde{Y} - 2s_{y \cdot x} = 22.2$ and $\tilde{Y} + 2s_{y \cdot x} = 54.2$. Therefore, in general, for students for whom the arithmetic score is 10, nearly all the midterm scores would presumably be below 54.2, a score only slightly higher than the mean score for the total group.

Consider now the conditional distribution for $X = 40$. Here $\tilde{Y} = 58.2$ and so $\tilde{Y} - 2s_{y \cdot x} = 42.2$ and $\tilde{Y} + 2s_{y \cdot x} = 74.2$. We would, therefore, expect nearly all students for whom the arithmetic score is 40 to be above the mean of the total group. In addition, the comparison of the distribution for $X = 10$ and for $X = 40$ suggests that the latter is so much higher than the former that groups having these X scores differ greatly.

These considerations show that knowledge of X provides much more information than would be available without it. Knowledge of the X scores of individuals is helpful in making selections for employment, or for school, when the goal is high achievement on certain Y scores.

Applications of the Regression Formula. The concept of conditional distribution of Y for a given X can now be used in the problem of estimation or prediction which was raised at the beginning of this chapter. The problem raised there was, "Given a value of X for an individual, what is the best estimate of Y for the same individual?"

The concept of conditional distribution states that $\tilde{Y}$ for a given X is the best estimate of this Y mean of individuals with that same value of X. For this reason it is a best estimate of the Y score of an individual with given X.

The concept of conditional distribution is useful beyond mere estimation since it provides a method of placing an individual with respect to an average, or expectation. Thus an individual with a given X who scores higher than the corresponding $\tilde{Y}$ exceeds his expectation, and he falls below his expectation if his score is below the appropriate $\tilde{Y}$.

To illustrate these concepts consider the regression of midterm scores on scores in arithmetic which was computed in Table 9.3 as $\tilde{Y} = 31.6 + .66X$. Suppose an individual has an X score of 33, as is the case of Student 1 in Appendix table VIII. By the regression formula the best estimate of the corresponding Y score is 53.4. Since his actual score was 58, he did better than he might have been expected to do in view of his mathematical ability.

A similar analysis shows that Student 2 performed more poorly than might have been expected.

Let us now apply the regression formula to the study of the groups of students in sections I, II, and III. For each of these groups we can compute the mean of the arithmetic test scores. Call this mean $\overline{X}_i$. From $\overline{X}_i$ a mean of estimated values of Y — namely, $\overline{\overline{Y}}_i$ — can be computed by the formula

(9.7) $$\overline{\overline{Y}}_i = a + b\overline{X}_i$$

a and b having the values already computed in the usual way. In Table 9.5 are shown the means on the arithmetic test, the means of estimated midterm scores, and, for comparison, the means of actual midterm scores. The closeness with which the means of

TABLE 9.5 Means of Arithmetic Test Scores, Midterm Test Scores, and Estimated Midterm Test Scores for Students in Sections I, II, and III

$$\overline{\overline{Y}} = 31.6 + .66\overline{X}$$

Student group	Mean of arithmetic test scores X	Mean of estimated midterm test scores $\overline{\overline{Y}}$	Mean of actual midterm test scores Y
Section I	35.85	55.26	55.05
Section II	30.07	51.44	52.78
Section III	26.32	49.0	48.18
All Students	31.38	52.3	52.46

estimated scores agree with means of actual scores is impressive. This approximation is far greater than for individuals. One might conclude, therefore, that the groups in the three sections performed on the midterm test very nearly in accordance with relative ability as shown on the arithmetic test. This agreement between means of expected scores and means of actual scores is shown also in Figure 9–5, where means of actual scores are plotted as small crosses.

Graphic Representation of the Regression Coefficient. The regression coefficient b, together with the two means $\overline{X}$ and $\overline{Y}$, fully determine the line of regression. Geometrically, b is the *slope* of the line of regression. If we take any two points on the line of regression, draw a horizontal line through the lower and a vertical line through the upper point, and continue these lines until they meet, a right triangle will be formed. The ratio of the vertical segment to the horizontal is the *slope of the line* and is b.

(9.8) $$b = \frac{\text{vertical segment}}{\text{horizontal segment}} = \frac{v}{h}$$

Figure 9–6 shows two regression lines and two such triangles drawn on each. For the left-hand figure, both h and v are considered positive, so b is positive and the line has *positive slope*. When b is positive, the regression line is directed in a general southwest to northeast direction. For the right-hand figure, v is considered

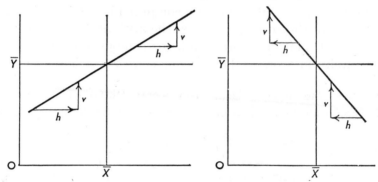

Fig. 9–6 Geometric Representation of the Slope of a Regression Line, $b = \dfrac{v}{h}$.

positive and h negative, so the quotient v/h is negative and the line has *negative slope*. When b is negative, the regression line has a general northwest to southeast direction. Readers who are unfamiliar with directed lines may find help in Chapter 8 of Walker, *Mathematics Essential for Elementary Statistics*. A further discussion of the slope of a line is found in Chapter 10 of the same book.

The Assumption of Linearity. The discussion in this chapter has restricted itself to fitting a straight line to a set of data and the reader is no doubt thinking of situations in which the trend is not linear. The graphs in Figure 9–7 are interesting in this respect. These curves were fitted by Henry A. Ruger to data originally collected by Sir Francis Galton, and show for about 7000 adult males the way in which certain physical measures change with age. Each of the little black dots shows the mean value of the measure for a group of men of the specified age. Consider the first of these, showing the trend of visual acuity. Apparently if we had a group with age range from about 20 to about 40 years, the regression would be nearly linear and with a slightly negative slope indicating a slow decrease in visual acuity with advancing age. But if the age range were from about 20 to 80 years, no straight line would fit the data very well.

A discussion of nonlinear curves is beyond the scope of this book. A more or less intuitive decision as to the appropriateness of fitting a straight line can be made from a scatter diagram in which there has been some grouping. If the means of the columns cluster about a straight line as they do in Figure 9–5, then a linear relationship may be presumed and a straight line should be fitted.

Origin of the Term "Regression." Most people think "regression equation" and "regression coefficient" rather queer terms unless they know the peculiar situation in which they were first used. Francis Galton, being profoundly impressed by *Origin of the Species* which his cousin Charles Darwin published in 1859, set himself to explore various aspects of heredity. In the process he gathered data on the stature of parents and their adult offspring and plotted a bivariate frequency distribution in which each entry represented one family, one axis being scaled for the average height of the two parents and the other for the average height of all the adult offspring. As might be anticipated, this chart showed clearly that taller parents tended to have taller children than did shorter parents. However, Galton also noted the surprising result that the children of very tall parents were, on the average, not quite so tall as their parents, while the children of very short parents were, on the average, not quite so short as their parents. In other words, extreme parents have children more mediocre than themselves. What is it, pondered Galton, which is dragging the human race back toward mediocrity? He commented that, "However paradoxical it may appear at first, it is theoretically a necessary fact, and one that is clearly confirmed by observation, that the stature of the adult offspring must on the whole, be more *mediocre* than the stature of the parents; that is to say, more near the *M* [the median] of the general population." In 1885 Galton published his famous paper on "Regression toward Mediocrity in Hereditary Stature" and introduced the term *lines of regression*.[1] The term still holds.

Not only is historical interest and clarification of meaning to be found in Galton's use of the term regression but there is also an important corrective for a certain kind of loose thinking. People

---

[1] For further discussion, see the following references: Francis Galton, *Memories of My Life*, London: 1908. Karl Pearson, "Notes on the history of correlation," *Biometrika*, **13** (1920), 25–45; *The Life, Letters and Labours of Francis Galton*, 3 vols., Cambridge University Press, 1914, 1924. Helen M. Walker, *Studies in the History of Statistical Method*, The Williams and Wilkins Co., 1929. The original works by Francis Galton are: "Regression towards mediocrity in hereditary stature," *Journal of the Anthropological Institute*, **15** (1885–86), 246–263; "Family likeness in stature," *Proceedings of the Royal Society*, **40** (1886), 42–63; "Co-relations and their measurement, chiefly from anthropological data," *Proceedings of the Royal Society*, **45** (1880), 135–145; and *Natural Inheritance*, 1889.

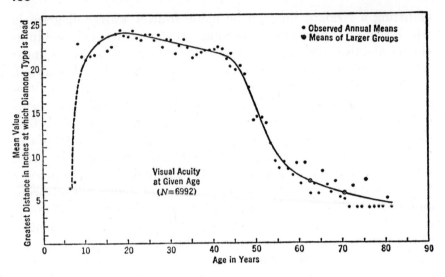

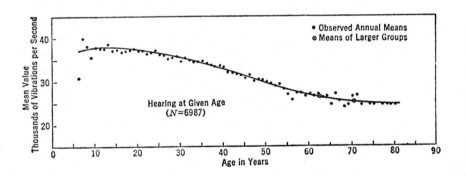

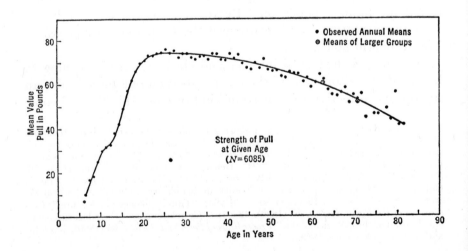

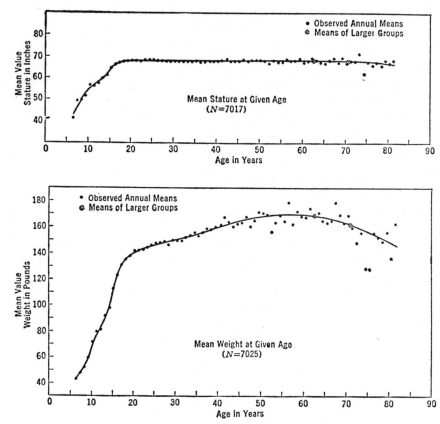

Fig. 9–7 Curvilinear Regression Curves of Various Physical Characters on Age for Males. (From H. A. Ruger, and B. Stoessiger, "On the growth curves of certain characters in man (males)," *Annals of Eugenics*, II, April, 1927, 76–110.)

are very prone to expect those who excel in one trait to excel in all others, whereas a proper understanding of the concept of regression would help them to be more realistic. There is, let us recognize, a tendency for high ability in reading to be associated with a high intelligence quotient. Therefore, if we select a group of children with high IQ, they will on the average read better than children with lower IQ, but their reading will not on the average exceed the mean reading score of their group by as many standard deviations as their intelligence quotients exceed the mean intelligence quotient of their group. This is an important lesson which many teachers fail to comprehend. And failing, they set unrealistic goals for their pupils. A clearer understanding of the concept of regression would make wiser teachers.

Routine for Computing Regression from a Scatter Diagram. This topic will be considered in the following chapter.

EXERCISE 9.1

1. Examine each of the curves in Figure 9–7 and describe relationships which seem to you to be nearly linear, stating for each the age range over which linearity appears to hold. Describe situations in which a relationship appears not to be linear. Interpret what you see in terms of the way physical change appears to be related to increasing age. Do you find any variable which cannot be estimated from age?

2. (a) From the data of Table VIII, the student with code number 30 has the scores $X = 25$, $Y = 52$. Is his Y value above or below what you would estimate by the regression equation $\tilde{Y} = 31.6 + .66X$? By how much?

    (b) Answer the same questions for student number 68 for whom $X = 39$ and $Y = 44$.

3. Is there any fallacy in the comment that the general level of intelligence appears to be rising because in several families where the parents are of very low intelligence the children are considerably brighter than their parents?

10

Correlation

In the previous chapter, the relationship between two variables was studied from the point of view of the line of regression and the variation about this line. In the present chapter, this relationship will be considered by use of the concept of the correlation coefficient. This coefficient can be viewed on one hand as providing a measure of the precision with which prediction is achieved by use of the line of regression, and on the other hand, as providing a measure of the mutuality of relationship between two variables.

The Correlation Coefficient. In the preceding chapter, prediction was achieved by means of the regression equation. When all actual values are on the regression line, prediction is exact and the relation between the two variables is perfect. We shall presently see that in such situations the correlation coefficient is either +1 or −1. When actual values are not identical with regression estimates, the prediction is not precise and the relation between the variables is not perfect. In such situations, the correlation coefficient is between −1 and +1.

We have seen in the preceding chapter that the degree of precision in estimating the variable Y from the variable X depends upon the sum of the squares of the residual errors, namely

$$\Sigma(Y - \tilde{Y})^2$$

However, this sum of squares cannot be used as a measure of the precision of estimate because its value depends not only on the closeness of the relationship of X and Y but also on the variability of Y and on the number of cases involved. To obtain a measure which would be free of this dependence on N and on s_y, we might divide $\Sigma(Y - \tilde{Y})^2$ by $\Sigma(Y - \overline{Y})^2$. The ratio

$$\frac{\Sigma(Y - \tilde{Y})^2}{\Sigma(Y - \overline{Y})^2}$$

is zero when prediction is exact, for then every $Y - \tilde{Y}$ is zero and so the numerator is zero. When knowledge of X contributes no information about Y, the numerator of the ratio is equal to the denominator and the value of the ratio is one. It should be noted that the numerator represents the sum of squares of the deviations of Y values from the regression line, while the denominator represents the sum of squares of deviations from the mean; and the numerator will *never* be larger than the denominator.

This ratio could serve as a measure of precision of regression estimates but, for reasons which are partly historical, the closely related coefficient of correlation is more commonly used for that purpose. The correlation coefficient, commonly denoted r, will now be defined by four algebraically equivalent formulas, each of which serves to reveal certain important aspects of this measure.

First, a formula which relates r to the sum of squares of residuals is

(10.1a) $$r^2 = 1 - \frac{\Sigma(Y - \tilde{Y})^2}{\Sigma(Y - \overline{Y})^2}$$

From this formula it can be seen at once that, when prediction is exact, $r^2 = 1$ because the ratio

$$\frac{\Sigma(Y - \tilde{Y})^2}{\Sigma(Y - \overline{Y})^2}$$

is 0; and when prediction fails entirely, $r^2 = 0$ because the ratio is 1. In other words, $r^2 = 0$ means no correlation and $r^2 = 1$ means perfect correlation. It can also be seen that r^2 can never be larger than 1 because the ratio cannot be negative. Thus r cannot be numerically larger than 1 but can have values between -1 and $+1$. This formula gives no clue as to whether correlation is positive or negative. It does not provide a convenient pattern of computation.

As correlation is a mutual relationship between two variables, you are probably thinking that if X had been predicted from Y, r should also be related to the precision of that prediction. You are correct, and the formula

(10.1b) $$r^2 = 1 - \frac{\Sigma(X - \tilde{X})^2}{\Sigma(X - \overline{X})^2}$$

is algebraically identical with (10.1a).

The best-known formula for the correlation coefficient is

(10.2a) $$r = \frac{\Sigma(X - \overline{X})(Y - \overline{Y})}{\sqrt{\Sigma(X - \overline{X})^2 \Sigma(Y - \overline{Y})^2}}$$

which becomes more vivid to the eye and consequently easier to remember when x and y are substituted for $X - \overline{X}$ and $Y - \overline{Y}$. Then

(10.2b) $$r = \frac{\Sigma xy}{\sqrt{\Sigma x^2 \Sigma y^2}}$$

Obviously, this formula has the same numerator as the formula for the regression coefficient. The denominator for r is positive and the denominator for b is positive and therefore r and b must have the same sign. When the regression line has positive slope, r and b are both positive, and there is a tendency for large values of the two variables to occur together and for small values to occur together. When the regression line has negative slope, r and b are both negative and there is a tendency for large values of one variable to occur in connection with small values of the other.

Neither formula (10.2a) nor formula (10.2b) provides a convenient routine for computation. The formula which provides the *easiest routine for computation* is considerably longer and looks more complicated than the easily remembered formula (10.2b). This formula can be derived from formula (10.2) by easy algebraic manipulation:

(10.3a) $$r = \frac{N\Sigma XY - (\Sigma X)(\Sigma Y)}{\sqrt{\{N\Sigma X^2 - (\Sigma X)^2\}\{N\Sigma Y^2 - (\Sigma Y)^2\}}}$$

The relation of this formula to formula (9.2) for b is obvious. It will be used to provide the computational pattern in later sections of this chapter.

Formula (10.3a) may be written in terms of coded deviations (x' and y') from an arbitrary origin instead of gross scores (X and Y), the general pattern of the formula remaining unchanged. The formula is then written as

(10.3b) $$r = \frac{N\Sigma f_{xy}x'y' - (\Sigma f_x x')(\Sigma f_y y')}{\sqrt{\{N\Sigma f_x(x')^2 - (\Sigma f_x x')^2\}\{N\Sigma f_y(y')^2 - (\Sigma f_y y')^2\}}}$$

This is the formula employed in the computational routine of Table 10.1 and Figure 10–1. The symbols used in this formula will be defined in the discussion of the computational procedure.

A fourth formula equivalent to those already presented shows the relationship between the correlation and regression coefficients:

$$(10.4a) \qquad\qquad r = b\,\frac{s_x}{s_y}$$

Since s_y and s_x are both positive, the formula shows once more that r and b must have the same sign. A formula equivalent to formula (10.4a) is

$$(10.4b) \qquad\qquad b = r\,\frac{s_y}{s_x}$$

When the two variables have equal variability so $s_y = s_x$, the correlation coefficient r is identical with the regression coefficient b. This was the situation in Francis Galton's study of hereditary stature. He used the letter r for the regression coefficient, but later it became almost universally used for the correlation coefficient instead of for the regression coefficient. We have already seen that r cannot be numerically larger than 1. There is, however, no such limitation on the size of b. If, for example, $r = .8$, $s_x = 3$ and $s_y = 12$, b would be 3.2.

Computation of the Correlation Coefficient without Plotting. The computation of the correlation coefficient is very similar to that of the regression coefficient and the two are usually obtained together. For a first illustration, let us turn to the data of Table 9.2 on page 126, where we already have $\Sigma(Y - \tilde{Y})^2 = 279.01$ and

$$\Sigma(Y - \overline{Y})^2 = 23{,}316 - \frac{(454)^2}{9} = 414.22. \text{ Therefore, by formula (10.1)}$$

$$r^2 = 1 - \frac{279.01}{414.22} = .326$$

and r is either $\sqrt{.326} = +.571$ or $-\sqrt{.326} = -.571$. Whether r is positive or negative we cannot tell from formula (10.1).

From Table 9.2 we also know that $N = 9$, $\Sigma XY = 13{,}013$, $\Sigma X = 253$, $\Sigma Y = 454$, $\Sigma X^2 = 7{,}577$, and $\Sigma Y^2 = 23{,}316$, and therefore by formula (10.3) we have

$$r = \frac{9(13{,}013) - (253)(454)}{\sqrt{[9(7{,}577) - (253)^2][9(23{,}316) - (454)^2]}} = .571$$

Although the two procedures are algebraically identical, formula (10.3) is better to use because it involves easier computation and less rounding error and because it indicates whether r is positive or negative.

To compute the correlation coefficient between midterm test scores and arithmetic test scores for all 98 cases, work in Table 9.3 on page 130 is extended to obtain the following values:

$$N\Sigma XY - (\Sigma X)(\Sigma Y) = 331,437$$

$$[N\Sigma X^2 - (\Sigma X)^2][N\Sigma Y^2 - (\Sigma Y)^2] = (499,313)(819,117)$$
$$= 408,995,766,521$$

$$\sqrt{[N\Sigma X^2 - (\Sigma X)^2][N\Sigma Y^2 - (\Sigma Y)^2]} = \sqrt{408,995,766,521} = 639,526$$

$$r = \frac{N\Sigma XY - (\Sigma X)(\Sigma Y)}{\sqrt{[N\Sigma X^2 - (\Sigma X)^2][N\Sigma Y^2 - (\Sigma Y)^2]}} = \frac{331,437}{639,526} = .518$$

The Second Line of Regression. In Chapter 9 and in the earlier parts of this chapter, regression has been treated as though there was only one regression line and Y was always estimated from X. In many situations only one prediction makes much sense. For example, it is often important to estimate performance on a job from score on an aptitude test, but no one wants to estimate aptitude score from job performance. However, in other situations the mutuality of relation is such that it is just as important to be able to predict X from Y as to predict Y from X. Suppose, for example, that after the data for Appendix Table IX have been analyzed, two new pupils appear. One of them has taken only the arithmetic computation test and the teacher wants to obtain an estimate of his score in arithmetic reasoning by a regression equation. The second has taken only the arithmetic reasoning test and a regression equation is needed to estimate what his arithmetic computation score would have been if he had taken that test also. There is nothing whatever in this situation to suggest that one regression equation is more important or more meaningful than the other.

The equation $\tilde{Y} = a + bX$, which we have been using, will now be changed slightly by attaching a subscript to each of the constants, making it

(10.5a) $$\tilde{Y} = a_{yx} + b_{yx}X$$

The analogous equation to estimate X from Y is

(10.5b) $$\tilde{X} = a_{xy} + b_{xy}Y$$

The order of letters in the subscript is the same as the order of variables in the equation. The first letter in the subscript names the variable to be estimated; the second letter in the subscript names the variable by means of which the estimation is made.

TABLE 10.1 Steps in the Computation of Correlation and Regression Coefficients from a Scatter Diagram

Step	Procedure
1	Plot the data on a bivariate frequency chart. This will ordinarily be done by tallies as in Figure 9–2 on page 124, and the result will be confusing to work from. If the number of cases is at all large, the tallies should be replaced by numerals before the next steps are taken. The symbol f_{xy} is used to represent the number of cases in a cell at the intersection of a row and a column.
2	Add across each horizontal row to obtain the marginal frequency for that row and record the result at the right in a column labeled f_y. Add down each vertical column to obtain the marginal frequency for that column and record the result below the chart in the row labeled f_x. Find Σf_y and Σf_x and verify that they are equal. Record that value as N. In Figure 10–1, $N = 98$.
3	In the column labeled y', record an arbitrary set of coded scores for the Y intervals. In the row headed x', record an arbitrary set of coded scores for the X intervals. If you are using a machine, it is convenient to place the arbitrary origin (coded 0) in the lowest interval in which a frequency occurs as in Figure 10–1, because then all deviation values will be positive. When working by hand, some computers prefer to place the arbitrary origin nearer the center of the distribution in order to have smaller numbers to work with. Then special attention must be paid to signs.
4	Compute $\Sigma f_y y'$ and $\Sigma f_y (y')^2$ exactly as you obtained similar values when computing a standard deviation. In Figure 10–1, these are 497 and 2849, respectively, and for ease of identification have been designated A and B. Turn the table around and compute $\Sigma f_x x'$ and $\Sigma f_x (x')^2$ in the same way. In Figure 10–1, these are 479 and 2551, respectively, and can be identified as C and E.
5	For each row separately, compute $\Sigma f_{xy} x'$ and enter the result in the column headed $\Sigma x'$. For example, the computation for the third row from the top is $4(4) + 3(5) + 10(6) + 4(7) = 119$. The sum of that column must agree with the $\Sigma f_x x'$ obtained in step 4 and will thus furnish a check on the correctness of the preceding step. In the example, the sum of this column is 479 and has been marked C to show its relation to the sum of the row C. In practice it is helpful to make a small movable scale exactly like the fixed horizontal scale of the correlation chart, with code numbers inserted, and to place this scale immediately below each row so you can easily multiply each f_{xy} by the corresponding x' and sum the products. Turn the table around and, in similar manner, find $\Sigma f_{xy} y'$ for each column and enter the results below the table in the row headed $\Sigma y'$. The sum of entries in this row must be identical with that previously obtained for $\Sigma f_y y'$. In the example, both sums are 497.
6	In the column $\Sigma x'$, multiply each entry by the corresponding y' and record in the final column of the table headed $y' \Sigma x'$. The first entry in the column $\Sigma x'$ is 13, actually obtained as $1(6) + 1(7)$. When this is multiplied by $y' = 9$, we have $9(13) = 117$ and $1(6)(9) + 1(7)(9) = 117$, which is the value of $\Sigma f_{xy} x' y'$ for the two cases in the top row of the table. The sum of all the entries in this final column will be $\Sigma f_{xy} x' y'$ for the entire table. Turn the table around. Multiply each entry in the row $\Sigma y'$ by the corresponding x' and enter in the final row of the table. The sum of the entries in this row will also be $\Sigma f_{xy} x' y'$ and thus provides a complete check on that part of the computation. In the example, these two numbers have been labeled D.
7	Complete the computation of $\overline{X}$, $\overline{Y}$, s_x, s_y, r, b_{yx} or b_{xy} by inserting the obtained sums into the appropriate formulas.

The regression coefficient b_{yx} is already familiar, but its formula will be repeated here in order that the similarity of form of b_{yx} and b_{xy} may be recognized:

$$(10.6a) \qquad b_{yx} = \frac{N\Sigma XY - (\Sigma X)(\Sigma Y)}{N\Sigma X^2 - (\Sigma X)^2}$$

(10.6b) $$b_{xy} = \frac{N\Sigma XY - (\Sigma X)(\Sigma Y)}{N\Sigma Y^2 - (\Sigma Y)^2}$$

Note that the two numerators are identical with each other and with the numerator of r. Compare the two denominators, and note that the square root of their product is the denominator of r.

The value of a_{yx} is already familiar. Note its relation to a_{xy} in the formulas

(10.7) $$a_{yx} = \bar{Y} - b_{yx}\bar{X} \quad \text{and} \quad a_{xy} = \bar{X} - b_{xy}\bar{Y}$$

Arithmetic Score

Midterm Score	5-9	10-14	15-19	20-24	25-29	30-34	35-39	40-44	f_y	y'	$f_y y'$	$f_y(y')^2$	$\Sigma x'$	$y'\Sigma x'$
70-74							1	1	2	9	18	162	13	117
65-69						1	1		2	8	16	128	11	88
60-64					4	3	10	4	21	7	147	1029	119	833
55-59				1	3	7	5	3	19	6	114	684	101	606
50-54				1	6	3	8		18	5	90	450	90	450
45-49	1		1	2	6	4	2	2	18	4	72	288	78	312
40-44		1	2		1	3	3		10	3	30	90	42	126
35-39				1	1	1	1		4	2	8	16	14	28
30-34					1	1			2	1	2	2	7	7
25-29			2						2	0	0	0	4	0
f_x	–	–	6	6	22	22	30	10	98		497 A	2849 B	479 C	2567 D
x'	0	1	2	3	4	5	6	7						
$f_x x'$	0	1	12	18	88	110	180	70	479 C					
$f_x(x')^2$	0	1	24	54	352	550	1080	490	2551 E					
$\Sigma y'$	4	3	12	22	106	113	174	63	497 A					
$x'\Sigma y'$	0	3	24	66	424	565	1044	441	2567 D					

$\bar{Y} = 27 + 5(\frac{497}{98}) = 52.36$

$\bar{X} = 7 + 5(\frac{479}{98}) = 31.44$

$s_y^2 = 84.66 \qquad s_y = 9.2$

$s_x^2 = 54.06 \qquad s_x = 7.4$

$b_{yx} = \frac{5}{5} \cdot \frac{13,503}{20,557} = .66$

$b_{xy} = \frac{5}{5} \cdot \frac{13,503}{32,193} = .42$

$N\Sigma xy = 98(2567) - (497)(479) = 13,503$

$N\Sigma y^2 = 98(2849) - (497)^2 = 32,193$

$N\Sigma x^2 = 98(2551) - (479)^2 = 20,557$

$(32,193)(20,557) = 661,791,501$

$r = \frac{13,503}{\sqrt{661,791,501}} = \frac{13,503}{25,725} = .53$

Fig. 10–1. Computation from a Scatter Diagram.

Computation of the Correlation and Regression Coefficients from a Scatter Diagram. In the previous chapter, we considered one method for obtaining the sums of squares and sums of products needed in the regression formula, and these same sums are the values needed in the correlation formula. The method described there is convenient to use when data are given in a list such as the lists of Appendix Tables VIII and IX and when a computing machine is available. If no machine is at hand and N is large, that method would be very time consuming. It would be difficult to use when data are presented in a scatter diagram such as that of Figure 10–1. We shall now consider a method of computation more appropriate for data displayed in a scatter diagram. This method provides a complete check on computation of ΣX, ΣY, and ΣXY but does not check the computation of ΣX^2 and ΣY^2.

Figure 10–1 shows a computation for the correlation coefficient between midterm test scores (Y) of 98 students in a first course in statistical method and scores on an arithmetic test taken at the beginning of the term. Table 10.1 describes in words the steps in that process. You should examine the two tables together, identifying in Figure 10–1 the outcome of each step described in Table 10.1.

In Figure 10–1 it happens that $i_x = i_y$. Usually these two step intervals are not equal and care must be taken to multiply by the proper numbers in computing regression coefficients. A summary of computation formulas using the letters A, B, C, D, and E to represent the results of specific operations performed in Figure 10–1 may be helpful.

$$(10.8) \qquad s_x = i_x \sqrt{\frac{NE - C^2}{N(N-1)}}$$

$$(10.9) \qquad s_y = i_y \sqrt{\frac{NB - A^2}{N(N-1)}}$$

$$(10.10) \qquad r = \frac{ND - AC}{\sqrt{(NE - C^2)(NB - A^2)}}$$

$$(10.11) \qquad b_{yx} = \frac{i_y}{i_x} \cdot \frac{ND - AC}{NE - C^2}$$

$$(10.12) \qquad b_{xy} = \frac{i_x}{i_y} \cdot \frac{ND - AC}{NB - A^2}$$

EXERCISE 10.1

1. Using the bivariate distribution of Figure 10–1, place the arbitrary origins at $A'_x = 27$ and $A'_y = 57$ and verify the following:

$$\Sigma f_x x' = 87 \qquad\qquad \Sigma f_y y' = -91 \qquad\qquad \Sigma f_{xy} x' y' = 57$$
$$\Sigma f_x (x')^2 = 287 \qquad\qquad \Sigma f_y (y')^2 = 413$$

Complete the computations until you obtain the same values of r and b_{yx} as are found in Figure 10–1.

2. With the same frequency distribution and with arbitrary origins at $A'_x = 32$ and $A'_y = 62$, carry out the same computations.

3. Verify the values of r indicated below Figures 10–2 to 10–7.

4. Find r and both regression equations if preliminary computations have yielded the following results:

$$N = 250 \qquad\qquad \Sigma x' = 160$$
$$A_x' = 15 \qquad\qquad \Sigma y' = -125$$
$$A_y' = 50 \qquad\qquad \Sigma (x')^2 = 812$$
$$i_x = 3 \qquad\qquad \Sigma (y')^2 = 914$$
$$i_y = 5 \qquad\qquad \Sigma x' y' = -34$$

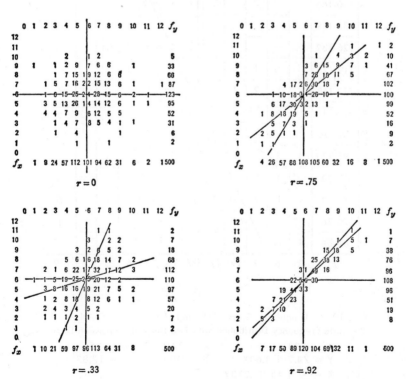

Fig. 10–2 Scatter Diagrams and Regression Lines for Four Distributions with Different Sizes of r.

Scatter Diagrams Illustrating Various Values of the Correlation Coefficient. No one can judge the size of a correlation coefficient precisely from the visual appearance of a scatter diagram, but persons who work extensively in correlational material acquire a background of experience which enables them to make a rough estimate. To help you acquire a little experience with correlations of various sizes, Figures 10–2 to 10–7 have been drawn up.

Look first at Figure 10–2 in which there are four distributions with correlation coefficients of 0, .33, .75, and .92. These are drawn from artificial data, primarily to show the positions of the two regression lines which are identical with the lines of the means when $r = 0$ and draw closer and closer together as r increases.

Figure 10–3 shows the joint distribution of language score and intelligence quotient for the 109 cases in Appendix Table IX.

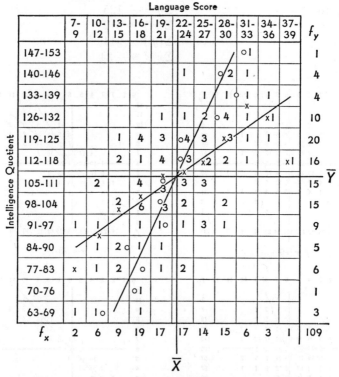

Language Score

Intelligence Quotient	7-9	10-12	13-15	16-18	19-21	22-24	25-27	28-30	31-33	34-36	37-39	f_y
147-153									o1			1
140-146						1		o2	1			4
133-139							1	1 o 1	1	1		4
126-132					1	1	2	o4	1	x1		10
119-125			1	4	3	o4	3	x3	1	1		20
112-118			2	1	4	o3	x2	2	1		x1	16
105-111		2		4	o3	3	3					15
98-104			2	x6	o3	2		2				15
91-97	1	1		1	1o	1	3	1				9
84-90		1	2o	1	1							5
77-83	x	1	2	o	1	2						6
70-76				o1								1
63-69	1	1o		1								3
f_x	2	6	9	19	17	17	14	15	6	3	1	109

$\overline{X}$

Fig. 10–3 Language Score (X) and Intelligence Quotient (Y). Bivariate Frequency Distribution with Two Lines of Regression Drawn.

$r = .583$	$\overline{X} = 22.0$	$s_x = 6.51$
$\hat{Y} = 74.9 + 1.60X$	$\overline{Y} = 110.1$	$s_y = 17.83$
$\hat{X} = -1.45 + .213Y$		

Circles mark means of horizontal rows.
Crosses mark means of vertical columns.

Here $r = .58$. To see more clearly the relation of the regression lines to the horizontal and vertical lines through the means of the marginal distributions (to which we shall refer briefly as the "lines of the means"), draw a red line horizontally across the chart at $\overline{Y} = 110.1$. Then mark in red the small crosses which represent the means of the various columns and also mark in red the straight regression line $\tilde{Y} = 74.9 + 1.6X$. You will now see vividly how this regression line straightens out the irregularities of the set of observed column means.

Now, with a blue pencil, mark the vertical line $\overline{X} = 22.0$, the small circles which represent the means of rows, and the regression line $\tilde{X} = -1.45 + .21Y$. You will notice that of the two regression lines, the one to predict Y is the one nearer to $\overline{Y}$ and the one to predict X is the one nearer to $\overline{X}$.

Figure 10–4 shows that for the 109 fourth-grade pupils in Table IX of the Appendix, the correlation of age with IQ was

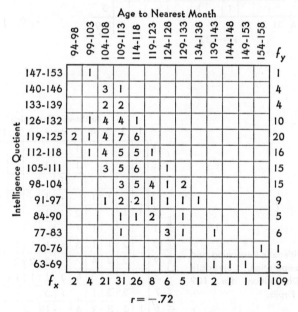

Fig. 10–4 Age and Intelligence Quotient. Bivariate Frequency Distribution for 109 Fourth-grade Pupils.

negative and fairly high, $r = -.72$. Experience tells you that this is reasonable, because in any single school grade the older pupils are, by and large, duller than the younger ones. If all pupils in an entire school were considered, the correlation of age with IQ would be nearly zero.

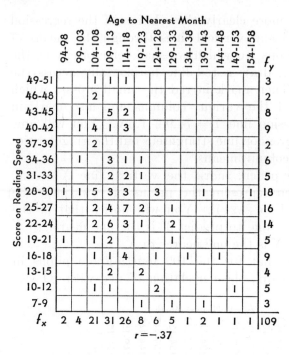

Age to Nearest Month

Score on Reading Speed	94-98	99-103	104-108	109-113	114-118	119-123	124-128	129-133	134-138	139-143	144-148	149-153	154-158	f_y
49-51			1	1	1									3
46-48			2											2
43-45		1		5	2									8
40-42		1	4	1	3									9
37-39			2											2
34-36		1		3	1	1								6
31-33				2	2	1								5
28-30	1	1	5	3	3		3			1			1	18
25-27			2	4	7	2		1						16
22-24			2	6	3	1		2						14
19-21	1		1	2				1						5
16-18			1	1	4		1		1		1			9
13-15				2		2								4
10-12			1	1			2					1		5
7-9					1			1		1				3
f_x	2	4	21	31	26	8	6	5	1	2	1	1	1	109

$r = -.37$

Fig. 10–5 Age and Reading Speed. Bivariate Frequency Distribution for 109 Fourth-grade Pupils.

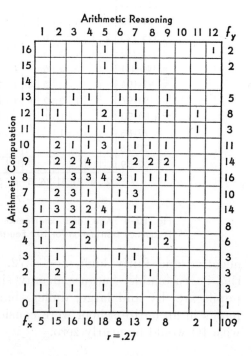

Fig. 10–6 Arithmetic Reasoning and Arithmetic Computation. Bivariate Frequency Distribution for 109 Fourth-grade Pupils.

Arithmetic Reasoning

Arithmetic Computation	1	2	3	4	5	6	7	8	9	10	11	12	f_y
16					1							1	2
15					1		1						2
14													
13			1	1		1	1		1				5
12	1	1			2	1	1		1		1		8
11						1	1				1		3
10		2	1	1	3	1	1	1	1				11
9		2	2	4			2	2	2				14
8			3	3	4	3	1	1	1				16
7		2	3	1		1	3						10
6	1	3	3	2	4		1						14
5	1	1	2	1	1		1	1					8
4	1			2				1	2				6
3		1				1	1						3
2		2						1					3
1	1		1	1									3
0		1											1
f_x	5	15	16	16	18	8	13	7	8		2	1	109

$r = .27$

Figure 10–5 shows a negative correlation (− .37) between age and reading speed for the 109 fourth-grade pupils in Appendix Table IX, and Figure 10–6 shows a low relationship ($r = .27$) between arithmetic reasoning and arithmetic computation. Figure 10–7 shows high positive correlation ($r = .66$) between midterm test and final examination for the 98 students of a first course in statistics.

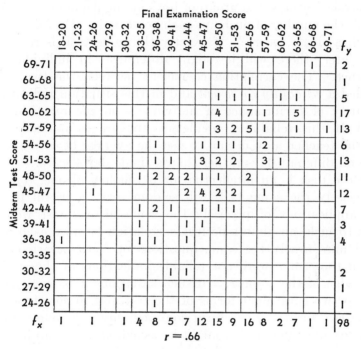

Fig. 10–7 Midterm and Final Examination Scores. Bivariate Frequency Distribution for 98 Students in a First-term Course in Statistics.

EXERCISE 10.2

Examine Figure 10–7 to obtain answers to the following questions:

1. Of the two persons scoring lowest on the midterm test, did either one make the lowest score on the final?
2. Compare the 8 persons with highest scores on the midterm and the 9 with highest scores on the final. How many persons were in both groups?
3. Do your answers to the preceding questions lead you to believe that, when $r = .66$, the persons who are at the extremes on one variable are almost certain to be equally extreme on the other?
4. Consider the 8 persons scoring lowest and the 8 scoring highest on the midterm. Do their scores on the final overlap at all?

5. Of the 30 persons who scored below 48 on the midterm, how many scored 48 or above on the final?

6. Of the 44 who scored above 50 on the final, how many scored 50 or below on the midterm?

Reliability of Measurement. A very important use of the correlation coefficient is to evaluate the reliability of measurements. Suppose a physical education teacher, wanting to measure the physical fitness of a group of boys at the beginning of a term, records the number of push ups each boy can do. How dependable is such a single record? If exactly the same task is repeated a week later, there will be slight differences in individual performance. The correlation coefficient between the two records is called a *reliability coefficient* and in this situation indicates the similarity of performance of individuals on the repetition of a task. If this reliability coefficient appears to be undesirably low, the teacher may decide to use the average of several scores made on different days rather than a single day's score.

If the task is an intellectual or psychological one, repetition of precisely the same task will seldom serve a useful purpose. Two applications of precisely the same history test would be likely to yield an almost perfect correlation because each person would miss nearly the same questions on both occasions, even though the scores were not reliable indications of the students' knowledge of the subject. In such situations it is customary to develop two equivalent forms of the test and to correlate scores on the two forms. Each form contains only a sample out of all the many questions which might be asked, and so is an imperfect measuring instrument. The correlation between scores on the two forms gives information about the similarity of those forms and measures the *reliability of the test*. If the two forms are administered on the same day, variation in the physical or emotional state of the pupils has little effect on the outcome and so this reliability coefficient is really descriptive of the test. If the two forms are administered on different days, the correlation between the scores on the two forms is affected both by the differences between the items in the two forms and by day-to-day changes in the persons who take the test.

Sometimes only one form is available and the items are divided into two half tests called "split halves." The correlation between scores on the two halves is, of course, lower than the correlation between two complete test forms, and it is the latter which is meant by "the reliability of the test." The reliability of the entire test can, however, be estimated from the correlation between the half tests.

Let R = correlation between two comparable test forms and
r = correlation between two half tests.

(10.13)   Then $$R = \frac{2r}{1 + r}$$

This formula is known as the Spearman-Brown Prophecy formula, because it was published by Carl Spearman and by William Brown, in two papers which appeared simultaneously.

The reliability coefficient is very easily affected by the range of scores. A reliability coefficient computed for pupils in grades seven to nine would be considerably higher than one computed for pupils in a single grade only.

EXERCISE 10.3

1. Suppose that a 40-item test has been divided into two half tests of 20 items each, and that the correlation between scores on the half tests, administered to 60 pupils, is $r = .52$.   (a) What would the correlation probably be between scores on two similar tests of 40 items each?   Would this value necessarily be achieved?   What may this correlation be expected to be between the two 20-item tests if given to 120 pupils instead of 60?
2. Suppose the correlation between two forms of a test has been found to be .45 and the test user feels this is too low a reliability coefficient to serve his purposes.   What reliability coefficient might he hope to achieve if he could add similar items to make the test twice as long? Do you think this result would be achieved if he lengthened the test by adding poorer items than those in the original test?

Validity. A common use of measurement is to predict scores on one variable from scores on another. Thus college entrance examinations, or high-school grades, may be used to predict performance in college. Attempts have been made to predict delinquency from factors in home environment. The accuracy with which a prediction of this sort can be made is called the *validity* of a measure in making a particular prediction. A validity, or validity coefficient, is usually expressed as a correlation coefficient between the measure used in making the prediction and the measure which is predicted.

Validity differs from reliability in that reliability is an evaluation of the consistency in repeated measures of the same sort, whereas validity is an evaluation of the relationship between measures on different variables. Reliability is an inherent characteristic of a measure, but validity is a relationship between two measures. Thus in reports on a mental test, the reliability will be reported as an aspect of the tests, but validities are reported separately for each of the variables the test may be used to predict. Thus a test in mathematics might have a validity of .50 in predicting success in engineering school and a validity near zero in predicting success as a salesman.

Validity itself is influenced by reliability and a test with low reliability will necessarily have low validity in all its predictions.

Personnel Selection. A very important application of the correlation coefficient is the standardization and evaluation of procedures used in selection of persons for employment or for admission to school. The selection procedure provides a measure by which subsequent performance on the job or in the school can be estimated.

The user of the test has two problems. He must select a score, or standard, such that all candidates who attain or surpass this score are selected and the remaining candidates are rejected. He must also check to ascertain whether the test is actually effective in selecting the more desirable candidates and in rejecting the less desirable.

The solution of both of these problems is accomplished by relating the scores of the selection test to those of a measure of achievement in the occupation or school for which applicants are selected. This new measure is commonly called the *criterion*, because it is the criterion against which the selection procedure is evaluated. Thus the selection procedure might be an entrance examination to a college and the criterion might be college grades. Another example is provided by a test which leads to employment in a position and ratings of job performances given by supervisors.

The correlation between a selection test and a related criterion is the *validity* of the test, or the *validity coefficient*, because this correlation measures the validity, or correctness, of the test in predicting criterion scores.

Table 10.2 has been prepared to demonstrate the effectiveness of several validity coefficients in a selection procedure. The table consists of six subtables, each of which represents a distribution of 100 individuals according to several levels of the test score and of the criterion. Consider, for example, the first subtable at the left. Suppose that the standard for this group has been set to select the higher scoring half of the candidate group. Of the 50 so selected, 17 are in the top third of the criterion group, 16 are in the middle third, and 17 are in the lowest third. We notice also that the rejected candidates have exactly the same distribution according to the criterion. We see, therefore, that when the validity coefficient is zero, choice of the higher group on test score provides no advantage. In fact, one is just

TABLE 10.2 Effectiveness of Selection Procedures for Three Different Validity Coefficients

100 candidates

Validity coefficient	Criterion score	Number of candidates with test score in				
		Lower half	Upper half *	Lowest third	Middle third	Top third †
$r = 0$	Top third	17	17	12	10	12
	Middle third	16	16	10	12	10
	Lowest third	17	17	12	10	12
$r = .50$	Top third	9	25	5	10	19
	Middle third	16	16	10	12	10
	Lowest third	25	9	19	10	5
$r = .80$	Top third	4	30	1	8	25
	Middle third	16	16	8	16	8
	Lowest third	30	4	25	8	1

* Upper half of candidates selected
† Upper third of candidates selected

as well off without using the test. When the validity is 0.50, if we choose the upper half of the group on test score, we find that fully 25 are in the top third of the criterion group, but only 9 are in the lowest third. It is clear, therefore, that here there is a distinct gain in using the test over using no test at all. A similar reading of the lowest subtable in the left column shows an even greater advantage in using the test when the validity coefficient is .80.

In the right-hand column of Table 10.2 it is assumed that we select only the top third of the group on the basis of test score. The first subtable in this column shows at once that the test is not helpful in selection when validity is zero. The second subtable shows that 19 of the 34 selected subjects are in the upper third of the criterion group. This is 56 percent of the selected group, whereas only 50 percent were in the upper third when half were chosen. Thus a choice of upper third rather than upper half provides a distinct improvement in selection when the validity coefficient is 0.50. A similar gain is demonstrated for the validity coefficient of 0.80.

The conclusion from this analysis of Table 10.2 is that a test is increasingly useful in selection as its validity coefficient increases. If the validity coefficient is positive, selection is improved if the standard for selection is set higher.

The situation is analogous when the validity coefficient is negative, but in that case we choose from the lower level of test score rather than from the upper level.

Phi Coefficient. Sometimes the scatter diagram consists of only two rows and two columns. If the frequencies in the four cells of such a table are indicated by the letters a, b, c, and d, placed as in the adjacent sketch, the correlation coefficient can be obtained by a very convenient short cut and the result is usually called ϕ (phi) to inform the reader that it was obtained from a four-fold table.

	0	1	
1	b	a	$a+b$
0	d	c	$d+c$
	$b+d$	$a+c$	

$$(10.14) \qquad \phi = \frac{ad - bc}{\sqrt{(a+b)(d+c)(b+d)(a+c)}}$$

Suppose that out of 60 men, 23 approve a particular proposition, while out of 80 women, 27 approve it. Is there a relation between sex and approval of the proposition?

$$\phi = \frac{37(27) - 53(23)}{\sqrt{50(90)(60)(80)}} = -.047$$

	Men	Women	
Approve	23	27	50
Disapprove	37	53	90
	60	80	140

The relationship is practically zero, certainly negligible.

Correlation among Ranks. Sometimes where there is no satisfactory device for scoring a trait, individuals can be placed in a rank order in respect to the degree of the trait they exhibit. In such a situation it is possible to say for any two individuals which one is higher on the scale for the trait, but not possible to say how much higher. The reader will readily think of many situations of this kind, as, for example, the attempt to place in order of merit the performances of contestants for an award in some contest or to rank persons on some intangible such as "friendliness" or "conscientiousness." If the group is large, even determining the order of individuals becomes difficult, so a correlation coefficient based on rank order is obviously most useful when samples are not large.

The correlation between two sets of ranks is called *rank order correlation*, or *Spearman's rank order coefficient* (because it was originally proposed by Carl Spearman), or sometimes *rho* (because he denoted it by Greek letter ρ). The formula is

$$(10.15) \qquad R = 1 - \frac{6\Sigma d^2}{N(N^2 - 1)}$$

where N is the number of individuals ranked and d is the difference in the ranks assigned to the same individual. In the computation, a useful check is provided by the fact that $\Sigma d = 0$. This formula is derived by applying the usual product moment formula to the ranks.

Suppose 12 cakes submitted in a competition at a country fair have been ranked by two judges with results as shown in Table 10.3. Then

$$R = 1 - \frac{6(40)}{12(144 - 1)} = \frac{123}{143} = .86$$

TABLE 10.3 Computation of Coefficient of Correlation among Ranks Assigned to 12 Cakes

Cake	Rank assigned by		d	d^2
	Judge I	Judge II		
A	7	6	1	1
B	8	4	4	16
C	2	1	1	1
D	1	3	−2	4
E	9	11	−2	4
F	3	2	1	1
G	12	12	0	0
H	11	10	1	1
I	4	5	−1	1
J	10	9	1	1
K	6	7	−1	1
L	5	8	−3	9
			$\Sigma d^2 = 40$	

$$R = 1 - \frac{6(40)}{12(143)} = 1 - \frac{20}{143} = \frac{123}{143} = .86$$

Now let the ranks assigned by Judge I be denoted X and those assigned by Judge II be denoted Y. Then

$$\Sigma X = 78 \qquad\qquad\qquad \Sigma Y = 78$$
$$\Sigma X^2 = 650 \qquad\qquad\qquad \Sigma Y^2 = 650$$

$$\Sigma x^2 = 650 - \frac{78^2}{12} = 143 \qquad \Sigma y^2 = 650 - \frac{78^2}{12} = 143$$

$$\Sigma XY = 630 \qquad\qquad \Sigma xy = 630 - \frac{(78)(78)}{12} = 123$$

and $$r = \frac{123}{\sqrt{(143)(143)}} = \frac{123}{143} = .86$$

This computation illustrates the fact that the rank order coefficient and the product moment coefficient applied to the ranks are identical. However, if scores are transformed to ranks, the product moment correlation of the ranks (which is the rank order coefficient) is almost certain to be different from the product moment coefficient of the original scores.

11

Circumstances Affecting the Size of Correlation and Regression Coefficients

The outcome of a correlational study is often difficult to interpret because the correlation between two variables not only reflects the strength of the intrinsic relation between those variables but may also be affected by other circumstances, such as the reliability with which the variables have been measured and the selection of subjects for the study. You can be more realistic about the meaning of coefficients you obtain if you are aware of such possible effects.

Effect of Changing Units. Some changes in data leave the correlation coefficient entirely unchanged.

1. Multiplying (or dividing) all the scores of either variable by the same number has no effect at all on r. However, if all the values of x are multiplied by the number a and all values of y are multiplied by the number c, the regression coefficient b_{yx} will be multiplied by c/a and the regression coefficient b_{xy} will be multiplied by a/c.

Thus the correlation between height and weight will have identically the same value (except for rounding errors) whether measurements are taken in inches and pounds or in centimeters and kilograms. The equations to predict weight from height will be different in the two situations, but the result in pounds of predicting the weight of a particular person from his height in inches will be equivalent to the result in kilograms of predicting his weight from his height in centimeters.

2. Adding the same number to all values of one variable has no effect on either r or b but will affect the constants in the regression equations.

Statements (1) and (2) call attention to the fact that, in computing the sums of products and of squares which are used in obtaining a correlation coefficient, no use whatever is made of the scales of the variables. However, the scales are needed for obtaining the regression equations since the step interval is required for finding the regression coefficient, and both means are required for finding the constant term in the equation.

Effect of Grouping Scores. Grouping scores into class intervals will not greatly affect the value of r or b provided the intervals are not made very large. While the most accurate results are achieved by use of ungrouped data, computations made by subdivision of the scales into 10 or 15 intervals give satisfactory results for many purposes. The extreme procedure of subdividing the scales into two or three intervals and then computing the correlation and regression coefficients should be avoided since the distortion would then be considerable.

Variable Errors of Measurement. By now you are aware that nothing can be measured with complete precision. Every good research worker eliminates all possible bias from his measures and reduces accidental errors of observation and measurement to a minimum, but he can never completely free his observations from accidental error. If these variable errors which remain are purely chance errors, they are as likely to be positive as to be negative, and to have only a negligible effect on measures of central tendency. They tend to increase measures of variability, and they tend to *decrease measures of relationship*. This is an important matter. It means that an observed correlation is almost always lower than the correlation between true measures of the same traits would be. It means that if measurement is made with unreliable instruments, the observed correlation coefficient may be very low even when the traits concerned are closely related.

The reduction in the size of r because of variable errors of measurement is called *attenuation*. To illustrate its effect, an experiment was performed in which purely random errors were attached to the language scores and the intelligence quotients of the 109 subjects in Appendix Table IX. A variable error was attached to each score in this way. Two decks of cards were shuffled together and a card was drawn. The number on the first card drawn was taken as the error to be added to the score of the first child, the number on the second card drawn as the error for the second child, etc. Red cards were considered to indicate positive errors; black cards, negative. After every tenth drawing the cards were reshuffled. For case 1, the original language score was 17, the first card drawn was a six of hearts, and so the score plus error is $17 + 6 = 23$. (It must not be supposed that the original scores were free from measurement error!)

Results of computing from the original scores and from the scores with random errors attached were as follows:

	Original Scores	Scores with Errors
Mean language score	21.98	22.08
Mean IQ	110.04	110.02
Standard deviation, language scores	6.5	10.3
Standard deviation, IQ	17.5	19.6
Correlation coefficient	.59	.20

The means have been changed so little by the variable errors that results have to be carried to four or five places before any difference appears. One mean has been very slightly increased, the other very slightly decreased. Both standard deviations have been noticeably increased. The correlation coefficient has been greatly decreased.

Effect of Number of Cases. The number of cases on which r or b is calculated does not influence the values of these coefficients in the sense of making them either larger or smaller. The number of cases does, however, affect the accuracy with which a relationship between two variables is determined. The matter of accuracy of the measurement of relationship is discussed more fully on the basis of statistical inference in Chapter 16.

Linearity of Regression. Sometimes the means of the arrays of one variable (or both) lie on a line which is not straight. (Either a row or a column is called an array. A straight line is called *linear* or *rectilinear*. A line that is not straight is called *nonlinear* or *curvilinear*.) Thus the regression on age for almost any physical measure of a person is nonlinear if taken over the entire life span. Several such curved regression lines have been shown in Figure 9–8 on page 138. When a measure of overhead expense is related to the number of individuals involved, the scatter diagram often resembles the adjacent sketch. In some psychological studies there are variables for which

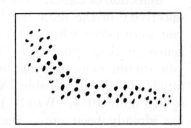

a rating at either extreme tends to be associated with low performance or poor adjustment, and a rating in the middle range to be associated with better achievement or more healthy adjustment. An extreme situation is represented in the sketch below where column means are represented by small crosses and row means by small circles. A curved regression line fitted to the small crosses would represent the data rather well, so that it would be possible to make a fairly good estimate of Y from X, but a line fitted to the row means would have little meaning.

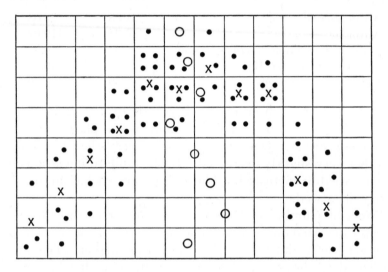

Since the correlation coefficient is based on the assumption of linearity of regression, it would be practically meaningless in data such as are sketched here; in fact, it could be nearly zero in such data, even if there were a decided relation between the variables. There is a measure of relation which is applicable in such situations, called the *correlation ratio*. It is equal to r when regression is precisely linear, and greater than r when regression is not linear. The computation of the correlation ratio will not be described in this book.

Selection of Cases. The effect on correlation of some particular selectivity in the data can be very perplexing. For example, if you were asked what is the correlation between age and intelligence quotient, you might say promptly that it is zero. Yet if you should compute that correlation for the 109 fourth-grade pupils of Appendix Table IX, you would discover that $r \equiv -.72$, as in Figure 10–4. Why? Because of selectivity of subjects. It has already been noted that within any single grade (here the fourth) the younger children tend to be brighter than the older ones, producing a negative correlation between age and a measure of intelligence. If all children in a school system are measured, that correlation would almost certainly be near zero.

It has already been noted that mere increase or decrease in the number of individuals, without any change in the nature of those individuals, has little effect on the size of r. However, if the form of distribution is considerably changed, r may also be considerably changed. Some of the ways in which this can occur will be discussed in the next four sections.

Eliminating Cases near the Mean. Sometimes a research worker gathers data on a large number of cases and then eliminates from consideration a block of cases near the center of the distribution. If he computes a coefficient of correlation from the two

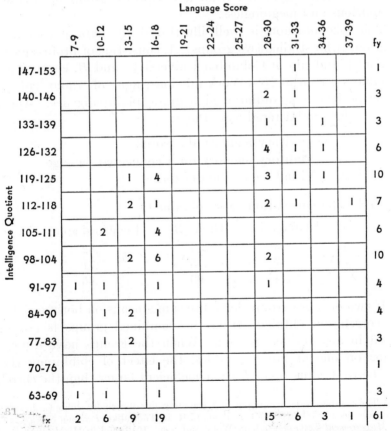

Intelligence Quotient	7-9	10-12	13-15	16-18	19-21	22-24	25-27	28-30	31-33	34-36	37-39	fy
147-153									1			1
140-146								2	1			3
133-139								1	1	1		3
126-132								4	1	1		6
119-125			1	4				3	1	1		10
112-118			2	1				2	1		1	7
105-111		2		4								6
98-104			2	6				2				10
91-97	1	1		1				1				4
84-90		1	2	1								4
77-83		1	2									3
70-76				1								1
63-69	1	1		1								3
fx	2	6	9	19				15	6	3	1	61

Language Score

Fig. 11-1 Distribution of Figure 10-3 after the Elimination of 48 Cases with Language Score between 19 and 27.

$$r = .69$$

extreme groups, he is likely to get a value numerically larger than if he had used the full distribution.

For example, consider Figure 11–1 in which, for all 109 cases, the correlation between intelligence quotient and language score has been found to be $r \equiv .58$. If you should eliminate the 48 cases with language score between 19 and 27, leaving the distribution of Figure 11–1, the correlation computed for the remaining 61 cases would be $r \equiv .69$. It is possible to make a good estimate of the correlation in an entire distribution from certain statistics computed from cases at the two ends of that distribution, but special tables are required for that purpose.[1]

Correlation in a Composite Group when the Subgroups Have Unequal Means. Sometimes two groups with widely separated means are thrown together to form one bivariate distribution. The correlations obtained from a composite group of this sort are spurious and meaningless.

This phenomenon is well illustrated by data gathered by Simpson,[2] who studied two groups: A, consisting of professors and advanced students in Columbia University; and B, consisting of unemployed men in New York missions, none of whom had ever held a position demanding a high grade of intelligence. Among the tests he administered were these:

x_1 — Auditory memory for words
x_2 — Auditory memory for a connected passage
x_3 — Visual recognition of forms

The following correlations were obtained:

	Group A	Group B	Combined groups
r_{12}	.23	.73	.82
r_{13}	.37	.15	.71
r_{23}	.14	.06	.66

If two or more groups have the same means on both variables, the correlation obtained from the combined groups is not distorted in any serious fashion. When the groups have different means on one or both variables, the effect of combining them may be to produce a correlation coefficient larger than the correla-

---

[1] These tables were computed and privately distributed by John C. Flanagan. They have been reproduced by permission in R. L. Thorndike, *Personal Selection, Test and Measurement Techniques*, John Wiley and Sons, 1949, and in H. M. Walker and J. Lev, *Statistical Inference*, Henry Holt, 1953.

[2] *Correlations of Mental Abilities*, New York, Teachers College Bureau of of Publications, 1912.

tion in the separate groups, as in the example just cited, or smaller, or even different in sign. Some such effects are schematically suggested in Figure 11–2.

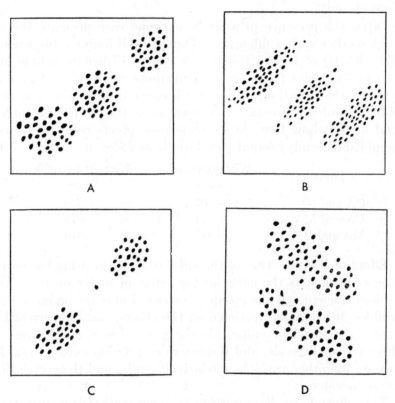

Fig. 11–2 Sketches to Illustrate How the Value of the Correlation Coefficient May Be Affected by the Combination of Two or More Groups with Unequal Means.

    A. In each group, *r* is near zero. In composite group, it is high and positive.

    B. In each group, *r* is positive. In composite group, it is negative.

    C. In each group, *r* is positive but low. In composite group, it is positive and much higher.

    D. In each group, *r* is negative. In composite group, it is near zero.

Two or more groups with unequal means may be pooled in order to obtain a common coefficient of correlation which will reflect the relation of the two variables within the groups and will not be affected by the differences between the groups. To do this formula (11.1) may be used

$$(11.1) \quad r = \frac{\Sigma X_1 Y_1 + \Sigma X_2 Y_2 + \Sigma X_3 Y_3 - \dfrac{(\Sigma X_1)(\Sigma Y_1)}{N_1} - \dfrac{(\Sigma X_2)(\Sigma Y_2)}{N_2} - \dfrac{(\Sigma X_3)(\Sigma Y_3)}{N_3}}{\sqrt{\Sigma X_1^2 + \Sigma X_2^2 + \Sigma X_3^2 - \dfrac{(\Sigma X_1)^2}{N_1} - \dfrac{(\Sigma X_2)^2}{N_2} - \dfrac{(\Sigma X_3)^2}{N_3}}\sqrt{\Sigma Y_1^2 + \Sigma Y_2^2 + \Sigma Y_3^2 - \dfrac{(\Sigma Y_1)^2}{N_1} - \dfrac{(\Sigma Y_2)^2}{N_2} - \dfrac{(\Sigma Y_3)^2}{N_3}}}$$

The formula as presented here is for a composite of three subgroups, but can easily be adapted to a different number of groups. Such expressions as ΣX_1, ΣY_2, etc., indicate summation for the subgroup only.

Often the presence of a single extreme case presents the research worker with a dilemma. Thus Rowell found a 14-year-old child with IQ of 45 in a third-grade class. Either to include him or to exclude him from her computations would obviously misrepresent the situation. Under such circumstances the best procedure is probably to state the situation so the reader can understand it and show how the extreme case affects results. Rowell (unpublished study) found correlations as follows:

Traits	With extreme case	Without extreme case
CA and IQ	$-.500$	$-.430$
CA and MA	$-.171$	$-.078$
MA and IQ	$-.917$	$-.919$

Effect of Range. One of the chief troubles in using the correlation coefficient is the effect of the range of scores on the value of this coefficient. If the group is restricted in range on one of the variables, it is also so restricted on the others, and the correlation is greatly reduced in value. If the group has a great range of values on one variable, and if nonzero correlation exists, then the range on the other variable is relatively great, and the correlation is large in value.

This effect is so disconcerting to some statisticians that they prefer not to use the coefficient of correlation at all. Instead, they use the regression formula and the related standard error of estimate as a description of the relation between two variables. The correlation coefficient is, nevertheless, generally used as a measure of relationship. The precaution must be taken, however, to keep the range of scores in mind when interpreting a correlation coefficient.

As an example of the effect of changing the range of scores, consider the correlation between IQ and language for the children listed in Figure 10–3 on page 150. For the entire group this correlation is .58, but when the IQ range is restricted by considering only children with IQ of 126 or higher from this group, the correlation is reduced to .20. When children with IQ less than 91 or IQ greater than 125 are excluded, the correlation is reduced to .24. See Exercise 11.1.

The matter of range in test scores is very important in evaluating validity and reliability coefficients. Such a coefficient based on a group which is highly homogeneous in ability is likely to be low for that reason alone, in comparison with such a coefficient for a group very diverse in ability.

A problem of restriction of range arises when only those who achieve high test scores are selected for employment and the later success of these people is used as a criterion for judging the validity of the selection process. Since the validity coefficient, the correlation between selection score and measure of success, is computed for a group which had attained or exceeded the selection standard, this group is restricted on the range of scores in the selection test. The validity coefficient is, therefore, much lower than if the entire candidate group could have been used in computing the coefficient. In other words, the accomplishment of the test in eliminating a large number of undesirable candidates is not made evident by the computation.

One way to recapture the information about the validity of the test for the entire candidate group merely by using data for the selected group is to estimate a correlation coefficient by extension. Suppose that, for the selected group, the standard deviation of test scores is s_x and the correlation with the criterion is r_{xy}. Since the entire candidate group was given the selection test, the standard deviation for this group is available. Call this S_x. Then the validity coefficient for the entire group R_{xy} can be estimated by the formula

$$(11.2) \qquad R_{xy} = \frac{r_{xy}S_x}{\sqrt{r_{xy}^2 S_x^2 + s_x^2(1 - r_{xy}^2)}}$$

EXERCISE 11.1

1. Verify the values of r, b_{yx}, b_{xy}, s_x, and s_y listed below which would be obtained from the data of Figure 10–3 if certain parts of the distribution were eliminated and computations were made from the cases indicated:

Cases retained	N	s_x	s_y	r	b_{yx}	b_{xy}
(a) Entire group	109	6.5	17.8	.58	1.60	.21
(b) Language score between 19 and 27 inclusive	48	2.4	14.4	.16	.93	.026
(c) IQ between 91 and 125 inclusive	75	5.8	9.6	.24	.40	.15
(d) Language score below 19	36	2.8	16.6	.39	2.28	.07
(e) Language score above 27	25	2.6	13.9	.13	.70	.025
(f) Language score below 19 or above 27	61	8.4	13.9	.69	1.65	.29

Cases retained	N	s_x	s_y	r	b_{yx}	b_{xy}
(g) IQ below 91	15	4.5	7.9	.26	.45	.15
(h) IQ above 125	19	4.0	6.8	.20	.34	.11
(i) IQ below 91 or above 125	34	7.8	28.9	.85	3.14	.23

2. In situation (b), the extreme values of x were removed. What did this removal do to s_x? s_y? r? b_{yx}? b_{xy}? Which was affected more, s_x or s_y?

3. In situation (c), the extreme values of Y were removed. What did this removal do to s_x? s_y? r? b_{yx}? b_{xy}? Which was affected more, s_x or s_y?

4. In situation (f), the middle of the distribution of x was removed. What did this do to s_x? s_y? r? b_{yx}? b_{xy}? Which was affected more, s_x or s_y?

5. In situation (i), the middle of the distribution of Y was removed. What did this removal do to s_x? s_y? r? b_{yx}? b_{zy}? Which was affected more, s_x or s_y?

Variation in a Third Trait. Sometimes part of the difficulty in interpreting a coefficient of correlation comes from the fact that both of the correlated variables appear to be related to a third variable in such a way that the intrinsic relation between the two correlated variables is either exaggerated or suppressed by variation in the third. For example, in 1877, long before the coefficient of correlation was known, an American named Bowditch made a study of the physical characteristics of 24,500 Boston school children, and prepared what today we would call regression lines of weight on height, weight on age, and height on age.[3] He was clearly looking for some way to express the relation between height and weight, and he nearly discovered the idea of correlation. However, he became confused by the possible influence of age on that relation and so failed to reach a satisfactory measure of relationship. Years later Ethel Elderton made body measurements of a large number of school children in Scotland. For girls ranging in age from 5 to 18, the correlation of height and weight was .91, but when the total group was broken up into smaller groups with an age range of only one year, the correlation was much lower. For children whose ages span a wide range, the correlation is affected by the fact that older children are, on the average, both taller and heavier than younger children, so the correlation $r_{hw} = .91$ actually involves age as well as height and weight. When age range is rigidly restricted, the correlation coefficient between height and weight averages in the low .80's,

---

[3] Henry Pickering Bowditch, "The Growth of Children," *Report of Board of Health of Massachusetts* (1877). Reprinted in *Papers on Anthropometry*, Boston, 1894.

though, of course, it would not be the same for infants as for older children.

The effect of a third variable, which we may call z, on the correlation between x and y can be removed by a formula which involves the three correlations, r_{xy}, r_{xz}, and r_{yz}. The result is called the *partial correlation of x and y, when z is held constant* and denoted $r_{xy.z}$ (read "rxy point z"). What this formula actually does is to describe the correlation of two residuals, one the residual $X - \tilde{X}$ where $\tilde{X}$ is predicted from Z, and the other $Y - \tilde{Y}$, when $\tilde{Y}$ is predicted from Z. The formula is

$$(11.3) \qquad r_{xy.z} = \frac{r_{xy} - r_{xz}r_{yz}}{\sqrt{(1 - r_{xz}^2)(1 - r_{yz}^2)}}$$

Thus if for the three variables height, weight, and age,

$$r_{hw} = .907, \quad r_{ha} = .70, \quad \text{and} \quad r_{wa} = .70$$

the partial correlation is

$$r_{hw.a} = \frac{.907 - (.70)(.70)}{\sqrt{1 - .49}\sqrt{1 - .49}} = .82$$

The computations are easy enough. In most situations the perplexing question is whether you are interested in the correlation r_{xy} (called a "zero order correlation") or $r_{xy.z}$ (called a "first order partial"). For that decision, the only guide is very careful thinking about the nature of the data.

To illustrate the complexity of the problem, we may consider some data gathered by Lander[4] in a study of factors related to juvenile delinquency. For each of 155 census tracts in Baltimore ($N = 155$), he obtained a measure of juvenile delinquency (y), of median education level of adults (x_1), of overcrowding in housing (x_2), of percent of residents who were nonwhite (x_3), and of percent of homes owned by their occupants (x_4). The following correlations were obtained among these variables:

	x_1	x_2	x_3	x_4	y
x_1 = median education	—	−.71	−.41	.39	−.51
x_2 = overcrowding		—	.69	−.72	.73
x_3 = percent nonwhite			—	−.76	.70
x_4 = percent homes owner occupied				—	−.80
y = juvenile delinquency					—

[4] Bernard Lander, *Toward an Understanding of Juvenile Delinquency*, Columbia University Press, 1954.

The correlations listed in the y column are all fairly large, but each requires interpretation in terms of the other variables. Suppose we had only the correlation $r_{y3} = .70$ and argued that this high correlation indicated that the presence of nonwhites is the chief cause of juvenile delinquency. We should be overlooking the fact that a census tract with a large percent of nonwhite residents is likely to be also a tract in which median education is low ($r_{13} = -.41$), overcrowding is prevalent ($r_{23} = .69$), and relatively few homes are owner occupied ($r_{43} = -.76$). If we should "partial out" one of these three other variables, we would obtain much smaller correlations:

$$r_{y3.1} = \frac{.70 - (-.51)(-.41)}{\sqrt{(.74)(.83)}} = .63$$

$$r_{y3.2} = \frac{.70 - (.73)(.69)}{\sqrt{(.47)(.52)}} = .40$$

$$r_{y3.4} = \frac{.70 - (-.80)(-.76)}{\sqrt{(.36)(.42)}} = .24$$

Here any interpretation of correlation values as indicative of *cause* is obviously fallacious. If, however, the goal is to select census tracts in which delinquency is very likely to be high and other tracts in which it is likely to be low, the data can be used effectively. Selection on the basis of x_4 alone would serve very well. It is possible to obtain what is known as a *multiple regression equation* to estimate y from all four of the other variables together, but this technique is outside the scope of this text. For the Lander data, the multiple regression equation to predict the juvenile delinquency measure for a Baltimore census tract would be

$$\tilde{y} = -.134x_1 + .163x_2 + .127x_3 - .534x_4$$

when y, x_1, x_2, x_3, and x_4 are deviations from the means of the respective variables. The correlation between the criterion variable y and the estimate of y obtained by the multiple regression equation is known as a *multiple correlation* or *multiple r*. In the Lander data this multiple r is .84 whereas $r_{y4} = .80$, and so the single variable x_4 provides nearly as good a selective device as the combination of all four variables.

EXERCISE 11.2

1. From the Lander data quoted above, confirm that $r_{14} = .39$ while $r_{14.2} = -.24$. Note, therefore, that a partial correlation may even be different in sign from the corresponding zero order coefficient.

2. Confirm that the negative correlation between median education and percent of nonwhite residents becomes very low but positive when the effect of variation in overcrowding is removed ($r_{13.2} = .16$).

3. We have already seen that the correlation between intelligence quotient and language score for the 109 fourth-grade children was .58. This correlation, however, is partly due to the fact that younger children in the fourth grade tend to have higher language scores and higher intelligence quotients than older children. Examine the subgroups based on age in Figure 11–3. Verify the correlations stated for the subgroups.

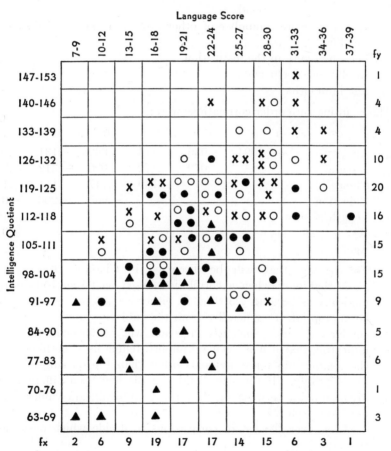

Fig. 11–3 Language Score and Intelligence Quotient Bivariate Distributions for Children of Varying Age.

X	Children aged 94–108 months	N = 27	r = .50
O	Children aged 109–113 months	N = 31	r = .42
●	Children aged 114–118 months	N = 26	r = .35
▲	Children aged 119–156 months	N = 25	r = .56

For entire group N = 109 and r = .58

4. For the 109 subjects in Appendix Table IX what would be the partial correlation between language score (x_1) and intelligence coefficient (x_2) with the influence of age (x_3) removed if the zero order correlations are as follows:

$$r_{12} = .583, \quad r_{13} = -.396, \quad r_{23} = -.723$$

5. In a study of 65 delinquent boys at the New York State Training School at Warwick, Trent obtained measures on the following variables:

x_1 Anxiety = score on questionnaire items related to manifest anxiety
x_2 L score = score on questionnaire items related to tendency to falsify
x_3 Choice score = number of other boys who indicated a preference for this boy as a friend
x_4 Rejection score = number of other boys who indicated dislike of this boy
x_5 Length of stay in the institution
x_6 Intelligence coefficient
x_7 Age in months

The resulting zero order correlations were:

		x_1	x_2	x_3	x_4	x_5	x_6	x_7
x_1	Anxiety	—	.094	−.036	.114	.082	−.131	.107
x_2	L scale		—	.079	−.172	.090	−.312	.751
x_3	Choice			—	.749	.147	−.111	.148
x_4	Rejection				—	−.066	−.206	−.040
x_5	Length of stay					—	−.182	.197
x_6	IQ						—	−.014
x_7	Age							

(a) For reasons that will be discussed in Chapter 16, we may agree that only when a correlation based on 65 subjects is numerically as large as .25 (that is, either $r - .25$ or $r + .25$) will it be appropriate to generalize from the subjects examined to other similar subjects. Such a correlation will be termed *significant*, indicating that it has a general import, telling us something about the relationship for individuals other than the 65 subjects used in this study. If the size of this sample had been different, the dividing point between significant and nonsignificant values would not have been .25.

Look over the list of correlations to decide which ones meet this criterion.

(b) Examine $r_{27} = .751$. Which of the following statements seems to you to be justified? What is wrong with each of the others?

(1) In general, delinquent boys have a tendency to falsify more as they grow older.

(2) In general, delinquent boys have a tendency to falsify less as they grow older.

(3) In general, all boys have a tendency to falsify less as they grow older.

(4) In general, older boys in an institution for delinquents tend to falsify more than younger boys.

(5) In general, older boys in an institution for delinquents tend to falsify less than younger boys.

(6) If the oldest and the youngest boys in the institution are given the L scale, the oldest boy will obtain the higher score.

(7) Among these 65 boys, the older ones made higher scores on the L scale, but the correlation was too small to permit generalization beyond the 65 subjects examined.

(c) Examine r_{26}. Which of the following statements seems to you to be justified? What is wrong with the others?

(1) Children who are brighter tend to falsify more than those who are duller.

(2) Having a low IQ is the reason delinquent boys falsify.

(3) In general, delinquent boys with a high IQ tend to have lower L scores (i.e., to falsify less) than those with a low IQ.

(4) For these 65 boys there was a negative relation between intelligence and L score, but the correlation was too low to warrant generalizing to other similar subjects.

(5) The correlation r_{26} is large enough so that the IQ will provide a good prediction of the tendency to falsify.

(d) Examine r_{34}. Did you expect it to be negative? Most people would assume that choice score and rejection score were practically opposite and should therefore show a high negative correlation. However, in such a group as has been studied here, a boy who is much sought after by the members of one clique may be much disliked by the members of another and so may score high on both x_3 and x_4, while a little-known boy may receive few choices and few rejections. This point is made to help you see how important it is to understand your data and to think about them, and how the person who merely computes but does not think about the data may misinterpret results that are numerically correct.

(e) For these 65 boys, which of the other variables was positively related to anxiety? Negatively related? Were any of the correlations large enough to have good predictive value? Were any of them large enough to justify generalization to other similar subjects?

Interpretation of the Size of a Correlation Coefficient. This problem is discussed in Chapter 16 and the reader is referred to that discussion.

12

The Normal Distribution

I know of scarcely anything so apt to impress the imagination as the wonderful form of cosmic order expressed by the "Law of Frequency of Error." The law would have been personified by the Greeks and deified, if they had known it. It reigns with serenity and in complete self-effacement amidst the wildest confusion. The huger the mob and the greater the apparent anarchy, the more perfect is its sway. It is the supreme law of Unreason. Whenever a large sample of chaotic elements are taken in hand and marshalled in the order of their magnitude, an unsuspected and most beautiful form of regularity proves to have been latent all along.

Sir Francis Galton

Almost every person trained in any of the sciences knows and uses the term "normal curve" but many use it incorrectly or at least without understanding. Social scientists sometimes assert that when enough cases are observed, every human trait is normally distributed. This is not so. The curve is esthetically beautiful and mathematically interesting and many people assume that mathematicians have proved it to have a universal cogency. Teachers sometimes talk foolishly about "grading on the curve" and deceive themselves into thinking they are being commendably scientific. However, in spite of popularly held misconceptions and all too frequent misuse, the normal distribution is a powerful statistical concept with extremely valuable practical applications.

The Normal Curve. Suppose you have measured the heights of 50 adult men and from those measures have constructed a histogram with step intervals of 1 inch. Try to imagine in a general way how that histogram might look. It would be somewhat irregular because the number of cases is small. Almost certainly the frequencies would pile up in the neighborhood of the mean and fall off at both ends of the distribution.

Suppose you increase the number of cases from 50 to 200, and construct another histogram. How would this differ from the first one? The range would be about the same, or possibly a little larger, the irregularity in the first distribution would tend to decrease, and the histogram would become more symmetrical.

Now suppose the number of cases is increased to 10,000 and the interval is made much narrower, say 0.1 of an inch. There will now be a great many narrow rectangles instead of a few broad ones so the steps will be smaller. Because the number of cases has been greatly increased, the distribution will be more regular. The piling up of frequencies around the mean is now very obvious, and we say the *density* is greater in that part of the distribution.

Imagine that the rectangles in this last histogram are outlined in heavy ink and that the graph is hung on a wall at some distance from you. The frequency distribution is still represented by a series of rectangles, but from a distance the tops of those rectangles may look to you like a smooth curve. Furthermore for the variable named — that is, the heights of adult men — the curve which this distribution suggests would strongly resemble the ideal mathematical curve known as *the normal curve.*

Figure 12–1 shows just such a histogram with many narrow step intervals and shows a normal curve superimposed on it. This

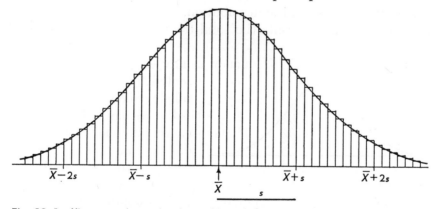

Fig. 12–1   Histogram Approximating a Normal Curve, with a Normal Curve Superimposed.

smooth curve is both interesting and important and in this chapter we shall discuss its characteristics and present some of its applications.

If, for any continuous variable, a histogram with narrow step intervals is drawn to show the frequency distribution for a very large number of cases, the tops of the rectangles will convey the

general impression of a smooth curve. However, that curve will
not necessarily resemble the normal curve you have seen in Figure 12–1. Suppose, for example, that the variable is the annual
dollar income of all families in some fairly large city. Toward
the lower end of the income scale, the density will be much greater
than toward the upper end, and the distribution will be considerably skewed, with its mean larger than its median and its median
larger than its mode. The smooth curve suggested by the tops
of the rectangles in this histogram would be similarly skewed and
would not bear much resemblance to the normal curve.

The Normal Distribution. The normal curve is a mathematical
construct based on an equation which was first derived as a mathematical exercise without any reference to concrete data. It is an
astonishing fact that many physical variables have frequency distributions which bear a striking similarity to this mathematical
curve.

The theoretical normal curve never actually touches the base
line and its range is unlimited, though it comes closer and closer
to the base line as you go farther out in either direction. For any
physical variable, such as height, the range must of necessity be
limited.

The area of all the rectangles which form a histogram represents
the total frequency in the distribution. Similarly, the area under
a normal curve represents the total frequency of a *normally distributed* variable.

In a histogram, the frequency in any class interval is repre-

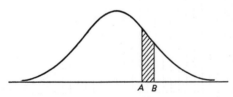

sented by the area of a rectangle which has that interval as its base. In a normal
curve, if one ordinate is
drawn at any point *A* on the
base line and another drawn

at a second point *B*, the area of the segment between those ordinates represents the frequency of values in the interval *AB*.

In graphing the distribution of a physical variable, it is impossible to make the intervals small enough for the distribution actually to become a smooth curve. Thus the graph of a set of
observed data will always be a step curve, or histogram. However,
if the normal curve appears to approximate closely the frequency
distribution of a variable in a set of data, we are inclined to generalize and to say that variable is *normally distributed*, or *has a
normal distribution*.

Mean and Standard Deviation of a Normal Distribution. On the histogram of the heights of 10,000 adult men discussed earlier in this chapter, the mean height would be represented by a point on the base line in the manner made familiar in earlier chapters, and the standard deviation would be represented by the length of a horizontal line segment. Thus for the histogram of Figure 12–1, the mean is located at the point marked $\overline{X}$; the standard deviation is the length marked s, the point one standard deviation above the mean is marked $\overline{X} + s$; etc.

The normal distribution also has a mean which is usually called μ (*mu*, the small Greek letter corresponding to the English m), and has a standard deviation which is usually called σ (*sigma*, the small Greek letter corresponding to the English s). These could be obtained approximately by computation in which the frequencies are represented by segments of area, but accurate solutions are obtained by the methods of integral calculus.

Principal Uses of the Normal Distribution. Though the content of such applications varies enormously, the principal applications of the normal distribution fall into the three general categories which follow:

1. Its most important and most interesting application is in connection with generalization from a limited number of measures on observed individuals to similar measures of a larger number of individuals that have not been observed. Much of the information basic to modern science, industry, education, and government depends upon investigations of this sort. As this use is discussed at some length in Chapters 13 to 16, it will not be elaborated on here.

2. Certain types of physical measurements have distributions which so closely approximate the normal that its use greatly facilitates their analysis. (a) The physical sciences furnish numerous distributions of this nature. The first tabulation of the normal distribution appeared in a book on the refraction of light near the horizon, published shortly before 1800. Another early work used it in relation to the determination of the position of the polar star. (b) The distributions of some measurements on human beings have a striking resemblance to the theoretical normal distribution; other measurements do not suggest normality. For example, in a large, unselected group of adults, homogeneous as to racial origin and living under fairly similar conditions, the distribution of height closely approximates the normal form. The distribution would probably not be normal if the group included both sexes,

or was made up of children of varying age, or included persons born in diverse parts of the globe and reared under different climatic and dietary conditions. The distribution of weight, on the other hand, is likely to be very far from normal because weight is not so directly dependent on heredity as height is, being partly controlled by individual preference. It takes little thought to recognize that many measures influenced by social customs have distributions very far from the normal form. Consider, for example, the distributions, for adults in the United States, of dollar income, number of years of education, average caloric intake per day, number of days illness in the past year, etc. About the middle of the nineteenth century, the great Belgian statistician, Adolph Quetelet, made studies of the heights of army recruits and decided that they followed the "normal law." In that period there were almost no other large-scale compilations of data available, but Quetelet was convinced, by analogy to height, that when such became available they too would "obey the normal law" and his ideas were widely disseminated. This historical accident may be the origin of the current superstition that all variable traits are normally distributed. There are statistical tests for normality of distribution but these are outside the scope of this book. One such test is described on pages 119–123 of the authors' *Statistical Inference.*

3. For some variables the true form of distribution is unknown, but it is convenient to scale the variable in such a way as to produce a normal distribution of scores. Consider intelligence, for example. It seems reasonable to assume that an unselected group of children of a given age would show a normal distribution of intelligence test scores and most of the intelligence tests are scaled in such a way as to produce that result. In some situations only categorical ratings are available — as, for example, when a teacher assigns grades of A, B, C, D, and F. As nothing is known about the form of the underlying distribution, it often seems not unreasonable to transform these categorical ratings to scores on the assumption that the underlying trait has a normal distribution. The procedure of "normalizing" will be taken up at the end of this chapter.

Drawing a Normal Curve. In order to make use of the normal distribution, one needs to be able to read values from such tables as Tables I and II in the Appendix and to have a clear understanding of what the tabular entries mean. An intuitive feeling for the shape of the curve is a real help. One of the best ways to develop such understanding is to make a drawing of the curve and to examine its properties.

Look once more at Figure 12–1. If X represents the score value of any point on the horizontal scale, then $\dfrac{X - \overline{X}}{s}$ would be the standard score of that point expressed in terms of the mean and standard deviation of a set of observed scores. In relation to a normal distribution, such a standard score would be denoted

$$(12.1) \qquad\qquad z = \frac{X - \mu}{\sigma} \quad \text{or} \quad z = \frac{x}{\sigma}$$

and called a *standard normal deviate*. We shall scale the horizontal axis of the curve we are about to draw in terms of z. On Figure 12–1 it is apparent that the normal curve comes very close to the base line at 2.5 standard deviations on each side of the mean, that is at $z = \dfrac{X - \mu}{\sigma} = 2.5$. Therefore, it would seem satisfactory to let our scale go from $z = -3$ to $z = 3$.

As a first step, lay off on a piece of graph paper a horizontal scale and mark on it points which you label −3, −2, −1, 0, 1, 2, and 3. It will be convenient to have the interval between two successive points subdivided into 5 or 10 small units in order that you can easily plot the values listed in Table 12.1. At the point marked 0, erect a perpendicular axis and mark on it the points .05, .10, .15, .20, .25, .30, .35, and .40 as in Figure 12–2. You may use a scale different from that in this figure but do not make your drawing too small.

For each pair of entries in Table 12.1 plot a point in the usual manner. Then plot a second point for which the value of z is

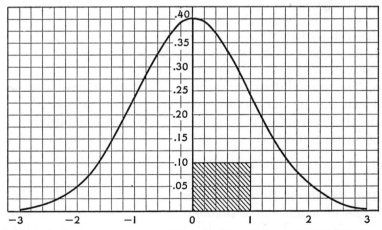

Fig 12–2 The Normal Curve. (Area of shaded rectangle is one tenth of total area under the curve.)

TABLE 12.1 Abscissas (z) and Ordinates (y) of the Standard Normal Curve

z	y	z	y
0	.399	1.6	.111
.2	.391	1.8	.079
.4	.368	2.0	.054
.6	.333	2.2	.036
.8	.290	2.4	.022
1.0	.242	2.6	.014
1.2	.194	2.8	.008
1.4	.150	3.0	.004

negative, thus producing a symmetrical pattern of dots as in Figure 12–2. Draw a smooth curve through the points you have plotted. If you find you cannot draw the curve *smoothly* and touch all the points marked, you may know you have estimated some values incorrectly and you should re-examine them.

Characteristics of the Normal Distribution. Certain general characteristics of the normal distribution will now be stated and you should try to visualize them in relation to the figure you have just drawn.

1. The curve is symmetrical. If the figure were folded along its vertical axis, the two halves would coincide.

2. The mean, median, and mode of the normal distribution are identical.

3. The range is unlimited, infinite, in both directions, but as the distance from μ increases the curve approaches the horizontal axis more and more closely. Theoretically, it never actually reaches the horizontal axis.

4. The curve is smooth in contrast to the histograms or step curves we have previously drawn from observed data.

5. The normal distribution has a standard deviation which we shall call σ. In the picture you have drawn, $\sigma = 1$. In other words, the horizontal scale has been laid off in standard deviation units, so that the horizontal variable is actually in standardized form. Then the horizontal variable is $\frac{X - \mu}{\sigma}$.

The Family of Normal Curves. We have said that the distribution of heights of a population of adult persons of one sex closely approximates the normal distribution. If we consider men and women as separate populations, the distribution of the heights of each population will also closely approximate the normal. However, the means of these two distributions of heights will surely differ, and there may also be a difference between the two standard deviations.

We see in this pair of normal distributions an example of the fact that there is not *a* normal curve, but a family of normal curves. A member of this family is fully defined when its mean, μ, its standard deviation, σ, and the number of cases, N, on which it is based, are known. Several members of the normal family are illustrated in Figures 12–3, 12–4, and 12–5. The curves in Figure 12–3 all have the same μ and σ, but are based on different values

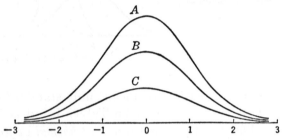

Fig. 12–3   Three Normal Curves All Having the Same Mean and Standard Deviation but different Total Frequencies.

    For curve A, $N = 300, \sigma = 1$
    For curve B, $N = 200, \sigma = 1$
    For curve C, $N = 100, \sigma = 1$

of N. The curves in Figure 12–4 all have the same N and μ but differ in their values of σ. The curves in Figure 12–5 all have the same N but differ in their values of μ and σ.

Parameters.   The values of μ, σ, and N which distinguish one member of the family of normal curves from other members of this family are called *parameters*. This term is borrowed from mathematics where it is used generally to distinguish one member of a family of curves from other members of the same family. We shall find in the next two chapters that the search for information about parameters plays a central role in statistical investigations.

Standard Normal Distribution.   When a normally distributed variable X is expressed in standard score form, $z = \dfrac{X - \mu}{\sigma} = \dfrac{x}{\sigma}$, the mean of these standard scores is 0, and the standard deviation is 1. The area, representing N, can also be considered to be unity; then we have a kind of standard curve convenient to tabulate, to which all normal curves can be reduced by changing scale or posi-

Fig. 12–4 Three Normal Curves All Having the Same Mean and Total Frequency
but Different Standard Deviations.
    For curve D, N = 300, σ = 1
    For curve E, N = 300, σ = 2
    For curve F, N = 300, σ = 3

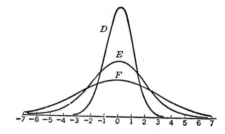

Fig. 12–5 Three Normal Curves with
Same Area but Different Values of μ
and σ.

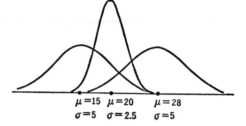

tion. Such a curve — with zero mean, unit standard deviation, and unit area — is the form to which Tables I and II in the Appendix relate. This form is called *standard normal* or *unit normal*. The equation for the general normal curve is

$$(12.2) \qquad y = \frac{N}{\sigma \sqrt{2\pi}} e^{-\frac{(X - \mu)^2}{2\sigma^2}}$$

In standard form, this equation becomes

$$(12.3) \qquad y = \frac{1}{\sqrt{2\pi}} e^{-\frac{z^2}{2}}$$

Formulas (12.2) and (12.3) have been presented for the information of those readers who are interested. These formulas will not be used in any subsequent portions of this book. The normal distribution has been so thoroughly tabulated that few persons ever need to make use of its formula.

Area Relationships under a Normal Curve. Ordinates are seldom needed for anything except for drawing the curve, and while there are some practical problems which call for knowledge of an ordinate you will not meet any such in this book. The area between two ordinates, on the other hand, is of great importance in a variety of problems, because such an area represents frequency. Before you can solve any problems of the kind presented in the latter part of this chapter and in the two following chapters, you must be able to obtain such proportions of area from Table I. In order that you may clearly understand the entries in this table, we shall first estimate certain areas from the graph you have drawn and then check these crude results against the tabulated values.

To obtain an estimate of the fraction of area between the ordinate at $\frac{x}{\sigma} = 0$ and the ordinate at any other point, you may count the number of small squares in that area — estimating as well as you can the parts of squares cut by the curve — then divide this number by the total number of squares in the entire area under the curve. The latter can be estimated fairly well by sheer counting but that is laborious and the area in the tails is hard to estimate. There is a much easier way. Draw a small rectangle with length equal to σ and height equal to the interval from 0 to .1 on the vertical axis. (See the shaded rectangle in Figure 12–2). Count the number of small squares in this rectangle, multiply that number by 10 and you will have the number of small squares in the entire area under your curve.

In the following examples, areas obtained by counting squares on the graph which you have constructed will be compared with areas read from Table I. Since the areas in Table I are based on the standard normal distribution which has total area unity, the areas in that table are in effect fractions of the total area. To get comparable readings from your graph you will need to divide the area in the specified segment by the total area.

The column headed *area* in Table I gives the areas between an ordinate at a specified value of $\frac{x}{\sigma}$ and the ordinate at $\frac{x}{\sigma} = 0$. Such an area is shaded in the adjacent sketch.

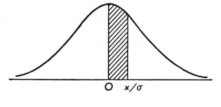

By counting squares on your graph, find the percent of area between the ordinates at 0, and at .2. This should be approximately 8. Now turn to Table I, find the value of .2 in the column headed $\frac{x}{\sigma}$ and read the corresponding entry in the column headed area. It is .0793 or approximately 8 percent.

Again, from your graph, find the fraction of area between ordinates at 0 and at −1.4. Check the outcome by finding the value 1.4 in the $\frac{x}{\sigma}$ column of Table I and noting that the corresponding area is given as .4192. As the curve is symmetrical, the area between ordinates at −1.4 and at 1.4 would be .4192 + .4192 = .8384 or .84.

Find the area to the left of the ordinate at 1.8. The area between ordinates at 0 and at 1.8 is .4641, and you know that half of the total area is to the left of the ordinate at 0. Therefore, the area to the left of the ordinate at 1.8 is .5000 + .4641 = .9641, or .96.

What area is to the left of an ordinate at −1.8? Reference to your graph will convince you that this is .5000 − .4641 = .0359, or .04.

What area lies outside the ordinates at −1.8 and at 1.8? This is the area to the left of −1.8 and the area to the right of 1.8, or .0359 + .0359 = .0718 or .07. It can, of course, also be computed as 1.0000 − 2(.4641) = 1.0000 − .9282 = .0718.

EXERCISE 12.1

(Some students will need to go through only a few of the exercises in each group in order to achieve mastery. Others will need much practice. It is suggested that you check your results with the answer key and stop work in each group as soon as you find you are making no errors.)

A. First, by counting squares on your graph and then by reading from Table I, find the area between an ordinate at the mean and an ordinate at a point for which $\frac{x}{\sigma}$ has the value indicated.

1. .60	3. 1.60	5. −2.00	7. 1.00
2. .40	4. −.10	6. 1.80	8. .70

B. What is the area between symmetrically placed ordinates at the indicated values of $\frac{x}{\sigma}$? Read answers from the table.

1. −.45 and .45	3. −1.00 and 1.00	5. −2.57 and 2.57
2. −.67 and .67	4. −1.96 and 1.96	6. −1.03 and 1.03

C. What is the area to the left of an ordinate at the indicated value of $\frac{x}{\sigma}$? Read answers from the table.

1. .15	3. 1.90	5. −1.85	7. .67
2. −1.32	4. 1.67	6. −1.65	8. −.67

D. What is the area outside ordinates at the indicated values of $z = \frac{x}{\sigma}$? Read answers from the table.

1. −1.96 and 1.96	3. −2.32 and 2.32	5. −.75 and .75
2. −1.64 and 1.64	4. −2.58 and 2.58	6. −2.81 and 2.81

Percentiles of the Normal Distribution. Suppose you have read from Table I that 73 percent of the area under the unit normal curve lies below — i.e., to the left of — an ordinate at $z = \dfrac{x}{\sigma} = $ .61. The same relationship may be stated in either of the following ways:

(a) $z = .61$ is the 73rd percentile of a unit normal distribution
(b) $z_{.73} = .61$

In earlier chapters the letter X with appropriate subscript was used to designate a percentile. As we are now using the letter z to denote a standardized deviate of the unit normal distribution, we shall use z with appropriate subscript to denote a percentile of that distribution. Thus $z_{.50}$ is the median (and also the mean). Whenever z has a subscript larger than .50, it represents a point to the right of the median and such points have positive values. Whenever z has a subscript smaller than .50, it represents a point to the left of the median and such points have negative values.

What is the value of $z_{.90}$? The subscript tells us that 90 percent of the area lies to the left of the desired point and, therefore, we know that 90 percent − 50 percent = 40 percent lies between that point and 0. In Table I we look along the area column to find the entry which is closest to .40. This is the entry .3997 corresponding to $\dfrac{x}{\sigma} = 1.28$. We conclude that $z_{.90} = 1.28$. This solution required some maneuvering but Appendix Table II would have given us immediately the statement that $z_{.90} = 1.282$.

What is the value of $z_{.10}$? Because the subscript is less than .50 we know the value must be negative. Since 10 percent of the area is to the left of $z_{.10}$, the area between $z_{.10}$ and the mean must be .50 − .10 = .40. As before, in Table I we find the number nearest .40 in the area column and read the corresponding value in the $\dfrac{x}{\sigma}$ column. As before, it is 1.28, but now we must attach a minus sign. Thus $z_{.10} = -1.28$. Now look in Table II. Here you read that $z_{.10} = -1.282$.

Since $z_{.10} = -1.282$ and $z_{.90} = 1.282$, the following relations hold:

$$z_{.10} = -z_{.90}$$
$$z_{.90} = -z_{.10}$$
$$z_{.10} + z_{.90} = 0$$

These statements might be generalized by using some letter, say, a, to represent one of the subscripts:

$$z_a = - z_{1-a}$$
$$z_{1-a} = - z_a$$
$$z_a + z_{1-a} = 0$$

If a normal distribution has $\mu = 72$ and $\sigma = 13$, what is its 40th percentile? From Table II we read that the 40th percentile of the standard normal curve is $-.253$. This tells us that $\dfrac{X_{.40} - \mu}{\sigma} = -.253$.

If $\mu = 72$ and $\sigma = 13$, then $\dfrac{X_{.40} - 72}{13} = -.253$

Therefore, $X_{.40} - 72 = -.253(13) = -3.289$
$$X_{.40} = 72 - 3.289$$
$$X_{.40} = 68.7$$

EXERCISE 12.2

In each group answer only as many questions as you need to achieve mastery. Be sure to go on to Group I as the questions in that group provide important background for Chapter 13.

A. What area is to the left of each value?

   1. $z_{.07}$ 2. $z_{.96}$ 3. $z_{.55}$ 4. $z_{.31}$ 5. $z_{.42}$

B. What area is to the right of each value?

   1. $z_{.99}$ 2. $z_{.05}$ 3. $z_{.40}$ 4. $z_{.995}$ 5. $z_{.95}$

C. Which of the values named in groups A and B are negative?

D. What area lies between the stated values?

   1. $z_{.01}$ and $z_{.99}$ 3. $z_{.25}$ and $z_{.75}$ 5. $z_{.025}$ and $z_{.975}$
   2. $z_{.005}$ and $z_{.995}$ 4. $z_{.02}$ and $z_{.08}$ 6. $z_{.60}$ and $z_{.71}$

E. By reference to Table II verify the following statements:

   1. $z_{.01} = -2.326$ 5. $z_{.75} = .6745$ 9. $z_{.999} = 3.090$
   2. $z_{.25} = -.6745$ 6. $z_{.80} = .842$ 10. $z_{.005} = -2.576$
   3. $z_{.12} = -1.175$ 7. $z_{.20} = -.842$ 11. $z_{.995} = 2.576$
   4. $z_{.70} = .524$ 8. $z_{.94} = 1.555$ 12. $z_{.975} = 1.960$

F. What area lies outside the stated values? (This area is the sum of the area to the left of the smaller value and the area to the right of the larger.)

   1. $z_{.01}$ and $z_{.99}$ 3. $z_{.025}$ and $z_{.975}$ 5. $z_{.05}$ and $z_{.95}$
   2. $z_{.005}$ and $z_{.995}$ 4. $z_{.02}$ and $z_{.98}$ 6. $z_{.10}$ and $z_{.90}$

G. Between which percentile values is the middle 30 percent of the area included? Solution: If 30 percent of the area is in a strip symmetrically placed around the mean, one half of 30 percent = 15 percent must lie on each side of the mean.   Therefore, the area below the lower edge of that strip must be

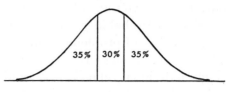

.50 − .15 = .35 and below the upper edge, .50 + .15 = .65. The strip, therefore, extends from $z_{.35} = -.385$ to $z_{.65} = .385$. These values were obtained by reading $z_{.34}$ and $z_{.36}$ from Table II and interpolating between them.

H. State the percentile values which would bound a middle strip of area symmetrically placed around the mean if that area is as follows:

1. .99   3. .50   5. .90   7. .25
2. .98   4. .95   6. .80   8. .999

I. In a normal distribution with $\mu = 64$ and $\sigma = 8$,

1. What is the value of the 10th percentile?
2. What is the value of the 70th percentile?
3. What proportion of cases would have scores larger than 70?
4. What proportion of cases would have scores less than 50?
5. Between what scores would the middle 50 percent of the cases lie?
6. Between what scores would the middle 95 percent of the cases lie?
7. Beyond what score would the highest 5 percent lie?
8. Outside what two scores, symmetrically placed in regard to the mean, would the most extreme 1 percent lie?

J. Answer the eight questions asked in Group I if $\mu = 91$ and $\sigma = 15$.

K. Answer the eight questions asked in Group I if $\mu = 59$ and $\sigma = 12$.

L. Answer the eight questions asked in Group I if $\mu = 6$ and $\sigma = 4$.

Probable Error. The values $z_{.25}$ and $z_{.75}$ are the first and third quartiles of the standard normal distribution, and one half the area under the normal curve lies between them. From Table II it can be seen that $z_{.25} = -.6745$ and $z_{.75} = .6745$. The value $.6745\sigma$ is called *the probable error.*[1] The term is rather unfortunate because it is somewhat misleading but it has been in use since 1815 and

[1] The term was introduced in 1815 by the great German astronomer and physicist, Friedrich Wilhelm Bessel, in a paper on the position of the pole star, published in the Berlin Astronomical Yearbook. (See Walker, *Studies in the History of Statistics*, p. 24). He used the term *der wahrscheinliche Fehler*. Almost at once the expression appeared in scientific journals all over Europe, as *error probabalis* in Latin, as *l'erreur probable* in French, as *l'errore probabile* in Italian, as *the probable error* in English. The roots of this term are deep and tenacious.

seems to survive all efforts to do away with it. Neither the term nor the idea will be used again in this book. It is mentioned here only because you are likely to meet it in your reading elsewhere.

Normal Probability. In certain very interesting and very important types of problems, some of which are treated more fully in Chapters 13 through 16, the task is to assess the likelihood that a single individual, chosen "at random" from a group of individuals, will come from a particular category of that group. In such problems the *proportional frequency in each category is called the probability of that category and the proportional frequency distribution is called a probability distribution.*

There are many forms of probability distribution; not by any means are all probability distributions normal. A probability distribution may have a continuous scale or may consist of discrete classes. It may consist of just two classes. For example, it is well known that about 51 percent of newborn babies are boys and about 49 percent girls. The two classes, boys and girls, and the relative frequencies .51 and .49 constitute a probability distribution. One may say that there is probability .51 that the first baby born in Chicago in the year 1975 will be a boy. In general, a probability distribution consists of a set of classes and the relative frequencies related to them. Many extremely useful probability distributions are described in more advanced texts. At this point our emphasis will not be on the topic of probability in general, but on the use of the normal distribution as a probability distribution in preparation for a better understanding of the important ideas taken up in the next four chapters.

First let us consider a rather artificial situation. Suppose that for each of 50,000 school children an intelligence quotient is available and that the distribution of these is approximately normal. If each child's IQ is recorded on a small ticket, all the tickets are thoroughly mixed in a huge lottery, and one ticket is drawn at random,[2] what is the probability that the IQ recorded on that ticket will be at least two standard deviations above the mean of the entire group of 50,000? Because the distribution has been described as normal, this question can be answered by merely finding the area under a normal curve above an ordinate at $z = \dfrac{X - \mu}{\sigma} = 2$. Table I shows this area to be .023. What is the probability that a ticket drawn at random will contain an IQ very

---

[2] Some discussion of what drawing "at random" means will be found in the next chapter. For the present the term will be left admittedly vague.

close to the mean — say, one lying within 0.1 of a standard deviation from the mean? Answer 2(.0398) = .08.

Now let us discard as irrelevant the fiction of writing the IQ's on tickets and physically drawing one by means of a lottery, but retain the idea of a very large normally distributed population of IQ's. Selecting at random an individual from such a population is a matter of some difficulty because people of widely different intelligence levels do not tend to frequent the same places. So let us again place a question with respect to an unborn infant. What is the probability that the first child born in Chicago in the year 1975 will have an intelligence quotient at least 3 standard deviations below the general mean? In other words, what is the area under the normal curve below $z = -3$? Table I shows this to be .0013.

In most physical populations it is difficult either to establish the normality of distribution or to select individuals at random, or both. The principal use of the normal curve as a probability distribution is in connection with sampling problems as described in the next chapter.

Classifying in Groups with Equal Range. Suppose a research worker is carrying out a study for which he needs a measure of job satisfaction (or interest in teaching, or conservatism-liberalism, or any other attitude difficult to measure objectively). This research worker has drawn up a list of 150 statements of opinion ranging from extreme satisfaction to extreme dissatisfaction and wants to place these on a scale. Ranking the 150 statements looks like a formidable undertaking but it does not seem too difficult to place them in ordered categories.

The number of categories is an arbitrary choice. Let us suppose the investigator decides to use 9 categories. Suppose also that he makes the assumption that his set of statements represents a normal distribution of job satisfaction and that he wishes to have each of the 9 categories cover the same range on the scale of the distribution. Strictly speaking this is impossible because the range of a normal distribution is infinite and $1/9$ of an infinite range would also be infinite. However, if he lets each category have a range of 0.5σ, the 9 categories will cover a range of 4.5σ, or the range from -2.25σ to 2.25σ.

Reference to the table of the normal distribution shows that only a little more than 1 percent of the area under the curve lies above 2.25σ or below -2.25σ. Consequently, the investigator may decide to make the end intervals open, so that all cases above

1.75σ constitute one category and all cases below -1.75 constitute another category. The following tabulation shows the 9 categories formed by such a subdivision of the scale, the corresponding percents of area under the curve, the number of statements in each category in accordance with the indicated percents, and code numbers ranging from 1 to 9 which are to be the scale values of the categories.

Category		Percent	Number	Code
Above	1.75	4.01 or 4	6	9
1.25 to	1.75	6.55 or 7	10	8
.75 to	1.25	12.10 or 12	18	7
.25 to	.75	17.47 or 17	26	6
−.25 to	.25	19.74 or 20	30	5
−.75 to	−.25	17.47 or 17	26	4
−1.25 to	−.75	12.10 or 12	18	3
−1.75 to	−1.25	6.55 or 7	10	2
Below	−1.75	4.01 or 4	6	1
		100.00	150	

The number of items to be placed in each of the nine categories is shown in the accompanying sketch as an area under the normal curve between ordinates drawn at the points indicated.

The statements must now be distributed in accordance with the frequencies shown in the tabulation. Each statement is written on a separate slip of paper and these slips are sorted into 9 piles of the size specified. The 6 statements (no more and no less) which are judged as expressing the greatest degree of job satisfaction (or interest in teaching, or whatever variable is under consideration) are placed at the extreme right and coded 9, while the 6 which are judged to express the greatest dissatisfaction are placed at the extreme left and coded 1. The other slips are assigned to intermediate piles in such a way as to form a set of ordered classes. The code numbers from 1 to 9 which are assigned to these classes are usually treated as constituting a scale.

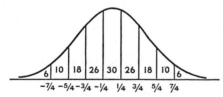

This is similar to the line of argument on which is based the *stanine scale* (Standard nine) employed by the United States Air Force in its testing and classification program.

This is also the general line of procedure for what is called the "Q-sort" used in many psychological studies. Each of the items to be sorted is written on a separate card, and the judges work independently. If they are told how many cards to place in each pile, every judge will achieve the same mean and standard deviation. If they are left free to decide how many cards to place in each pile, there may be considerable discrepancy from judge to judge as to mean and as to standard deviation of the distribution of cards. The purpose of having more than one judge to do the sorting is twofold: (a) to ascertain how well different judges can agree on the placement of items and (b) to improve measurement by eliminating those items on which a prescribed degree of agreement was not reached. Thus the investigator in this problem might intend to reduce his original 150 items to 50 by first throwing out each one which was so ambiguous that the judges did not place it in the same category, and then by random selection (discussed in the next chapter) eliminating enough others so that the frequencies in the categories were $\frac{1}{3}$ as large as for the original 150 items, namely 2, 3, 6, 9, 10, 9, 6, 3, 2.

EXERCISE 12.3

Verify enough of the following statements to be sure you understand them.

1. If individuals are classified in 5 categories each with range of 1σ, the division points will fall at -1.5, $-.5$, $+.5$, and 1.5 and the relative frequencies in each category will be .0668, .2417, .3830, .2417, and .0668, or roughly .07, .24, .38, .24, and .07.

2. If individuals are classified in 5 categories each with range of 1.2σ, the division points will fall at -1.8, $-.6$, $.6$, and 1.8, and the relative frequencies in the categories will be .0359, .2384, .4514, .2384, and .0359.

3. If 6 categories are used with range of 1σ each, the division points will be at -2, -1, 0, 1, and 2, and the relative frequencies will be roughly .02, .14, .34, .34, .14, and .02.

4. If 11 categories are used with range of $.4\sigma$, the division points will be -1.8, -1.4, -1.0, $-.6$, $-.2$, $.2$, $.6$, 1.0, 1.4, and 1.8, and the relative frequencies will be .036, .045, .078, .116, .146, .158, .146, .116, .078, .045, and .036.

5. If 11 categories are used with range of $.5\sigma$ each, the division points will be -2.25, -1.75, -1.25, $-.75$, $-.25$, $.25$, $.75$, 1.25, 1.75, and 2.25, and the relative frequencies will be approximately .01, .03, .07, .12, .17, .20, .17, .12, .07, .03, and .01.

Transforming Ordered Categories into Scaled Scores. Let us suppose that a wealthy citizen has given a sum of money to a high school for scholarships, with the stipulation that the recipients shall be chosen on the basis of average class marks. This presents a problem because the school's records are in the form of letter grades and now it must average these letter grades in some way which will appear fair and objective to all concerned. One member of the selection committee proposes to use the arbitrary code: A = 10, B = 9, C = 8, D = 7, E = 6, F = 5. Another member points out that reducing each code number by 5 so that A = 5, B = 4, C = 3, D = 2, E = 1, and F = 0 would simply reduce each pupil's average by 5, thus leaving pupils in the same relative order, but would somewhat lessen the work of obtaining averages. The committee is about to adopt this latter code when someone calls attention to the marks given over a period of several terms by three teachers in the same department, teaching students who are presumably similar in ability. These three teachers, Smith, Jones, and Brown, have assigned marks as indicated in Table 12.2. One member of the committee objects to the code on the ground that the letters do not seem to have exactly the same meaning as used by these three teachers, that an A given by Brown does not present as strong evidence of high achievement as one given by Smith. Another objection he makes to the code is that it is based on the assumption that the 6 letters represent 6 evenly spaced points on

TABLE 12.2 The Number and Percent of Students to Whom Each of Three Teachers Has Assigned the Specified Letter Mark

	Number of marks given by			Percent of marks given by		
Mark	Smith	Jones	Brown	Smith	Jones	Brown
A	24	36	106	9.6%	12.0%	26.5%
B	130	78	152	52.0	26.0	38.0
C	68	95	96	27.2	31.7	24.0
D	12	55	36	4.8	18.3	9.0
E	8	12	6	3.2	4.0	1.5
F	8	24	4	3.2	8.0	1.0
Total	250	300	400	100.0%	100.0%	100.0%

a scale, that A is assumed to be as much better than B as B is better than C, etc. This he says is unrealistic. This committee member proposes an alternate plan of scaling, based on the assumption that there was really a normal distribution of performance for the students taught by each teacher. He admits that this assumption may not be true — that it can neither be established nor refuted because there is no evidence. He thinks the assumption of normality is at least as acceptable as the assumption that increments between consecutive letters represent equal scale intervals. In order to place the categorical ratings (the letter grades) on a scale, it is necessary either to make an assumption concerning the scale interval (i.e., assign an arbitrary code), or to make an assumption concerning the form of distribution and to derive the scale equivalents from that distribution.

The committee member who argued in favor of making the assumption of normality carried out the appropriate computations and presented the following transformation code for the marks of Smith, Jones, and Brown:

Mark	Smith	Jones	Brown
A	67	66	61
B	54	57	51
C	43	49	43
D	36	42	35
E	33	37	29
F	29	32	24

He admitted, however, that the application of his method might be difficult to explain to the public, who were much interested in the allotment of the awards, and that it would require a considerable amount of work to make such a transformation for the grades of every teacher in the school and then to average the transformed scores of individual pupils.

The method used in making the transformation may be illustrated for Jones' set of 300 marks. A normal distribution is assumed to be divided into 6 segments with areas corresponding to the percents of frequency shown in Table 12.2. For each segment of area there must be found a value of the normal deviate z which will serve as typical value for that category. Either the median value

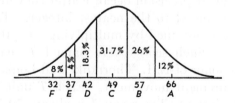

of the category or the mean value can be used, but the median is easier to obtain and so we shall use it. Consider category A. The median of that category is a point which has one half of the area of the segment on either side and, therefore, has .06 of the total area of the curve above it (to the right) and $.08 + .04 +$ $.183 + .317 + .26 + .06 = .94$ of the total area below it. Table II gives 1.555 as the value of $z_{.94}$. If we let $T = 10z + 50$, the transformed value for grade A will be $15.55 + 50 = 66$.

Now consider the median of category B. The area below it will be $.08 + .04 + .183 + .317 + .13 = .75$ and the area above it $.13 + .12 = .25$. The value of $z_{.75}$ is $.6745$ and $T = 50 + 6.7 = 57$.

TABLE 12.3 Computations Used in Transforming a Set of Ordered Categories to Scaled Scores (T) on the Assumption of Normality of Distribution

Category	Frequency	Percent in category	Percent below median of category	z	$T = 50 + 10z$
A	36	12.0%	94.0%	1.56	66
B	78	26.0	75.0	.67	57
C	95	31.67	46.17	−.10	49
D	55	18.33	21.17	−.80	42
E	12	4.0	10.0	−1.288	37
F	24	8.0	4.0	−1.75	32
	300	100.0%			

The computations leading to the transformation are presented in Table 12.3. Here the first two columns provide the data. The third column is obtained by dividing each frequency by the sum of all the frequencies (300 in this case). The percent below the median of the category for category C is $8.0 + 4.0 + 18.33 + \dfrac{31.67}{2} = 46.17$, and similarly for the other categories. The z values are read from either Table I or II and need not be recorded with great precision because after they are multiplied by 10 they will be rounded to the nearest integer. The entries in the final column are obtained by multiplying z by 10 and adding 50.

Such scores were named T scores by William A. McCall in honor of E. L. Thorndike and Louis Terman, pioneers in the measurement movement. Each T unit is one tenth of a standard deviation. The mean T is always 50 except as it may be affected by rounding errors. These transformed T scores must not be confused with the transformed standard scores, $Z = 50 + 10 \dfrac{X - \overline{X}}{s}$, used in Chapter 7. There are three important distinctions. In the first place, Z scores cannot be obtained from ordered categories but only from scaled scores. In the second place, in order to obtain Z scores, one computes a mean and a standard deviation and then

$Z = 50 + 10 \dfrac{(X - \overline{X})}{s}$; whereas to obtain T scores one computes percentile ranks (the percent below the midpoint of the category), reads the corresponding values of z from a table of normal probability, and then $T = 50 + 10z$. Only the final step of the two procedures is the same. In the third place, T scores have a normal distribution regardless of the form of the original distribution; Z scores do not have a normal distribution unless the original variable had a normal distribution.

EXERCISE 12.4

1. Verify the T score values given for the grades of Smith and Brown on page 195.
2. Suppose a supervisor has placed a group of 200 teachers in 6 qualitative categories as follows:

Excellent in every way	20
Superior in most traits	30
Above average	64
Fair	48
Poor but not subject to dismissal	30
Very poor subject to dismissal	8

What transformed scores correspond to these classes?

Profile Chart. When an individual is to be evaluated relative to a group on several traits at once, it is customary to plot his scores on a graph known as a *profile chart*.

A profile chart of Pupil Number 1 of Table IX appears in Figure 12–6. The bars represent the percentile ranks of this individual on the five variables named at the left of the graph. To read the bars it is necessary to refer to the horizontal scale at the bottom of the graph. The values of this scale are percentile ranks referred to the standard normal distribution. A bar originates at the 50th percentile rank and extends to the scale value representing the individual's percentile rank on a particular test. Thus we see from the bars that Pupil Number 1 has percentile rank 26 in IQ, percentile rank 88 on arithmetic computation, and so on.

In addition to its value in showing the relationship of an individual to the group, the profile chart is useful in comparing individuals to each other. Figure 12–7 shows profiles of Pupils 1, 2, 3 from Table IX set side by side for ready comparison. It is immediately apparent from the figure that Pupil 3 has the highest

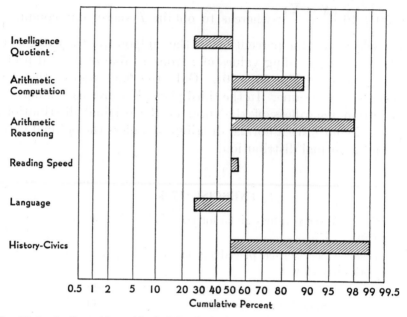

Fig. 12–6   Profile on Normal Probability Scale for Pupil No. 1 of Table IX.

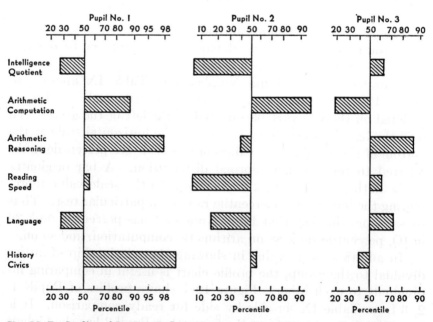

Fig. 12–7   Profiles of Pupils with Code Numbers 1, 2, and 3 in Appendix Table IX.

IQ and the highest scores on the verbal tests of reading speed and language, but is lowest in computation and history-civics.

A profile chart like that shown in Figure 12–6 can be made most simply by plotting percentile ranks on specially printed paper, which can be purchased as "arithmetic probability paper." If such paper is not available, the percentile ranks can be converted to T scores and these can then be plotted on an arithmetic scale.

The use of bars is a departure from the common practice of drawing line segments to connect the plotted percentile ranks. That common practice makes a profile chart look like a line graph, and emphasizes especially the relationship of a variable to its immediate neighbors. In a profile chart the order in which the variables are listed is usually arbitrary, so that the appearance of a line graph of a profile might be greatly changed if the order of listing were changed. The use of bars rather than connecting lines does away with the false impression of a trend, and simplifies both the evaluation of the individual on each variable and comparison of his standing on any one variable with his standing on all other variables.

A profile chart is sometimes made up by plotting percentile ranks directly on an arithmetic scale. This usage is unsatisfactory because it makes the distances on the scale for a difference between two percentiles near the middle the same as the distance for a like difference near the ends of the distribution. Most distributions ordinarily considered are less dense at the ends of the distribution than at the middle.

Another common practice is to make a profile chart by plotting the standard scores described in Chapter 7. The usefulness of this practice is limited when the shape of distribution differs from trait to trait. Consider, for example, two traits, one of which is measured by an easy test and the other by a difficult test. On the easy test, the top score might be only one and a half standard deviations above the mean, whereas on the difficult test the top score might be three standard deviations above the mean. Clearly a standard score of one and one half means something quite different on the two tests.

Transforming Ranks to Normal Deviates. The use of ranks in computing a correlation coefficient was described in Chapter 10. It often seems reasonable to assume that the underlying variable represented by the ranks is normally distributed. Appendix Table X may be used to transform a set of ranks into a set of scores from a normal distribution in which $\mu = 50$ and $\sigma = 10$, for samples in which $5 \leqq N \leqq 30$. To find the normal equivalent of a rank R when $N > 30$, first find the proportion

$$(12.4) \qquad\qquad p = 1 - \frac{R - 0.5}{N}$$

then read in Table II the normal deviate z_p in a unit normal curve corresponding to the proportion p. The corresponding normal deviate when $\mu = 50$ and $\sigma = 10$ is

$$Z_p = 10z_p + 50$$

Discovery of the Normal Curve.[3] The curve which we now call "normal" is the curve of normal probability or curve of error which attracted the interest of most of the great mathematicians and astronomers of the first half of the nineteenth century. More than two centuries ago, Abraham De Moivre (1667–1754), a refugee mathematician living in London, making his living partly by solving problems for wealthy gamblers, recognized that the random variation in the number of heads appearing on throws of n coins corresponds to the terms of the binomial expansion of $(.5 + .5)^n$, and that as n becomes larger this distribution approaches a definite form. In 1733 De Moivre derived the equation for this curve and presented it privately to some friends. To him it was only a mathematical exercise, utterly unconnected with any sort of application to empirical data.

At that time there were no collections of empirical data at hand for study. As yet no one had made any measurements of any large number of individuals. A Swiss mathematician named Jacques (or James) Bernoulli (1654–1705, eldest of the very remarkable family of mathematicians by that name) had suggested that the theory of probability might have useful applications in economic and moral affairs, but he, himself, was too near death to investigate the applications, and, moreover, he had no numerical data which he could have used for that purpose. The idea must have seemed fantastic to his contemporaries. In 1713, his great book on probability, *Ars Conjectandi*,[4] was published posthumously under the editorship of his nephew Nicolas, who seems to have tried in vain to induce other mathematicians to develop the

---

[3] For a more extended treatment, see H. M. Walker, *Studies in the History of Statistical Method*, Baltimore, The Williams & Wilkins Co., 1929, Chapter II; "Bi-centenary of the normal curve," *Journal of the American Statistical Association*, **29** (1934), 72–75; "Abraham de Moivre," *Scripta Mathematica*, **2** (1934), 316–333.

[4] Conjecto = to throw together, therefore, to gamble, therefore, to guess at or surmise.

argument further. Nearly a century passed before any scientific worker began to gather large masses of concrete data and to study the properties of distributions. The application of the normal curve in studies of concrete data begins with the work of the great mathematical astronomers who lived at the beginning of the nineteenth century, chiefly Laplace (1749–1827) in France, and Gauss (1777–1855) in Germany, each of whom derived the law independently and presumably without any knowledge of De Moivre's derivation.

The probability curve is often called the Gaussian curve, because until recently it was supposed that Gauss had been the first person to make use of its properties. However, in 1924, Karl Pearson discovered a hitherto unknown derivation by Abraham De Moivre.[5]

The idea that this curve could be used to describe data other than errors of observation in the physical sciences seems to have originated with the great Belgian statistician Adolphe Quetelet (1796–1874), who first popularized the idea that statistical method was a fundamental discipline adaptable to any field of human interest in which mass data were to be found. He was convinced that the measurement of mental and moral traits waited only for the collection of sufficient and trustworthy data, and was sure that when such measurement was feasible, the distribution of these traits would be found to be in accordance with the "law of error."

[5] Pearson, K., "Historical note on the origin of the normal curve of error," *Biometrika*, **16** (1924), 402–404.

13
Introduction to Statistical Inference

In an investigation which deals with matters of general interest, the findings are usually applied to a much larger number of cases than were actually observed in the sample of cases. This use of samples in statistics is probably the most important and certainly the most intriguing aspect of this science. The idea that information obtained from the examination of a relatively small number of cases can be used to throw light on the characteristics of a vast and unexamined universe is an exciting idea. That the sample not only furnishes an estimate of some characteristic of an unknown population, but also furnishes a measure of how much faith can be placed in that estimate, is still more remarkable.

Situations in Which Samples Are Employed. Statistical sampling plays a part in almost all statistical studies on which decisions for future action are to be based. Sometimes sampling is necessary because the universe, or population, about which information is desired is infinite and could never be examined in its entirety. This situation is typical of most psychological experiments. Some populations, even though finite, are so vast or so inaccessible that it would not be feasible to examine all their members. Sometimes, as in Example 1 below, it is important to process the results more quickly than would be possible if a complete count (or census) of the entire population were made. In certain kinds of research, measurement means the destruction of the individual measured. This is the typical situation in industrial studies where the strength of material or the length of life of some product is measured. To measure the tensile strength of cloth, pieces of cloth must be destroyed; to measure the breaking load of steel, steel must be broken; to measure the effective life of a battery or a light bulb or an automobile tire, it must be used until it is worthless. Consequently, in much industrial research the idea of studying an entire population is fantastic, and even the use of large samples is prohibitive.

Population. A sampling study is characterized by the fact that its objective is not simply to describe those individuals observed in the sample, but rather to search for information about the population from which the sample was drawn.

The statistical concept of a *population*, also called a *universe*, is an abstract concept fundamental to statistical inference. "It refers to the totality of numbers that would result from indefinitely many repetitions of the same process of selecting objects, measuring or classifying them, and recording the results. A population is, thus, a fixed body of numbers about which we would like to know. What we actually know is the numbers of a *sample*, a group selected from the population." [1] The reader must not think of a population in this sense as necessarily consisting of people or even of measurements of people. The three examples which follow happen all to be situations in which the population consists of observations on persons; they were chosen not because of but in spite of that peculiarity. A population might consist of observations on schoolhouses, on books, on cities, on shoes, on carloads of grain, on manufactured items, and so on.

To appreciate the nature of such studies, let us examine a few examples more closely.

1. *Estimating the number of unemployed in the United States.* In order to obtain current information on the state of the labor market, the United States Bureau of the Census conducts periodic sampling studies from which it calculates an estimate of the number of persons unemployed in various kinds of work and in different parts of the country. For the purpose of this investigation, each person in the labor market is placed in one of two classes: employed and unemployed. A two-class population is called a *dichotomous* population. The sample is necessarily obtained by selecting individual persons from the total number in the labor market. For the purpose of this investigation, when John Jones is drawn into the sample, we are not interested in all the personal attributes of John Jones as a human being, but only in whether he belongs in the class of the employed (E) or the unemployed (U). Thus the population is the totality of all observations U and E, and the sample consists of the number of observations of U and of E among the individuals selected. This particular example

---

[1] W. Allen Wallis and Harry V. Roberts, *Statistics, a New Approach*, The Free Press, Glencoe, Ill., 1956, page 126.

was chosen because it illustrates a dichotomous population and because it illustrates a situation in which the processing of a sample can be done rapidly enough to provide information while it is fresh and useful. The processing of a complete census would require so long that, by the time the findings could be published, they might no longer be applicable.

2. *Standardizing a test.* Standardized tests of achievement, of ability, of attitudes, or of preferences, etc., are used to determine the status of an individual person relative to a population, or of a subgroup relative to a population. (Such tests are also used to compare subgroups, but for this purpose it is not usually necessary that they be standardized.)

Consider for example the use of the Stanford Binet Test to provide information concerning the intelligence of an 8-year-old child. The child's test score would be useless in this connection without information about the distribution of the Binet scores of 8-year-old children in general to provide a standard against which an individual score could be rated. But the administration of the Binet test to *all* 8-year-old children is manifestly impossible, partly because of expense and partly because the class of persons who are ultimately to be measured by this test extends on into the future and includes children who are not now members of the population of 8-year olds. The desired norms can be developed only on the basis of sample data.

In this example the population of Binet scores for 8-year olds may be presumed to have a normal distribution, whereas in the first example the population was composed of two classes. While in this example it is impossible to obtain a complete census, in the first example it was merely inexpedient.

3. *Testing the effectiveness of a new drug.* When a new drug or vaccine is developed in a laboratory, its effectiveness must be tested by using it on live subjects. The first tests may be made on animal subjects, but, if it is intended for human use, later tests of its effectiveness must be made on human subjects.

A naive research worker might assume that all he needs to find to prove the effectiveness of a new drug is the proportion of subjects who recover from the malady in question when they are treated with the given drug. Thus he would be thinking in terms of a two-class population of observations; each person who had had the malady and been treated by the drug would be labeled either "recovered" or "did not recover." The proportion who recover under the given treatment would indeed provide some measure of the effectiveness of the drug but would not provide a basis for deciding whether to advocate its use. That decision can be made only after the results are compared with some alternative treatment, which may be some other drug or no drug at all.

The research worker must, therefore, consider two populations: (1) observations on persons who have the malady and are treated by drug *A*, and (2) observations on persons who have the malady and receive treatment *B*. Each of these populations is composed of two classes, those cured and those not cured. Presumably the decision to use drug *A* would be made only if the first population has a larger proportion of cures than the second.

To sum up, we speak of *a population as the collection of all possible measures of a certain kind, and we associate with that population a frequency distribution.* For convenience, the individuals themselves are often spoken of as a population, but this is a loose use of the term. Each individual may be measured on many different traits so that the collection of individuals is related to many different populations of measures. It is not the individuals themselves but some measure of those individuals which has a frequency distribution. Consider, for example, all the colleges in the continental United States. When these are classified as men's colleges, women's colleges, or coeducational, there is a population of three classes; when they are rated according to the state (or District of Columbia) in which they are located, there is a population distribution of 51 classes; when they are scored as to age or present enrollment or endowment or rate of tuition, there are populations of quite different natures.

Randomness. It should be fairly clear at this stage of the discussion that it is ordinarily not possible to study a population in its entirety. Usually information about the population can be obtained only by the selection of a limited group of individuals from the population. The manner in which these individuals are selected is a very important consideration.

All statistical theory involving the use of samples is based on the notion of randomness. *By randomness we mean that any group of individuals is as likely to be chosen as any other group of the same size.* Randomness is required because this procedure permits us to apply the laws of chance to the theory of samples. This matter will be discussed more fully below.

Achieving randomness in the selection of subjects is often one of the most difficult aspects of a statistical investigation. Such investigations have probably been criticized more often for failing to achieve randomness than for any other shortcoming. The well-known Kinsey studies of sexual behavior are an example of studies which have been criticized severely in this respect. The problem of achieving randomness is solved differently in each field of endeavor and becomes an element of study in that field. However, some indications of methods for achieving randomness will be pointed out here.

Suppose, for example, it is proposed to set up an experiment to study three methods of teaching statistics. For the purpose of the study, suppose the 98 students listed in Table VIII are to be divided into three groups, each of which is to be taught by one of these methods. It becomes, obviously, a matter of considerable importance to make sure that the groups to be taught by different procedures do not basically differ in other ways which will influence their learning. Assigning students to the different groups in a random manner is the best way to eliminate this difficulty.

To make such random assignment, slips of paper may be numbered 1 through 98, thoroughly shuffled, and then divided into three groups, just as playing cards might be dealt to three players.

A less cumbersome way to achieve the same result is the use of a table of random numbers like the one in Table XI of the appendix. This table consists of digits which have been previously randomized, so that their use has the same effect as the shuffling just described. To facilitate keeping track of one's position while using the table, the subdivisions of the numbers in Appendix Table XI are presented in blocks of five rows and five columns. Random numbers of any size can be obtained from this table.

For making a selection among the 98 students, we find their code numbers by choice of consecutive pairs of digits beginning with any row or any column. If we use the first 20 digits in line 1, we find the following pairs of digits: 10, 48, 01, 50, 11, 53, 60, 20. This selection gives us 8 students after eliminating duplicates. If we continue in this way until 33 students have been selected, the first list of randomly selected students is available. Should the number 99 occur, it would be passed over because no student has that code number. The table may be entered at any point and read in any direction — to right, to left, up the column, down the column, or diagonally. Use of a different starting point and reading plan will produce a different but equally good random selection. Had there been, for example, 4200 students in the population to be sampled, it would have been necessary to read four-digit instead of two-digit numbers and to discard all such larger than 4200.

EXERCISE 13.1

1. Suppose you want to choose 10 students at random from a group of 260. You decide to begin in the upper left-hand corner of Table XI, reading downward. Verify that you would select the code numbers 104, 223, 241, 94, 103, 71, 23, 10, 70, and 24.

2. Suppose you had decided to begin in row 31 and block 6 and to read downward. Verify that you would have selected code numbers 183, 170, 257, 244, 45, 219, 214, 130, 221, and 25.

3. Suppose you have 18 cases which you want to divide randomly into two groups of 9. You decide to begin at the extreme left of row 40 and read to the right. That row would yield numbers 14, 12, 7, 18, 1, and 3, all other numbers being larger than 18. You should have decided in advance what to do in case this row did not provide enough numbers. One course would be to go to row 41, reading from the left and picking up numbers 4, 2, and 9. These 9 numbers then form one group and the remaining 9 the other,

> Group I: Students 14, 12, 7, 18, 1, 3, 4, 2, and 9
> Group II: Students 5, 6, 8, 10, 11, 13, 15, 16, 17

Sample. The group of subjects selected from a population for the purpose of obtaining information about that population is called a sample. For the purpose of the analysis which is described below, it is necessary that the sample be selected by a process involving randomness. When the population is considered as a single group and a sample is selected from it by some random method, as by use of a table of random numbers, the sample is called a *simple random sample*.

Sometimes it is more appropriate to subdivide a population into several subpopulations, say into occupational or geographic groups, and then to sample randomly from the subpopulations. The subpopulations are called *strata*, and the sample selected from them is called a *stratified random sample*. Other variations on random sampling are described in advanced statistical literature. The expression *parent population* is often used in describing the relationship of a population to a sample drawn from it.

What is wanted, of course, is a *sample of measures drawn from a population of measures*, but usually the only practicable way of obtaining such measures is to obtain a sample of subjects from the collection of subjects loosely called a population of subjects, and then to measure the subjects in this sample. If the subjects have been selected at random, the measures of those subjects will constitute a random sample from the population of measures.

Parameter and Statistic. A statistical population always has a definite distribution but ordinarily the characteristics of that distribution are unknown. If the observations are on a scaled trait, the distribution has a mean, a median, percentiles, a standard deviation, etc. If the distribution is not scaled, it is characterized by the proportion of individuals in its various classes. The characteristics of a population are called *parameters;* the corresponding characteristics of a sample are called *statistics.*

The symbols used in this text for the parameters which we shall discuss and the related statistics are as follows:

Characteristic	Population parameter	Sample statistic
Mean	μ (mu)	$\overline{X}$
Standard deviation	σ (sigma)	s
Variance	σ^2	s^2
Correlation coefficient	ρ (rho)	r
Proportions in the two classes of a dichotomous distribution	P, Q	p, q

Statistical Inference. Ordinarily, the only information available to an investigator is contained in the statistics which he obtains from a sample. From this information he makes inferences about the population parameters.

Statistical inferences are usually of two kinds. One is *estimation of parameters* of a single population. The other is *comparison of populations.* Simple examples of both kinds of inference will be described below.

Law of Large Numbers. The basic justification for statistical inference is that the distribution which is obtained from a random sample tends to resemble the distribution of the population from which it was drawn. This tendency increases as the size of sample increases. Consequently, certain statistics computed from the sample tend toward corresponding values of parameters of the parent population. Thus the mean of a large random sample tends to be close to the mean of its parent population. This tendency of distributions of random samples to resemble the distributions of their parent population more closely as sample size increases is called the *law of large numbers.*

The importance of randomness in the operation of the law of

large numbers can hardly be exaggerated. Mere size without randomness may not provide the necessary approximation of sample to population.

Sampling Variability. Two extreme views, both incorrect, are often expressed by statistically untrained persons in respect to inferences from samples to population. One view is to regard the sample as an exact reproduction of the population and to speak of statistics computed from the sample as if they were actual values of parameters. The other view is to hold that information from samples is quite valueless as a basis for inference about population values because so much depends upon what sample one happens to have chosen. It is the purpose of the discussion which follows to evaluate the reliability, or credibility, of information obtained from samples.

As a first step in this discussion, we shall set up an artificial situation in which we have a population with a fully known distribution. From this population we shall draw random samples and see how the statistics computed from these samples agree with the corresponding known parameters.

For the artificial population with which we are going to work, we have chosen a set of scores on the Cooperative Service English Test of 447 college students. The scores have a distribution which is very nearly normal, with parameters $\mu = 121.6$ and $\sigma = 37.15$. The list of scores, together with code numbers of students to whom each applies, appears in Appendix Table XXIV of the authors' *Statistical Inference*.[2] However, understanding of what follows is in no way dependent on reference to the set of original scores.

We now continue the fiction by supposing that 20 people separately seek information about the parameter μ by random sampling. Each of these people draws randomly a sample of 1, a sample of 5, and a sample of 25, and computes the sample mean $\overline{X}$ for each sample.

In Table 13.1, the column headed $N = 1$ shows the distribution of the means of 20 random samples of 1 case each. Obviously, the mean of a sample of 1 case is merely the value of the observation itself. The mean and standard deviation of this column would therefore be expected to approximate μ and σ but to differ somewhat from them because of random sampling errors. You should note that this is what happened. However, an attempt to estimate μ from information about a single individual would expose the investigator to risk of a very large error. While the mean of

---

[2] H. M. Walker and J. Lev, *Statistical Inference*, Henry Holt, 1953, page 486.

TABLE 13.1   Distribution of Means of 20 Samples Drawn from a Normal Population with $\mu = 121.6$ and $\sigma = 37.15$ when $N = 1$, $N = 5$, $N = 25$

Score interval	Number of samples		
	$N = 1$	$N = 5$	$N = 25$
165–169	2		
160–164	1		
155–159	1		
150–154	3		
145–149	1	1	
140–144	2	2	
135–139		1	
130–134	1	2	1
125–129		2	5
120–124	1	1	6
115–119		2	5
110–114	1	1	3
105–109	1	4	
100–104	2	2	
95–99			
90–94			
85–89		1	
80–84		1	
75–79			
70–74	1		
65–69	1		
60–64			
55–59	1		
50–54			
45–49			
40–44			
35–39	1		
Total	20	20	20
* Mean of 20 means	122.5	119.0	121.7
* Standard deviation of 20 means	39.5	18.0	5.9

* Computed from ungrouped values

the column for $N = 1$ comes close to μ, one sample had a value of only 36 and one had a value of 169. The range of estimates of μ based on these 20 samples was therefore $169 - 36 = 133$.

Now examine the column headed $N = 5$. The observed means of the 20 samples recorded here have considerably less variability than those in the column $N = 1$, the lowest being 84.1 and the highest, 144.2, so that the range is $144.2 - 84.1 = 59.8$. Obviously, the error made in estimating μ from 1 sample of 5 cases is likely to be numerically smaller than the error made in estimating

μ from a single case. However, a person might happen to draw a single case with score almost exactly equal to μ and then might happen to draw a sample of 5 cases with a fairly extreme value of $\overline{X}$.

Look now at the column headed $N = 25$. Here the smallest mean in the 20 samples was 112.9 and the largest was 128.0, so that the range was only $128.0 - 112.9 = 15.1$.

The three distributions in Table 13.1 suggest certain generalizations about the validity of an estimate of μ made from a sample value of $\overline{X}$. These generalizations can be obtained by mathematical reasoning and are supported by many empirical studies. They apply only on the assumption that sampling is random. These generalizations are:

(1) The value of $\overline{X}$ obtained from a sample can be expected to differ somewhat from μ.

(2) In computations from many samples, the errors $\overline{X} - \mu$ are both positive and negative and the average error tends toward zero. In other words, the average value of $\overline{X}$ in many samples tends toward μ, regardless of sample size.

(3) As sample-size increases, the variability of the distribution of $\overline{X}$ decreases, and, consequently, there is smaller probability of making a large error in using $\overline{X}$ as an estimate of μ.

The third generalization is suggested both by the ranges and by the standard deviations of $\overline{X}$ in the three distributions of Table 12.1, which are:

	$N = 1$	$N = 5$	$N = 25$
Range of $\overline{X}$	133	59.8	15.1
Standard deviation of $\overline{X}$	39.5	18.0	5.9

Sampling Distributions. The 20 individual observations in Table 13.1 had a mean and a standard deviation similar to those of the parent population, μ and σ. If sampling were continued indefinitely, that mean and standard deviation would tend to approach μ and σ more and more closely. The 20 means of samples of 5 cases also had a mean (119.0) similar to the mean of the parent population, and if more and more samples were drawn, the mean of their means would tend to approach μ more and more closely. A similar statement can be made for the samples of 25 cases. However for samples larger than one, the standard deviation of the set of means was smaller than the standard deviation, σ, of the parent population, and would remain so even if the number of samples were vastly increased.

The mean actually has a distribution of its own which can be ascertained if the distribution of the parent population is known. In the previous paragraph we have noted that the variability of the distribution of the mean appears to depend on sample size, and that relationship will presently be made explicit.

For the samples used to obtain Table 13.1, many other statistics might have been computed and recorded. Thus, a distribution of medians might have been obtained, a distribution of variances, a distribution of ranges, a distribution of standard deviations, etc. In referring to such distributions, it is customary to refer to the statistic in the singular. Thus, the "distribution of the means of indefinitely many random samples of size N" is called "the distribution of the mean," just as the distribution of a set of heights is called the distribution of height rather than heights. Every statistic has a distribution which depends upon the distribution of the parent population and on sample size, but the distributions of different statistics are not the same. *The distribution of a statistic is called the sampling distribution of that statistic.*

A sampling distribution is itself a population. It differs from the parent population by the fact that its elements are values of a statistic rather than single observations. The individuals on which a sampling distribution is based are samples rather than individuals of the parent population. A sampling distribution has parameters which are related to the parameters of the population of observations from which the sampling distribution is derived and to the number of cases in the samples.

The Normal Distribution for Statistics. When the parent distribution is normal, the distribution of the mean is also normal. When the parent distribution is not normal, the sampling distribution of means is not normal for small samples but becomes very nearly normal as sample size increases. For many (but not for all) statistics the sampling distribution is approximately normal for large samples. For this reason the normal distribution is very important in statistical inference. However, for many purposes the normal distribution is insufficient for the needs of statistical inference, and several very important non-normal distributions are used extensively in more advanced work. Even the elementary problems considered in this chapter will require the use of certain non-normal distributions.

When the sampling distribution of a statistic is normal, or approximately normal, the mean of that sampling distribution is either a parameter of the parent population or an expression mathematically derivable from the parameters of that population. The same is true of the standard deviation of the distribution of the statistic.

The Standard Error. *The standard deviation of the distribution of a statistic is called the standard error of the statistic.* The standard error is especially important in dealing with statistics which are normally distributed. For such statistics the standard error provides information concerning the probability that a statistic will deviate from its parameter by a specified amount. The standard error of the mean will be denoted $\sigma_{\bar{x}}$ and is given by the formula

$$(13.1) \qquad\qquad \sigma_{\bar{x}} = \frac{\sigma}{\sqrt{N}}$$

To illustrate the meaning of $\sigma_{\bar{x}}$ let us look again at the data of Table 13.1. Since the standard deviation of the parent population was known to be $\sigma = 37.15$, we can compute $\sigma_{\bar{x}}$ for each of the three sample sizes and compare that value with the observed standard deviation of the 20 samples, thus:

Size of sample	$\sigma_{\bar{x}}$	Observed standard deviation
$N = 1$	$\dfrac{37.15}{\sqrt{1}} = 37.15$	39.5
$N = 5$	$\dfrac{37.15}{\sqrt{5}} = 16.6$	18.0
$N = 25$	$\dfrac{37.15}{\sqrt{25}} = 7.4$	5.9

Even for as few as 20 samples, the correspondence between the expected value $\sigma_{\bar{x}}$ and the observed value is notable. Now let us see what we might have predicted about the three distributions of Table 13.1 from knowledge of the fact that $\mu = 121.6$ and $\sigma = 37.15$ for the parent population. Since the parent population was approximately normal, the distribution of the sample mean may be assumed to be normal. We know that 95 percent of the area under a normal curve lies between -1.96σ and $+1.96\sigma$. Therefore, if a great many samples are drawn from this parent population, we should expect about 95 percent of them to have means lying between $\mu - 1.96\sigma_{\bar{x}}$ and $\mu + 1.96\sigma_{\bar{x}}$. Now let us compare the observed distributions with these expected values.

Size of sample	Value of $1.96\sigma_{\bar{x}}$	Range from $\mu - 1.96\sigma_{\bar{x}}$ to $\mu + 1.96\sigma_{\bar{x}}$	Observed means outside range Number	Percent
$N = 1$	72.8	48.8 to 194.4	1	5
$N = 5$	32.5	89.1 to 154.1	2	10
$N = 25$	14.5	107.1 to 136.1	0	0

EXERCISE 13.2

Assume that random samples are drawn from a normal population for which μ and σ have the values shown below. For samples of the size indicated, what would be the mean and the standard error of the sampling distribution of $\overline{X}$? Within what range would the middle 95 percent of the sample means fall? The middle 50 percent?

Population parameters μ	σ	N	Distribution of $\overline{X}$ Mean	Standard error	Range of middle 95 percent of sample means	Range of middle 50 percent of sample means
1. 60	12	9	60	4	52.2 to 67.8	57.3 to 62.7
2. 60	12	64	60	1.5	57.2–62.8	58.99–61.01
3. 40	12	36	40	2.0	36.08–43.92	38.65–41.35
4. 40	18	36	40	3.0	34.22–45.88	38.98–42.02
5. 92	8	100				
6. 53	25	100				
7. 39	15	900				
8. 39	15	144				

Estimation by a Single Value. In a previous paragraph of this chapter, we indicated two extreme views toward statistical inference, one that a sample provides an exact reproduction of the population, and the other that a sample provides little or no information about a population.

We have now reached a stage where we can discuss this problem somewhat rationally. We have found that the mean of a random sample is likely to be not far from the population mean, provided the sample is not too small. On this basis we feel justified in calling the sample mean an estimate of the population mean. We have used here the expression "estimation by a single value" in order to distinguish it from estimation by an interval which we shall describe later on. An estimate by a single value is also called a *point estimate*, because it represents a point on a scale of possible estimates.

The reasoning by which we have justified using $\overline{X}$ as an estimate of μ can also be used to justify using s as an estimate of σ, using a sample percentile as an estimate of a population percentile, and using other statistics as estimates of other parameters.

Some questions about point (single value) estimates remain to be answered. We note, for example, that for a normal population μ is not only the mean but is also the median. One may, therefore, raise the question as to the possibility of using the sample median as a basis for estimating μ for a normal population. Another question of some interest is the proper estimate for σ^2. Shall it be the estimate $\dfrac{\Sigma(X - \overline{X})^2}{N - 1}$ which is used in this text, or the estimate $\dfrac{\Sigma(X - \overline{X})^2}{N}$ used by most of the older books and by a few of the newer ones?

Two criteria for choosing estimates will now be discussed.

Unbiased Estimate. *An estimate is unbiased if the mean of its distribution is equal to the value of the parameter which it estimates.* Thus, no matter what the size of a sample may be, its mean is an unbiased estimate of the population mean. For the normal population, the sample median is also an unbiased estimate of the population mean. This relation is to be expected, since in a normal population the mean and the median are the same.

The formula, $s^2 = \dfrac{\Sigma(X - \overline{X})^2}{N - 1}$, gives an unbiased estimate of σ^2, but the alternative formula, $\dfrac{\Sigma(X - \overline{X})^2}{N}$, does not. This is the chief justification for the use of $N - 1$ rather than N in the denominator. For example, suppose a great many samples of 9 cases each were drawn from a normal population in which $\sigma^2 = 144$. If for each sample s^2 were computed with $N - 1 = 8$ as the denominator, the mean of all the sample variances would be approximately equal to $\sigma^2 = 144$. However, if $N = 9$ were used as the denominator, the mean of the sample variances would be approximately $\dfrac{\sigma^2(N - 1)}{N} = \dfrac{8(144)}{9} = 128$ instead of 144.

Table 13.2 presents distributions of sample means and sample medians for 20 samples of $N = 5$. Means and medians were computed for the same samples. We find that the means of the two distributions of statistics are very nearly the same and are close to μ. This illustrates the statement that the sample mean and the sample median are both an unbiased estimate of μ for a normal population.

Efficient Estimate. An interesting feature of the two distributions in Table 13.2 is that the medians are much more variable than the means. This is a reflection of the fact that the standard error of the median is greater than the standard error of the mean.

TABLE 13.2   Distributions of Means and Medians of Random Samples of Five from a Normal Population with $\mu = 121.6$ and $\sigma = 37.15$

Score interval	Number of sample means	Number of sample medians
160–164		1
155–159		1
150–154		1
145–149	1	1
140–144	2	1
135–139	1	1
130–134	2	
125–129	2	2
120–124	1	2
115–119	2	1
110–114	1	2
105–109	4	2
100–104	2	1
95–99		
90–94		2
85–89	1	1
80–84	1	
75–79		
70–74		1
Mean of distribution	119.0	119.5
Standard deviation of distribution	18.0	25.3

Because of this difference in standard errors, the mean of a sample is likely to be nearer to μ than its median, or, in other words, the error in using the sample mean as an estimate of μ is likely to be less than the error in using the sample median for this purpose.

Since the standard error of the mean is less than the standard error of the median, the sample mean is said to be a more *efficient statistic* for estimating μ in a normal population. When two statistics are available for estimating the same parameter, the one with the lesser standard error is the more efficient.

It should be pointed out that in a population in which the mean and median are presumed to differ, the sample median should be used for estimating the population median, and the sample mean used for estimating the population mean. This conclusion is based on consideration of bias.

The Standard Score for Means. In Chapter 7 the standard score for an observation was defined as

$$(13.2) \qquad z = \frac{X - \overline{X}}{s}$$

This expression is entirely in sample terms.

In Chapter 12 the corresponding expression in terms of parameters was given as

$$(13.3) \qquad z = \frac{X - \mu}{\sigma}$$

We learned that, if X is normally distributed, the latter expression has the standard (or unit) normal distribution.

Corresponding to formula (13.3) for observations, the standard score for means is

$$(13.4) \qquad z = \frac{\overline{X} - \mu}{(\sigma/\sqrt{N})}$$

Regardless of the size of N, the standard score in formula (13.4) is a standard normal deviate if $\overline{X}$ is distributed normally with mean μ and standard deviation σ. Unless N is very small, this standard score is distributed approximately normally even if the distribution of X is not normal. It may be helpful to the reader to notice that for means based on 1 observation ($N = 1$) formula (13.4) would be identical with formula (13.3).

Because of the normality of distribution of the standard score for means, we can apply the table of the normal distribution to answer questions like the following:

(1) Assume that we are drawing samples of size 25 from a population with $\mu = 60$ and $\sigma = 8$. For what percent of these samples will $\overline{X}$ exceed 61 if the number of samples is very large? Solution:

$$z = \frac{61 - 60}{(8/\sqrt{25})} = \frac{1}{1.6} = .625$$

In a normal distribution, the area above the point $z = .625$ is $.5 - .2340 = .2660$. Hence $\overline{X}$ may be expected to exceed 61 in about 27 percent of samples. A better statement is that there is probability .27 that $\overline{X}$ will exceed 61.

(2) Assuming the same situation as in the preceding question,

between what two limits will the values of $\overline{X}$ for the middle 80 percent of samples be contained?

Solution:

The middle 80 percent of the area under a normal curve is contained between $z_{.10} = -1.282$ and $z_{.90} = +1.282$. For the sampling distribution of $\overline{X}$, the corresponding points are obtained from the two equations $\dfrac{\overline{X} - 60}{8/\sqrt{25}} = -1.282$ and $\dfrac{\overline{X} - 60}{8/\sqrt{25}} = 1.282$. The solutions of these equations for $\overline{X}$ are 57.95 and 62.05 which are the required limits, and we may say there is probability .80 that $\overline{X}$ will not be less than 58 nor more than 62.

The expression for the standard score for means (13.4) which uses the population value σ is of great theoretical interest. Its direct application to data is limited to those situations where an estimate of σ is available from earlier experience. In the most common situations, σ is not known and s must be used as a substitute. The standard score for means is then called t rather than z.

(13.5)
$$t = \frac{\overline{X} - \mu}{(s/\sqrt{N})}$$

This t is not normally distributed, but for large samples its distribution is sufficiently like the normal so that the tables of the normal distribution may be used. Questions which arise in this situation are how large a sample should be in order to make the normal approximation applicable and how to deal with problems for which it is not applicable. These questions will be taken up on page 221.

EXERCISE 13.3

1. If random samples of size 36 are drawn from a normal population for which $\mu = 57$ and $\sigma = 12$, what proportion of such samples will have a mean
   (a) Greater than 57?
   (b) Greater than 60?
   (c) Smaller than 59?
   (d) Between 55 and 59?

2. In the situation described in Question 1, what is the probability that the mean of a random sample will be
   (a) Greater than 53?
   (b) Between 54 and 60?

3. Suppose random samples of 64 cases are drawn from a normal population for which $\mu = 90$ and $\sigma = 18$. Consider the 5 percent of samples with means which deviate most widely from μ. Outside what values will these means fall?

Solution: For half of them $\dfrac{\overline{X} - \mu}{\sigma/\sqrt{N}}$ will be larger than $z_{.975}$ and for half it will be smaller than $z_{.025}$.

$$\frac{\sigma}{\sqrt{N}} = \frac{18}{\sqrt{64}} = 2.25$$

$$z_{.025} = -1.96 \quad \text{and} \quad z_{.975} = 1.96$$

If $\dfrac{\overline{X} - 90}{2.25} = -1.96,\ \overline{X} = 90 - 1.96(2.25) = 85.6$

If $\dfrac{\overline{X} - 90}{2.25} = 1.96,\ \overline{X} = 90 + 1.96(2.25) = 94.4$

Therefore the most extreme 5 percent of the samples will have $\overline{X}$ either smaller than 85.6 or larger than 94.4.

4. Suppose random samples are drawn from a normal population for which $\mu = 75$ and $\sigma = 12$. Between what two values will the middle 99 percent of sample values of $\overline{X}$ fall if N is
   (a) 9?   (c) 36?   (e) 400?
   (b) 16?   (d) 100?   (f) 900?

5. Suppose a random sample of 200 cases is drawn from a population for which $\mu = 75$. Between what two symmetrically placed values is there probability .95 that $\overline{X}$ will fall if σ is
   (a) 4?   (c) 12?   (e) 20?
   (b) 10?   (d) 15?   (f) 24?

The Confidence Interval. Estimation of a parameter by a single number is valuable because the estimate is likely to be close to the value of the parameter. Because that estimate will almost never be exactly the same as the value of the parameter, however, it is somewhat unsatisfactory. Such point estimation does not sufficiently tie down our information about the parameter.

Another type of estimate is obtained by computing from the same sample two statistics and using the interval between these statistics as an interval estimate for the parameter. These two statistics are computed in such a way that the interval between them usually contains the parameter. By "usually" we mean that for some preassigned percentage of samples the interval between the computed values contains the parameter. In other words, *for any given sample the interval may or may not contain the parameter, but the computation of the interval is of such nature that for some preassigned percent of samples the interval contains the parameter.* An interval obtained in this way is called an *interval estimate* or a *confidence interval;* the two statistics which determine the limits of the interval are called *confidence limits;* and the pre-assigned percentage of samples is called a *confidence coefficient.* These concepts will be clarified and made more precise when we develop them for the problem of obtaining a confidence interval for μ.

Confidence Interval for the Mean when the Sample Is Large. The method of obtaining this interval for a sample of 50 or more cases will first be described, and then a justification will be given for the method.

Suppose we have drawn a random sample of 125 cases and we wish to compute a confidence interval for μ with confidence coefficient .99. In other words, we wish to compute a confidence interval of such nature that in 99 percent of similar computations the interval will contain the parameter. We compute $\overline{X}$ and s from the sample, and find $z_{.995}$ and $z_{.005}$ from the table of the normal distribution. From these values we compute the two statistics,

$$\overline{X} + z_{.995}\frac{s}{\sqrt{125}} \text{ and } \overline{X} + z_{.005}\frac{s}{\sqrt{125}}.$$ These are the two *confidence limits.* The interval between them is the *confidence interval.*

Suppose, in the above example, $\overline{X} = 93.5$ and $s = 14.2$. In Appendix Table II of the normal distribution, we find $z_{.995} = 2.576$ and $z_{.005} = -2.576$. Then the limits are

$$93.5 - 2.576\left(\frac{14.2}{\sqrt{125}}\right) = 93.5 - 3.3 = 90.2$$

and

$$93.5 + 2.576\left(\frac{14.2}{\sqrt{125}}\right) = 93.5 + 3.3 = 96.8.$$

Consequently the interval between 90.2 and 96.8 is the required confidence interval, and we state, with confidence coefficient .99, that $90.2 < \mu < 96.8$. This is read "μ is greater than 90.2 and less than 96.8" or "μ is between 90.2 and 96.8."

In more general terms, suppose the sample size N is sufficiently large to permit use of the normal approximation, and the confidence coefficient is c, then confidence limits for μ are

$$(13.6) \qquad \overline{X} + z_{\frac{1-c}{2}}\frac{s}{\sqrt{N}} \quad \text{and} \quad \overline{X} + z_{\frac{1+c}{2}}\frac{s}{\sqrt{N}}$$

The following justification for the limits in (13.6) is somewhat mathematical and may be skipped by a reader who wishes to do so. We know from the discussion of the tables of the normal distribution that the percentage of samples between $z_{1-c \over 2}$ and $z_{1+c \over 2}$ is $\dfrac{1+c}{2} - \dfrac{1-c}{2} = c$. In terms of the standard score for means, the percentage of samples for which $\dfrac{\overline{X} - \mu}{(s/\sqrt{N})}$ is between $z_{1-c \over 2}$ and $z_{1+c \over 2}$ is c. The statement can be put mathematically by saying that the inequality

$$(13.7) \qquad\qquad z_{1-c \over 2} < \frac{\overline{X} - \mu}{(s/\sqrt{N})} < z_{1+c \over 2}$$

is true for a proportion c of samples. By simple algebra, inequality (13.7) can be transformed into inequality,

$$(13.8) \qquad\qquad \overline{X} + z_{1-c \over 2}\frac{s}{\sqrt{N}} < \mu < \overline{X} + z_{1+c \over 2}\frac{s}{\sqrt{N}}$$

and this latter inequality is true whenever the former is true. Therefore c is also the proportion of samples for which inequality (13.8) is true.

It is important for the reader to realize that the probability expressed by (13.8) is about the intervals containing μ. It is not a statement about possible value of μ in the given interval. In other words, the inequality (13.8) might mislead a reader to think that there is a collection of populations, each with some value of μ and that a proportion c of these populations has values of μ in the interval indicated by the inequality. This is an incorrect interpretation of the inequality. The correct interpretation is that there is one population with a unique μ. There are, however, as many possible intervals as there are possible samples. Some of these intervals satisfy the inequality because they actually contain μ between their limits. Some do not. By the theory stated, the proportion of intervals which satisfy (13.8) is c.

Student's Distribution. We have stated above that, if the population has a normal distribution, the sample values $z = \dfrac{\overline{X} - \mu}{(\sigma/\sqrt{N})}$ also have a normal distribution, and that if N is sufficiently large the values $t = \dfrac{\overline{X} - \mu}{(s/\sqrt{N})}$ have a distribution which approximates the normal. For small samples, say $N = 40$ or less, the normal approximation for t is inadequate, and its exact distribution must be used. This distribution is called either "Student's"[3] distribution or the t distribution. It is a symmetrical distribution, with mean zero, but its form differs for different values of N.

A difficulty in using Student's distribution, one not met in using the normal distribution, is that we need a separate probability table for each sample size. The situation is somewhat further complicated by the fact that the tables are not stated directly in terms of numbers of cases, but in terms of a related value called *degrees of freedom* which we shall denote by n. The relationship between number of cases and number of degrees of freedom differs from one type of problem to another, and must be ascertained separately for each type. The concept of degrees of freedom is discussed in the authors' advanced book. A general understanding of that concept is not needed at this time. It is enough now to know that for $t = \dfrac{\overline{X} - \mu}{s/\sqrt{N}}$, the number of degrees of freedom is one less than the number of cases, or $n = N - 1$.

Tables of areas for Student's distribution are found in Appendix Table V. Each row is really a separate table corresponding to the number of degrees of freedom indicated in the left-hand column. The reader will notice that the heading of this column is n, which is our customary notation for number of degrees of freedom. Tabular entries are values of t. In the column headed $t_{.90}$, each entry is the 90th percentile of the distribution to which it belongs. A similar description applies to the other columns. Since the distributions are symmetrical with mean zero, it is not necessary to tabulate percentiles below the 50th. Instead we use the relationships $t_{.10} = - t_{.90}$, $t_{.005} = - t_{.995}$, etc. The entries in the bottom row are percentiles of the normal distribution.

EXERCISE 13.4

READING A TABLE OF STUDENT'S DISTRIBUTION

1. By examination of Appendix Table V, verify enough of the following statements to be sure you are reading the table correctly.

[3] "Student" was a well-known British statistician named William Sealy Gosset (1876–1947) who was adviser to the Guinness brewery in Dublin. A ruling of that firm forbidding their employees to publish the results of research was relaxed to allow him to publish mathematical and statistical research under a pseudonym. His paper on "The Probable Error of a Mean," published in *Biometrika* in 1908, which first called attention to the fact that the normal curve does not properly describe the distribution of the ratio of mean to standard error in small samples, is now a classic.

(a) The 95th percentile of Student's distribution is
   (1) $t = 2.35$, when $n = 3$.
   (2) $t = 1.94$, when $n = 6$.
   (3) $t = 1.74$, when $n = 17$.
(b) The 5th percentile of Student's distribution is
   (1) $t = -2.35$, when $n = 3$.
   (2) $t = -1.94$, when $n = 6$.
   (3) $t = -1.74$, when $n = 17$.
(c) For Student's distribution with $n = 5$,
   (1) 10 percent of the area lies to the right of an ordinate at $t = 1.48$.
   (2) 25 percent of the area lies to the right of an ordinate at $t = .73$.
   (3) 1 percent of the area lies to the right of an ordinate at $t = 3.36$.
   (4) 80 percent of the area lies to the right of an ordinate at $t = -.92$.
   (5) 99.5 percent of the area lies to the right of an ordinate at $t = -4.03$.
(d) For Student's distribution with $n = 12$,
   (1) 50 percent of the area lies between $t = -.70$ and $t = .70$.
   (2) 80 percent of the area lies between $t = -1.36$ and $t = 1.36$.
   (3) 90 percent of the area lies between $t = -1.78$ and $t = 1.78$.
   (4) 95 percent of the area lies between $t = -2.18$ and $t = 2.18$.
   (5) 98 percent of the area lies between $t = -2.68$ and $t = 2.68$.
   (6) 99 percent of the area lies between $t = -3.05$ and $t = 3.05$.

2. In the following questions you may assume that we are considering $t = \dfrac{\bar{X} - \mu}{s/\sqrt{N}}$ and that the number of degrees of freedom is $n = N - 1$.

(a) If $N = 10$, at what point on the scale of the t distribution would you draw an ordinate so that
   (1) 5 percent of the area would lie above it (i.e. to the right)?
   (2) 10 percent of the area would lie below it (i.e. to the left)?
   (3) 80 percent of the area would lie above it?
   (4) 99 percent of the area would lie above it?
(b) Answer the same four questions, if $N = 16$.
(c) If $N = 7$, at what two points on the scale of the t distribution would you draw ordinates so that they would include between them
   (1) The middle half of the area?
   (2) The middle 80 percent of the area?
   (3) The middle 90 percent of the area?
   (4) The middle 95 percent of the area?
   (5) The middle 99 percent of the area?

3. Answer the same five questions, if $N = 20$.

4. What percent of samples of size $N = 15$ would have values of $\dfrac{\bar{X} - \mu}{s/\sqrt{N}}$ between -2.14 and 2.14? Does your answer depend on the value of μ? Of s? Of N?

Confidence Interval for the Mean when the Sample Is Small.
The reasoning which led to the confidence limits given in formula
(13.6) for large samples leads also to the confidence limits for small
samples, with the only modification being that z is replaced by t
and that reference is made to the t distribution instead of to the
normal. For a small sample, the confidence limits for μ can,
therefore, be obtained as follows:

Suppose that a random sample of size N is drawn from a
normally distributed population, and that the confidence coefficient
is to be c, then the confidence limits for μ are

$$(13.9) \qquad \overline{X} + t_{\frac{1-c}{2}}\frac{s}{\sqrt{N}} \quad \text{and} \quad \overline{X} + t_{\frac{1+c}{2}}\frac{s}{\sqrt{N}}$$

Values of $t_{\frac{1-c}{2}}$ and $t_{\frac{1+c}{2}}$ are read from Appendix Table V with
$n = N - 1$.

In Table 13.3 is shown the confidence interval for each of the
20 samples of 25 cases which have been previously discussed and
for which the distribution of means was given in Table 13.1. We

TABLE 13.3   Confidence Interval for μ with Confidence Coefficient .90,
for Each of 20 Random Samples of 25 Cases from a Normal
Population with $\mu = 121.6$ and $\sigma = 37.15$

Sample number	$\overline{X}$	s	Lower limit $\overline{X} + t_{.05}\dfrac{s}{\sqrt{N}}$	Upper limit $\overline{X} + t_{.95}\dfrac{s}{\sqrt{N}}$	Includes μ?
1	123.7	36.9	111.1	136.3	Yes
2	116.0	31.9	105.1	126.9	Yes
3	117.9	25.6	109.1	126.7	Yes
4	126.7	35.9	114.4	139.0	Yes
5	128.0	41.4	113.8	142.2	Yes
6	124.5	38.1	111.5	137.5	Yes
7	112.9	38.7	99.7	126.1	Yes
8	123.8	34.3	112.1	135.5	Yes
9	118.8	39.0	105.5	132.1	Yes
10	127.6	39.7	114.0	141.2	Yes
11	128.3	37.0	115.6	141.0	Yes
12	122.1	41.7	107.8	136.4	Yes
13	125.6	36.0	113.3	137.9	Yes
14	111.0	30.1	100.7	121.3	No
15	111.4	39.6	97.9	124.9	Yes
16	123.8	31.8	112.9	134.7	Yes
17	117.8	37.2	105.1	130.5	Yes
18	117.3	37.8	114.4	130.2	Yes
19	133.6	34.7	121.7	145.5	No
20	123.0	41.4	108.8	137.2	Yes

recall that these samples were drawn randomly from a population for which μ and σ are known, which is, of course, a fictitious situation, because parameters are ordinarily not known.

Entries in the column at the extreme right show that 18 of the 20 confidence intervals include $\mu = 121.6$ and 2 do not. Inclusion of μ in the interval is indicated by "Yes" and noninclusion by "No." Here the proportion of samples ($\frac{18}{20} = .90$), in which μ is included between the computed confidence intervals, is exactly equal to the confidence coefficient of .90. However, one must not expect such perfect agreement of experience and theory every time an interval estimate is made. The value $c = .90$ applies to the totality of computations from a very large number of samples rather than to any fixed number of them. It is interesting to note in Table 13.3 that, even when the confidence interval missed the true value of μ, it missed it only slightly.

It will be of interest to the reader to check some of the computations in Table 13.3. We shall describe the first of these:

As the confidence coefficient is stated to be $c = .90$

$$\frac{1 - c}{2} = \frac{.10}{2} = .05 \quad \text{and} \quad \frac{1 + c}{2} = \frac{1.90}{2} = .95$$

To use Student's distribution, we first note that $n = 25 - 1 = 24$.

Referring to Student's distribution with $n = 24$, we read $t_{.05} = -1.71$ and $t_{.95} = 1.71$. Hence the confidence limits for sample 1 are

$$\overline{X} + t_{.05} \frac{s}{\sqrt{N}} = 123.7 + (-1.71) \frac{36.9}{\sqrt{25}} = 111.1$$

and

$$\overline{X} + t_{.95} \frac{s}{\sqrt{N}} = 123.7 + (1.71) \frac{36.9}{\sqrt{25}} = 136.3$$

EXERCISE 13.5

1. A sample of 16 cases has yielded $\overline{X} = 23.5$ and $s = 12$.
   Make an interval estimate for μ with confidence coefficient
   (a) $c = .99$,   (b) $c = .95$,   (c) $c = .90$.
2. A sample of 400 cases has yielded $\overline{X} = 23.5$ and $s = 12$.
   Make an interval estimate for μ with confidence coefficient
   (a) $c = .99$,   (b) $c = .95$,   (c) $c = .90$.
3. A sample of 16 cases has yielded $\overline{X} = 23.5$ and $s = 4$.
   Make an interval estimate for μ with confidence coefficient
   (a) $c = .99$,   (b) $c = .95$.

14

Testing Hypotheses

That aspect of statistical inference which deals with estimation of unknown parameters of a population was discussed in the preceding chapter. Of the three examples involving the use of samples described at the beginning of that chapter, the first two illustrate problems in which the main task is the estimation of parameters. The problem presented in the third example differs from those in the first two in that it requires a choice between two alternatives: (1) continued use of the medical treatment now in use, or (2) substitution of the new kind of treatment which is under consideration. These alternatives can be reduced to statistical considerations if we say that the old method will be continued if the new method does not cure a larger proportion of sick persons than the old. However, if the new method does produce a larger proportion of cures, then it will replace the old method.

The approach to this problem is to formulate a *hypothesis* that some particular relation between the proportions of cures is true, and then to test the hypothesis experimentally. On the basis of the outcome of the experiment, a conclusion is drawn about the relative effectiveness of the two methods of treatment.

Methods of statistical inference involving proportions will be described in the next chapter. In this chapter we shall develop methods required in dealing with hypotheses about means. Two applications will be discussed.

A Problem Involving a Hypothesis about Means. Suppose the question has been raised as to whether people who are deaf and those with normal hearing differ in motor abilities. By now the student should have developed far enough in statistical thinking to be unwilling to accept a generalization about this matter based only on a few personal experiences, "I know several deaf persons who . . ." He should also be unwilling to accept a generalization based only on general theories of physiology. Although one should recognize that either abstract theorizing or personal experience may lead to a formulation of a useful though tentative generalization, an appeal to empirical data is essential to establish that generalization.

In a research reported by Long,[1] deaf and girls having normal hearing were compared on a number of motor abilities. Inasmuch as motor ability increases with age, if one group had been older than the other, a difference might erroneously have been interpreted as related to deafness. For fear that the motor traits studied might be related to intelligence or that performance might be affected by the ability to concentrate and follow directions, it also seemed important to control intelligence. There are several ways to arrange an experiment for the purpose of controlling the effect of background traits which might bias the outcome.[2] Long paired each deaf girl with a girl having normal hearing of the same age and intelligence quotient. Such pairing is usually laborious and not always the most efficient device, but it is very frequently employed. The data which Long reported on 37 pairs are presented in Table 15.1, but for the purpose of the present discussion, only the first ten pairs have been used. Long presented findings on several traits of which only balance will be reported here. The method of obtaining a score for each child on a test of balance is important for the research but extraneous to the analysis of the data, which is our present concern.

For each pair, the score of the deaf child is subtracted from that of her hearing mate, leaving a difference score which may be denoted X. It should be recognized that X is a measure *of the pair*, that the matched pair is the individual in our sample, and that we shall generalize to a *population of matched pairs*.

The work of pairing has presumably eliminated gross differences related to age and intelligence. Differences related to training or experience will presumably be eliminated by selecting for measurement those tasks the children are not likely to have practiced specifically. It is never feasible to control *all* sources of variation, but sources which might seriously bias the outcome must be controlled. Differences related to individual performance will always remain. Deaf children are not uniform in motor

---

[1] John A. Long, *Motor Abilities of Deaf Children*, Teacher's College, Columbia University, Bureau of Publications, New York, 1932.

[2] See, for example, H. M. Walker and J. Lev, *Statistical Inference*, Henry Holt, 1953, page 382.

ability, nor are children with normal hearing. Even if deaf and hearing children are generally equal in balance, very few pairs will have zero difference. Sometimes a deaf child whose balance is better than average is mated with a hearing child whose balance is poorer than average, producing a negative difference score. Sometimes the accidents of pairing will produce a positive difference. The population of such differences may be assumed to have a normal distribution with mean μ. If there is no difference between deaf and hearing in general, $\mu = 0$. If hearing children have better balance than deaf, $\mu > 0$, although for many pairs the difference X may be negative. If hearing children have poorer balance than deaf, $\mu < 0$, although for many pairs the difference X may be positive.

A Statistical Hypothesis. A hypothesis about μ is a tentative statement that μ has some particular value or that μ has some one of a set of values. After it is formulated, the hypothesis is subjected to an experimental check known as a *test of the hypothesis*.

Suppose your knowledge of physiology inclines you to believe that μ is greater than zero; however, you are not inclined to guess how much greater. You might set up the statistical hypothesis $\mu = 0$ and test it against the alternative $\mu > 0$. If then the statistical hypothesis $\mu = 0$ is found to be unacceptable, you would have grounds for asserting your original belief; if the statistical hypothesis is found to be acceptable, you would be warned that you could not safely assert your belief that $\mu > 0$.

Suppose that a researcher is unaware of the connection between balance and the semicircular canals in the ears, and has no prior opinion as to the value of μ. He merely wants to find out whether any general difference exists. He will then set up the hypothesis $\mu = 0$ and test it against the alternative "μ is not 0."

The statistical hypothesis tested is often called the *null hypothesis*. A hypothesis is always a hypothesis about a parameter (or sometimes about more than one parameter) of a population, never about a statistic of a sample. It is stated in the present tense, that some general state of affairs is now existent. It should not be stated in future tense ("the mean will be zero," "the correlation will be positive" etc.), because that phraseology suggests a kind of fortune telling about the outcome of a particular sample.

Test of Hypothesis that $\mu = 0$. To test this hypothesis a random sample must be drawn; in the present problem that will be a

TABLE 14.1 Scores on Balance for 10 Pairs of Deaf and Hearing Girls *

Pair Number	Balance score for		X Hearing-deaf
	Hearing	Deaf	
1	2.3	2.0	0.3
2	1.0	2.0	−1.0
3	3.7	2.7	1.0
4	3.3	2.7	0.6
5	10.0	3.0	7.0
6	2.7	2.7	0
7	8.3	3.7	4.6
8	6.0	1.3	4.7
9	4.3	2.0	2.3
10	7.7	4.3	3.4
Total	49.3	26.4	22.9
$\overline{X}$			2.29
s			2.56
$s/\sqrt{N}$			0.810

* Source of data: Long, *op. cit.*

sample of matched pairs. The data for 10 such pairs will be found in Table 14.1. Each pair-difference has been denoted X and the statistics $\overline{X} = 2.29$, $s = 2.56$, and $s/\sqrt{N} = 0.810$ have been computed. The standard score for means is

$$t = \frac{\overline{X} - \mu}{s/\sqrt{N}} = \frac{2.29 - 0}{0.810} = 2.83$$

with $N - 1 = 9$ degrees of freedom. Referring $t = 2.83$ to Student's distribution, we find it slightly larger than $t_{.99}$. This means that, if the hypothesis $\mu = 0$ is true, we have accidentally drawn a sample which is in the 1 percent of samples with the largest values of t. We are inclined, therefore, to say that this sample is exceptional, or unusual, for samples from a population in which $\mu = 0$.

Now μ is not known. Only $\overline{X}$, s, and N are known, and from these statistics evidence must be extracted about the reasonableness of the hypothesis, $\mu = 0$. Since that hypothesis leads to a value of t that would occur only rarely in a random sample, it does not seem a reasonable hypothesis to entertain. Hence we *reject* the hypothesis that $\mu = 0$. When we have made this decision, our test of the hypothesis is completed.

The reader may feel that the hypothesis $\mu = 0$ should be rejected whenever a value of $\overline{X}$ different from zero is obtained in a sample. Such a policy would be mistaken because it fails to take account of sampling variability. Even if μ is actually zero in the population from which samples are drawn, the sample values of $\overline{X}$ will vary so that almost none of them will be precisely zero; most of them will deviate from zero by a small amount in one direction or the other, and only a few will show large deviations from zero. Consequently, values of $\overline{X}$ near zero do not throw suspicion on the hypothesis, $\mu = 0$.

In a general sense (this point will be clarified in further discussion), one tends to accept a hypothesis about μ whenever the value of $\overline{X}$ computed from a sample is close to the value specified by the hypothesis, and to reject that hypothesis whenever the value of $\overline{X}$ is far from the specified value. In either accepting or rejecting a hypothesis, an investigator may make the wisest decision possible in view of the data and still be in error. However, the nature of the procedures which will be now described are such that at least the probability of making large errors is kept at a low level.

Level of Significance. To this point the word "exceptional" applied to the size of $\overline{X}$ has been treated rather vaguely. Actually, the decision as to what is to be regarded as exceptional is arbitrary. For a small sample like the one we have been considering, it is customary to regard the 5 percent of samples having the most extreme values of $\overline{X}$ as exceptional and to reject the null hypothesis when one of these samples has been drawn. This arbitrary value (here selected as 5 percent) is called a *level of significance*, because it sets apart certain differences between sample mean and hypothetical population mean as being sufficiently significant to lead to rejection of the hypothesis.

Having decided upon a level of significance, it is still necessary to decide how to use it. Shall we apply it to the right tail of the distribution and reject the hypothesis $\mu = 0$ only when $\overline{X}$ is exceptionally large, or to the left and reject only when $\overline{X}$ is exceptionally small, or shall we regard both extremely large and extremely small values of $\overline{X}$ as exceptional?

The answer to these questions depends upon what alternatives seem particularly important to guard against in view of the problem situation. If the investigator has started out with no opinion concerning the relative balance scores of the deaf or hearing children, he will wish to reject the hypothesis that $\mu = 0$ should he find a value of t that is numerically very large, whether it is positive or negative. In other words, the alternative he will wish to consider is simply: μ is different from zero. Suppose he has selected .05 as the level of significance at which he will work. He will then decide to reject the hypothesis, $\mu = 0$, if he obtains a sample for which t exceeds $t_{.975}$ or a sample for which t is less than $t_{.025}$. The decision then is to reject the hypothesis $\mu = 0$ if a sample of 10 cases shows a value of $t = \dfrac{\overline{X} - \mu}{s/\sqrt{N}}$ which is smaller than -2.26 or larger than 2.26. This set of values of t is called the *region of rejection,* or the *region of significance,* or the *critical region.* The probability .05 corresponding to that region is the *level of significance.* The test we have just used is called a *two-sided test* or a *two-tailed test* because the region of rejection is on both sides of the probability curve (or in both tails of the curve).

One-sided Test. Now if the investigator has enough prior information to entertain a strong belief that the mean balance score for hearing children exceeds that for deaf children, he may wish to reject the hypothesis, $\mu = 0$, should his sample show a large positive value of t. He will not consider it important, however, to reject the hypothesis if a large negative value appears in the sample. (You will recall that, in Table 14.1, X is positive for a pair if the score of the hearing child exceeds that of the deaf child.) Therefore, his region of rejection will consist of those values of t larger than $t_{.95} = 1.83$. This region is a one-sided or one-tailed region, and the test is a one-sided test. Note that the level of significance is .05 in both situations, but that the location of the critical region differs.

The steps in formulation and testing a statistical hypothesis are stated in Table 14.2, first in general terms and then in terms specific to the problem of comparing deaf and hearing persons in regard to balance.

Comparing the Means of Two Populations. Pairing cases as described for deaf and hearing children is very laborious and time consuming and often requires elimination of cases for which no mates can be found. It is employed only when the investigator fears that a random sample from each of the two populations he wishes to compare might differ in respect to some extraneous variable which would introduce bias into the comparison. Fortunately, in many problems this danger is not crucial, and it is satisfactory merely to draw a separate random sample from each population.

Suppose, for example, the question is whether sophomore men in a certain university are more familiar with contemporary

TABLE 14.2 Steps in Formulating and Testing a Statistical Hypothesis

Step	General procedure	Application to comparison of deaf with hearing
1	Select the measures on which the investigation will be based.	Choose as a measure the balance score of a hearing girl minus the balance score of the deaf girl with whom she is paired.
2	Specify the general nature of the population and the parameter or parameters needed for the investigation.	The population of differences can be assumed to be approximately normal, and the parameter in question is its mean μ.
3	Formulate a hypothesis about the population and decide on the alternatives.	The hypothesis is $\mu = 0$ and the alternatives are μ is not equal to 0.
4	Determine a statistic by which the hypothesis is to be tested.	$$t = \frac{\overline{X} - 0}{(s/\sqrt{N})}.$$
5	Ascertain the distribution of the statistic.	Student's distribution with $n = N - 1$ degrees of freedom.
6	Choose a level of significance.	5 percent.
7	Determine the region of rejection on the basis of the level of significance and the alternatives to the hypothesis.	Reject $\mu = 0$ when t is larger than $t_{.975}$ or is smaller than $t_{.025}$.
8	Draw a random sample of size N from the population.	Determine differences in balance for a random sample of matched pairs.
9	Compute for this sample the value of the previously specified statistic.	Compute t from the sample in Table 14.1 obtaining $t = 2.83$.
10	Determine whether the computed value of the statistic is in the region of rejection.	Ascertain that t is in the region of rejection because $t_{.975} = 2.26$ and the sample value $t = 2.83$ is larger than $t_{.975}$.
11	Reject the hypothesis if the value of the statistic is in the region of rejection; otherwise accept it.	Reject the hypothesis $\mu = 0$.

science than sophomore women. A random sample of men is drawn from the sophomore class and given the Science Section of the *Contemporary Affairs Test* of the Cooperative Test Service. By this device what may be presumed to be a random sample of science scores of sophomore men is obtained. Let us use N_1, $\overline{X}_1$, and s_1 to denote the number of cases, the mean and the standard deviation of this sample.

A random sample of sophomore women is also drawn and given the same test. Let us use N_2, $\overline{X}_2$, and s_2 to denote the corresponding statistics of this sample.

If μ_1 represents the mean of the population of science scores achieved by sophomore men and μ_2 that of science scores of sophomore women, the hypothesis to be tested is $\mu_1 - \mu_2 = 0$.

The statistic by means of which this hypothesis is to be tested is the standard score for the mean difference $\overline{X}_1 - \overline{X}_2$. To obtain this standard score, the standard error of the mean difference is required. Advanced texts give several different formulas for this standard error, applicable under different experimental conditions. The one given in formula (14.1) can be used only if N_1 and N_2 are fairly large, for example, neither one less than 25. If the standard error of $\overline{X}_1 - \overline{X}_2$ is denoted $s_{\overline{X}_1 - \overline{X}_2}$, then for large values of N_1 and N_2,

$$(14.1) \qquad s_{\overline{X}_1 - \overline{X}_2} = \sqrt{\frac{s_1^2}{N_1} + \frac{s_2^2}{N_2}}$$

and the standard score for the mean difference is

$$(14.2) \qquad z = \frac{(\overline{X}_1 - \overline{X}_2) - (\mu_1 - \mu_2)}{\sqrt{\dfrac{s_1^2}{N_1} + \dfrac{s_2^2}{N_2}}}$$

This standard score has been denoted z rather than t because it is always referred to tables of the normal distribution. If values of N_1 and N_2 are so small that the investigator feels he should use Student's distribution, then he needs an entirely different formula and should consult a more advanced text.

Aside from the fact that the statistic of formula (14.2) is used instead of that of formula (13.5) and that we have two independently chosen samples instead of one sample of matched pairs, the test of the hypothesis $\mu_1 - \mu_2 = 0$ proceeds by the same 11 steps which were outlined in Table 14.2.

Suppose that a two-sided test and a significance level of .01 have been chosen, and the pertinent sample data are found as follows:

	Men	Women
N	120	130
$\overline{X}$	7.57	6.40
s^2	23.05	21.49
s^2/N	.1921	.1653

Then
$$\sqrt{\frac{s_1^2}{N_1} + \frac{s_2^2}{N_2}} = \sqrt{.3574} = .598$$

and
$$z = \frac{(7.57 - 6.40) - 0}{.598} = 1.96$$

The region of rejection is obtained from the normal distribution and consists of those values of z larger than $z_{.995} = 2.576$ or smaller than $z_{.005} = -2.576$.

Clearly, the obtained value $z = 1.96$ does not fall in the region of rejection. Consequently, the hypothesis that $\mu_1 - \mu_2 = 0$ must be considered tenable, reasonable, and not contradicted by the data.

A word of caution is needed at this point. To retain a hypothesis does not prove it true but merely indicates that it is not inconsistent with the observed data of a sample. Similarly, to reject a hypothesis does not prove it false but merely indicates that the sample data obtained are improbable if the hypothesis is true. Furthermore, if the hypothesis is not rejected, it is inappropriate for the investigator to discuss why one sample had a higher mean than the other. The failure to reject the hypothesis $\mu_1 - \mu_2 = 0$ means simply that the difference in sample means may well have arisen through accidents of sampling from populations with the same mean. It is wrong to say, "There was a tendency for men to have the higher mean but the difference was not significant." Failure to reject the null hypothesis means that there is no convincing evidence of a tendency for the scores of men and women to be different.

EXERCISE 14.1

1. The same 10 pairs of deaf and hearing girls whose balance scores were presented in Table 14.1 had scores on strength of grip as follows:

Pair	1	2	3	4	5	6	7	8	9	10
Hearing	16	12	17	18	15	21	16	22	18	16
Deaf	10	14	12	21	19	12	19	17	19	25

Test the hypothesis that deaf and hearing do not differ in respect to strength of grip, the alternative being that they do differ, and .05 the level of significance.

2. For all 37 pairs in Long's study, $\Sigma X = 87.1$ and $\Sigma X^2 = 363.17$, where X is the balance score of a hearing child minus the balance score of her deaf mate. Test the hypothesis $\mu = 0$, the alternative being $\mu > 0$, and .01, the level of significance.

3. For all 37 pairs, the corresponding data for strength of grip are $\Sigma X = 86$ and $\Sigma X^2 = 2072$. Test the null hypothesis, $\mu = 0$, when the alternative is $\mu > 0$ and .01 the level of significance.

4. For all 37 pairs, the corresponding data for rate of tapping with best hand are $\Sigma X = 5.9$ and $\Sigma X^2 = 982.55$. Test the null hypothesis, $\mu = 0$, the alternative being $\mu \neq 0$ and .02 the level of significance.

5. For all 37 pairs, the corresponding data for rate of tapping with right hand are $\Sigma X = 28.8$ and $\Sigma X^2 = 1595.52$. Test the null hypothesis $\mu = 0$ against the alternative $\mu \neq 0$, using the .05 level of significance.

Effectiveness of a Test of Hypothesis. In this section the various problems involved in testing a hypothesis such as choice of level of significance and choice of region of rejection will be reconsidered from the point of view of the relation of the hypothesis to its alternatives.

The reader will recall that the decision to reject or to accept a hypothesis involves a degree of arbitrariness. There is always a risk that a hypothesis may be rejected when it is true or accepted when it is false. The error in rejecting a hypothesis when it is true is known as an error of the first kind, or a Type I error. The error of accepting a hypothesis when it is false is known as an error of the second kind, or a Type II error.

What is called the level of significance is the probability of rejecting a hypothesis when it is, in fact, true. In the long run, during the course of a great many experiments in which he is testing a true hypothesis, an investigator who is employing the .05 level of significance will falsely reject 5 percent of those true hypotheses. If he is employing the .01 level of significance, he will falsely reject 1 percent of the true hypotheses he tests. The level of significance is, therefore, the probability of a Type I error. Naturally one would like to make the probability of a Type I error as low as possible; in other words, to make the level of significance as low as possible. At first thought this seems easy because the choice of this level is arbitrary. However, the possibility of reducing the level of significance is limited by the need for rejecting the hypothesis when it is false. To see this need, suppose the level of significance is set at zero, so that there is no possibility of an error of Type I. If this is done, however, there is no possibility of rejecting the hypothesis even when it is false. There is then no point to the study at all, because the essence of hypothesis testing is the utilization of experimental evidence as a basis for a choice between the acceptance of a hypothesis and its rejection.

In addition to the choice of level of significance for a test of a hypothesis, the statistical analyst is concerned with the location of the region of rejection. Shall it be in one tail of the sampling distribution, or the other, or in both tails?

The choice of *level of significance* and the choice of location of the *region of significance* (which is also the region of rejection) can be evaluated in terms of the need for rejection of the hypothesis when it is false.

The problems just posed can be approached directly in terms of the need for reducing the probability of a Type II error; that is, of reducing the probability of accepting a hypothesis when it is false. In the following discussion we approach the matter from the mathematically equivalent view of increasing the probability of rejecting the hypothesis when it is false.

The Power of a Test.   This discussion will involve comparison of statistical tests. It will be necessary to define the sense in which one test may be said to be better than another. To make this discussion clear, it will be necessary to state explicitly what is meant by a test of hypothesis. For the purpose of the following discussion, a test is defined when the following have been specified:

(1) A statistic,
(2) Sample size,
(3) Level of significance,
(4) Region of rejection.

The reader should note that a test thus defined is only one of a variety of test types. It is known as a fixed-sample-size, two-decision test. One different type of test is the sequential type in which sample size is not specified in advance of the experiment. In another type of test, known as a multiple-decision test, there are more decisions than the two of acceptance and rejection considered here.

For the fixed-sample-size, two-decision test with which we are dealing, a change in any one of the four elements constitutes a change in the test. Consider now a hypothesis and an alternative; for example:

Hypothesis H: $\mu = 0$
Alternative A: $\mu = 1$.

Suppose a test has been selected to test hypothesis H. It is possible to determine the probability that this test will lead to the rejection of H in case H is false and A is true, that is in case $\mu = 1$. Now consider a second test obtained by changing the level of significance or changing sample size, or both. It is also possible to compute the probability that this second test will lead to the rejection of H: $\mu = 0$ if $\mu = 1$. If the second probability is greater than the first, we say that the second test is more *powerful* than the first for rejecting H when A is true. For each test separately the probability of rejecting H when A is true is called the *power* of the test in that relationship between H and A.

Table 14.3 shows the power of eight different tests for rejecting $\mu = 0$ when $\mu = 1$, and of the same eight tests for rejecting $\mu = 0$ when $\mu = -1$. Consider first the alternative $\mu = 1$ and the

TABLE 14.3 Power of Several Tests of the Hypothesis $\mu = 0$ against the Alternatives $\mu = 1$ and $\mu = -1$

$$s = 10$$

Alternative	Level of significance	Power of the test			
		Two-tailed test		Upper-tailed test	
		$N = 100$	$N = 400$	$N = 100$	$N = 400$
$\mu = 1$	.05	.17	.52	.26	.64
	.01	.06	.28	.09	.37
$\mu = -1$	.05	.17	.52	.00	.00
	.01	.06	.28	.00	.00

four tests with sample size 100. Of the two-tailed tests, the one with level of significance .05 is more powerful than the one with level of significance .01; the situation is similar for the two tests with critical region in the upper tail. These comparisons illustrate the principle that an increase in probability of a Type I error leads to an increase in power. In other words, a decrease in the probability of a Type I error can be bought at the price of an increase in the probability of a Type II error.

Another principle can be discovered by comparing the power of the two upper-tailed tests with the power of the corresponding two-tailed tests for testing the hypothesis $\mu = 0$ against the alternative $\mu = 1$. In this situation the upper-tailed tests are clearly the more powerful. The two-tailed tests are equally powerful for the alternatives $\mu = 1$ and $\mu = -1$, but the upper-tailed tests have almost no power against the alternative $\mu = -1$. In fact, if the hypothesis $\mu = 0$ is tested by use of this upper-tailed test when μ is actually equal to -1, the false hypothesis $\mu = 0$ is almost sure to be accepted. This important point will be developed more fully below.

If sample size is increased from 100 to 400, the power is increased regardless of level of significance and regardless of the alternative value of μ. However, for the alternative $\mu = -1$, the power is still so small that several more decimal places would be required to distinguish the value from zero.

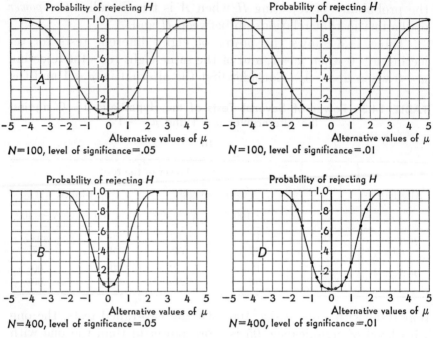

Fig. 14-1 Power Functions of Two-tailed Tests of Hypothesis $H : \mu = 0$ for Two Levels of Significance and Two Sizes of Sample with $s = 10$.

Power Function. The relationships in Table 14.3 are developed more fully in Figures 14–1 and 14–2. From these figures it is possible to read the probability of rejecting the hypothesis $\mu = 0$ if some particular alternative is true. For each curve, possible alternative values of μ are given on the horizontal scale. For each such alternative (as, for example, the alternatives $\mu = 1$ or $\mu = -1$ shown in Table 14.3), the probability of rejecting the hypothesis $\mu = 0$, has been computed and a point has been plotted with the alternative value of μ as abscissa and the corresponding probability of rejection (or power) as ordinate. Examining these graphs, the reader should note that on each of them, when $\mu = 0$, the probability of rejection is exactly equal to the level of significance. He should also identify on the appropriate graph the point corresponding to each entry in Table 14.3.

Certain general principles which are of importance in deciding whether to use a larger or a smaller significance level, a larger or a smaller sample, or a one-tailed or a two-tailed test, can now be made clear through further examination of these graphs.

Look first at Figure 14–1 and verify the following probabilities of rejection when $N = 100$:

	For test at .05 level	For test at .01 level
If $\mu = 0$	.05	.01
If $\mu = .05$ or $\mu = -0.5$	.08	.02
If $\mu = 1$ or $\mu = -1$	.17	.06
If $\mu = 2$ or $\mu = -2$	.52	.28
If $\mu = 3$ or $\mu = -3$	.85	.66
If $\mu = 4$ or $\mu = -4$	.98	.92

From the probabilities thus verified and from the corresponding probabilities for samples of 400, the following conclusion should now be clear. In general, when a two-tailed test is used, *the probability of rejection increases as the true alternative deviates more widely from the value under the hypothesis.* If μ is near zero, though not precisely zero, there is small probability of rejecting H: $\mu = 0$, but, when the actual value of μ departs considerably from

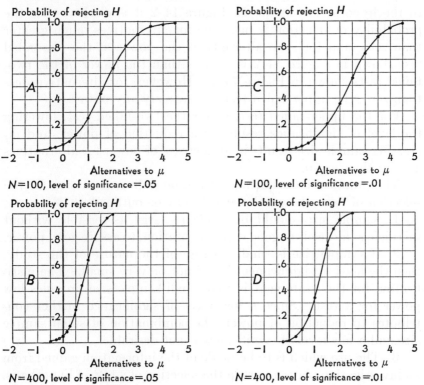

Fig. 14–2 Power Functions of Upper-tailed Tests of Hypothesis $H : \mu = 0$ for Two Levels of Significance and Two Sizes of Samples with $s = 10$.

zero, the test makes rejection of $H: \mu = 0$ almost a certainty. This is a quite satisfactory state of affairs, for obviously in a practical situation it may be essential to reject a hypothesis about μ when the hypothesized value is very wrong, and not essential to reject it when it is only slightly wrong. Now compare the probabilities of rejection shown above for the two levels of significance. For each alternative stated, the power is less when .01 is used as the level of significance than when .05 is used. In general, reducing the level of significance causes a reduction in the power of the test. In other words, an investigator who demands a very low probability of rejecting a true hypothesis must pay for that caution by incurring a larger probability of *not* rejecting it when some other hypothesis is true.

Now compare the probabilities of rejection listed above for $N = 100$ with corresponding probabilities read from the graphs for $N = 400$. *For a fixed level of significance, power is increased as sample size is increased*, and this relation holds for all alternatives to the hypothesis tested. In Figure 14–2 it is obvious that the probability of rejection is near one for alternatives much greater than zero, and for such alternatives the power of the one-tailed test shown in Figure 14–2 is greater than the power of the two-tailed tests shown in Figure 14–1. However, for alternatives less than zero, the upper-tailed test has scarcely any power.

For the upper-tailed test, as for the two-tailed test, lowering the level of significance results in a reduction of power, and increasing sample size results in an increase of power for alternatives greater than $\mu = 0$.

The practical consequences of the preceding discussion for the selection of tests of hypotheses will now be outlined.

1. Sample size should be made as large as feasible without sacrificing the needs of good experimentation, to assure good power.

2. If sample size is small because of the nature of the study, then the level of significance should not be very small. The justification for this statement is that small sample size provides low power for a test. Since a low level of significance further contributes to reduction of power, the combination of small sample size and a low level of significance is not desirable.

3. The use which is to be made of the information gained from an investigation plays a part in the selection of a test of hypothesis. Ordinarily, the hypothesis which is being tested is rather noncommittal. It consists, for example, of a statement that two groups do not differ. If the purpose of the study is to arrive at a scientific truth, one would be reluctant to reject a noncommittal

hypothesis and thereby accept a more positive alternative, unless the evidence is strongly in favor of the alternative. In these circumstances, one is likely to adopt a low level of significance, say .01 rather than .05.

However, if the purpose of the study is to choose some remedial action, the investigator would not wish to reject a method which may be helpful, even if the evidence in favor of the method is slight. Under such circumstances, the investigator would use a higher level of significance — for example, .05 in preference to .01.

4. In the choice between a one-tailed test and a two-tailed test, it is necessary to weigh the gains and losses involved from this choice. On the one hand, the one-tailed test gives greater power against certain alternatives. On the other hand the two-tailed test provides assurance that the hypothesis $\mu = 0$ will be rejected for all alternatives differing considerably from zero, whenever the one-tailed test does not provide such assurance.

The one-tailed test is chosen when certain alternatives are either of no importance or no interest. For example, suppose a new medical treatment is being compared with one already in general use. The hypothesis "old and new treatments are equally effective" should certainly be rejected if the alternative "new treatment is more effective" is true, because a change of practice would then be indicated. However, the hypothesis and the alternative "old treatment is more effective" call for the same action — namely, retaining the old treatment. Consequently, this alternative is of no importance and a one-tailed test may be used. However if two new treatments are under comparison, a difference in favor of either one is of interest, and the two-tailed test should be used.

Computing the Power of a Test. This section is intended for those readers who want to know how the power of a test is computed and it may be disregarded by others. In Figure 14–3, the solid line gives the sampling distribution of $t = \dfrac{\overline{X} - \mu}{s/\sqrt{N}}$ under the hypothesis $\mu = 0$ when $N = 100$ and $s = 10$. The region of rejection has been placed in the upper tail. In the picture, the shaded area represents the level of significance .05; the segment of line extending to the right from $A = 1.645$ and marked ⌇⌇⌇ includes values of $\dfrac{\overline{X} - 0}{10/\sqrt{100}} = \overline{X}$ which are larger than 1.645, and is the region of significance; the segment extending to the left from $A = 1.645$ and marked ××× includes all values smaller than 1.645, and is the region of acceptance.

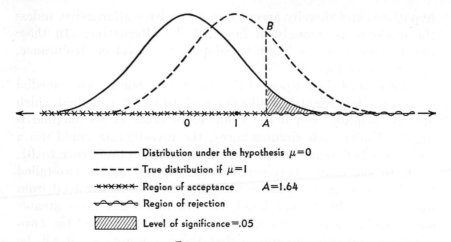

Fig. 14–3 Distribution of $t = \dfrac{\bar{x} - \mu}{s/\sqrt{100}}$ under the Hypothesis that $\mu = 0$ and True Distribution if $\mu = 1$. Region of Rejection Based on a One-tailed Test $N = 100$, $s = 10$.

Suppose, however, that the true value of μ is actually $\mu = 1$ and not, as hypothesized, $\mu = 0$. Then the actual sampling distribution is the distribution of $\dfrac{\bar{X} - 1}{10/\sqrt{100}} = \bar{X} - 1$, and is given by the dotted line in Figure 14–3. The regions of rejection and acceptance, being based on the hypothetical distribution, are the lines marked $\sim\!\sim$ and $\times\times\times$ as already described. The probability that a sample will show a value of $\bar{X}$ in the region of rejection is represented by the area under the actual sampling distribution (the dotted line) to the right of the ordinate AB. But the point A is $1.64 - 1.0 = .64$ units above $\mu = 1$, and so the probability sought is the area under a normal curve to the right of an ordinate at $z = .64$. (The sample size is large enough to make the use of the normal probability distribution appropriate.) This area is .26. Hence, the probability of rejecting the hypothesis $\mu = 0$, when μ is actually 1, is .26. This is the power of the one-sided test against the alternative $\mu = 1$. In Figure 14–2, the test for $\mu = 0$ at significance level .05, when $N = 100$ and $s = 10$, is shown in Section A. The ordinate at $\mu = 1$ can be read as .26.

In similar fashion, the power against the alternative $\mu = 1.5$ can be computed as .44, against the alternative $\mu = 2.0$ as .63 and against $\mu = 3.5$ as .97.

The computation shown above was made particularly simple because $s/\sqrt{N}$ came out so conveniently as $10/10 = 1$, but in Section B of Figure 14–2 $s = 10$ and $N = 400$. Then the region of

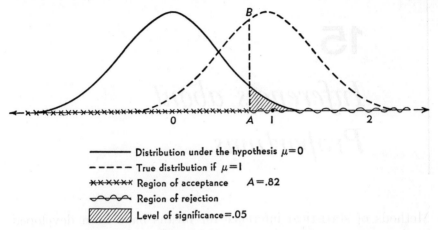

Fig. 14-4   Distribution of $t = \dfrac{\bar{x} - \mu}{s/\sqrt{N}}$ under the Hypothesis that $\mu = 0$ and True Distribution if $\mu = 1$.   Region of Rejection Based on a One-tailed Test $N = 400$, $s = 10$.

significance consists of values of $\dfrac{\bar{X} - 0}{10/\sqrt{400}} = \dfrac{\bar{X}}{.5}$ greater than 1.64, which means values of $\bar{X}$ greater than .82.   The hypothetical and actual distributions now appear like Figure 14-4, and the probability sought is the area under the actual curve to the right of the ordinate at A.   But the point A is $\dfrac{.82 - 1.00}{10/\sqrt{400}} = \dfrac{-.18}{.5} = -.36$ standard deviation units from the alternative $\mu = 1$.   The area under a normal curve to the right of $z = -.36$ is .64.   Compare this result with the ordinate at $\mu = 1$ of the power curve in Section B.

For that same one-tailed test of $\mu = 0$ ($N = 400$, $s = 10$, and significance level of .05), you may wish to verify by computation that the power against the alternative $\mu = .25$ is .13; against the alternative $\mu = .75$ is .44; against the alternative $\mu = 1.5$ is .91.

15

Inferences about Proportions

Methods of statistical inference for means have been developed in the two preceding chapters. Now we shall consider similar procedures applicable to proportions.

Meaning of Proportion. The word *"proportion* [1]*"* is used here to mean the fractional part of a group of *discrete individuals*. Thus, if a survey of 800 dwelling units should find 128 units substandard, the proportion of substandard units could be expressed as $\frac{128}{800}$ or as any other equivalent fraction such as $\frac{4}{25}$ or $\frac{16}{100}$ or .16. The percent of substandard units, however, can be expressed in only one way, namely as 16 percent, since percent means literally per hundred (per centum).

In ordinary speech the term "proportion" is also applied to the fractional part of a continuous quantity, as, for example, the proportion of milk sold in New York City which is supplied by a particular distributor, or the proportion of a teacher's time which is spent on routine tasks. The methods described in this chapter *are not applicable* to proportions of this sort.

One other correct use of the term "proportion" to which the methods of this chapter cannot be correctly applied should be mentioned. Consider a psychological test in which subjects make free responses which are then classified by judges into categories. Suppose these results have been obtained:

Number of subjects examined	150
Number of responses made in all categories	3000
Number of responses in category A	420
Number of subjects who gave no responses in category A	48

[1] The word "proportion" is used here with a meaning somewhat different from that given to it in textbooks in mathematics where it is defined as the equality of two ratios. The meaning attributed to the word here has become standard usage in statistical writing.

It is possible to make inferences about the proportion of subjects who give no responses in category A and to use as datum the statistic $\frac{48}{150} = .32$. It is not possible to use the methods of this chapter to make inferences about the proportion of responses falling into category A based on the statistic $\frac{420}{3000} = .14$, because such responses are not independent individuals subject to the processes of random sampling. Samples are not drawn from a population of responses but from a population of subjects.

Conversion of Dichotomous Data to Measurement Data. Methods of statistical inference for proportions are very similar to those for means, which are already familiar. The reason for this similarity will be clarified if we note how a dichotomy can be transformed into a special kind of measurement by assigning numerical values to the two classes in the dichotomy.

Consider, for example, the data reported in Appendix Table VIII. The six test scores reported are scaled data, and sex is a dichotomy. We shall assign the numbers 0 and 1 to the two sex categories. It is immaterial which number is assigned to which category, but, as some choice must be made, we shall score women as 0 and men as 1. The value 1 indicates presence in a class (males) and 0 means absence from that class. For the first 10 students from Table VIII we have the following tabulation:

Code number of student:	1	2	3	4	5	6	7	8	9	10
Sex of student:	M	M	M	M	F	F	M	M	M	F
Value of X	1	1	1	1	0	0	1	1	1	0

By counting entries in the second line we see that there are 7 males among the 10 students so the proportion of males is .7. By adding entries in the third line we obtain $\Sigma X = 7$ and $\overline{X} = \dfrac{\Sigma X}{N} = \dfrac{7}{10} = .7$. Clearly the arbitrary assignment of the numbers 0 and 1 to the two categories of this dichotomy shows that a proportion can be regarded as analogous to a mean.

The reader will notice that the proportion of women among the 10 students is .3 and that, if female sex is scored $X = 1$ and male $X = 0$, then $\Sigma X = 3$ and $\overline{X} = .3$.

Symbolism for Proportions. The symbol p will be used here to represent the proportion of individuals in a sample which have a specified characteristic (that is, the proportion which are in a given class) and $1 - p$ to represent the proportion which do not have that characteristic (are not in the given class). The letter q is often used in place of $1 - p$. If there are N individuals in a sample, then Np is the *number* which have the given characteristic and $N(1 - p)$ or Nq is the number which do not have it.

For the population from which the sample is presumed to be drawn, we shall use capital P to represent the proportion in the given class and $1 - P$ or Q to represent the proportion not in the class. The Greek letter π which is analogous to p will not be used for two reasons: (1) it is in familiar use to mean the number 3.1416 and, (2) the Greek alphabet has no letter analogous to our Q.

Statistical Inference about Proportions. The parameter P of a dichotomous population is analogous to the parameter μ of a population defined on a continuous variable. Therefore the four main problems of inference about μ described in Chapters 13 and 14 suggest the following analogous problems about P:

(1) To find a point estimate for P;

(2) To find an interval estimate, or confidence interval, for P;

(3) To test the hypothesis that P has some specified value;

(4) To test the hypothesis that two populations have the same value of P, regardless of what that value may be.

Population Distribution. In making inferences about means, it was assumed that there was a population distribution of some variable X with population parameters μ and σ. The sample statistic $\overline{X}$, which will vary from sample to sample, must provide the basis for inferences about μ, as μ itself is almost always unknown. In the problems of Chapters 13 and 14, the variable X was always a scaled variable and always treated as if continuous.

In the problems of our present discussion, the population distribution is a dichotomy in which the proportion of individuals in one class is P and in the other, $1 - P$. This population has a mean and a standard deviation also, and it can be shown by a little mathematics that these are

(15.1)	Mean	$= \mu = P$
(15.2)	Variance	$= \sigma^2 = P(1 - P)$
(15.3)	Standard deviation $= \sigma = \sqrt{P(1 - P)}$

One notable difference now appears between the populations considered previously and the two-class populations which we are now considering. In the former, μ and σ are quite unrelated, knowledge of one gives no information as to the value of the other. However, in these two-class populations, σ depends completely on P.

Figure 15–1 illustrates a dichotomous population in which $P = .5$ and consequently $\sigma = \sqrt{.5(.5)} = .5$. Figure 15–2 illustrates a dichotomous population in which $P = .8$ and consequently $\sigma = \sqrt{.8(.2)} = .4$.

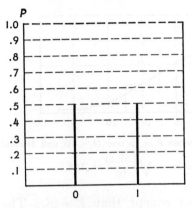

Fig. 15–1 Population Distribution when $P = .5$.

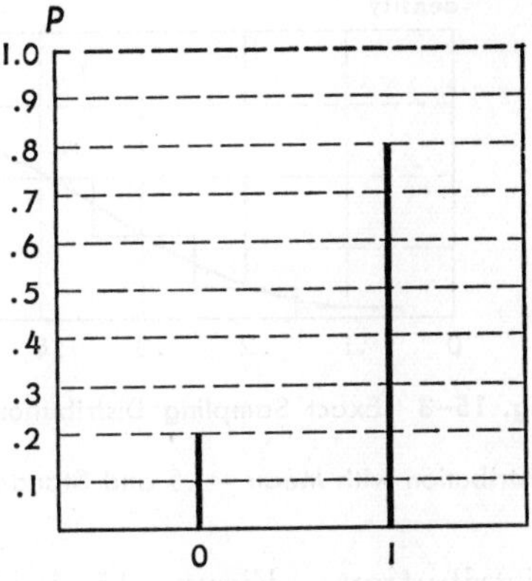

Fig. 15–2 Population Distribution when $P = .8$.

Sampling Distribution of a Proportion. Suppose we draw a random sample of 2 persons out of a population in which the proportion of men is $P = .5$. The sample may have no men, 1 man, or 2 men, and the corresponding proportions will be $p = \frac{0}{2} = 0$, $p = \frac{1}{2} = .5$, and $p = \frac{2}{2} = 1.0$. Thus if $N = 2$, p can take one of three different values and the sampling distribution of p is a distribution with three classes. The probabilities attaching to those classes can be obtained mathematically from the value of P, either from a known value of P or a hypothesis about P.

In general, if there are N cases in a sample, p can take any one of $N + 1$ values ranging from $p = \frac{0}{N} = 0$ to $p = \frac{N}{N} = 1.00$, and so the sampling distribution of p is a distribution of $N + 1$ discrete classes. The probabilities attaching to these classes can be obtained exactly by mathematical formulas which are available in all advanced texts but will not be reproduced here.[2]

Life is made much simpler for statisticians because the normal distribution provides an approximation to the sampling distribution of p. This approximation is good enough for most practical

[2] See the authors' more advanced text *Statistical Inference*, Henry Holt, 1953, pages 19–30.

purposes unless N is small or P is near 0 or near 1. Figure 15–3 shows the exact sampling distribution for p when $P = .5$ and $N = 10$, and also shows a normal curve placed over the exact

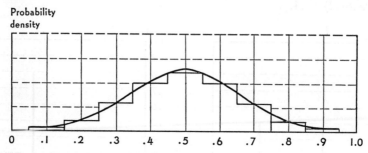

Fig. 15–3 Exact Sampling Distribution for p when $P = .5$ and $N = 10$ and Normal Distribution with Mean $= .5$ and Standard Deviation $= \sqrt{\dfrac{(.5)(.5)}{10}} = .158$.

distribution. Figure 15–4 is similar except that $P = .8$. The relationship between the normal distribution and the sampling distribution for proportions suggests that areas of the former

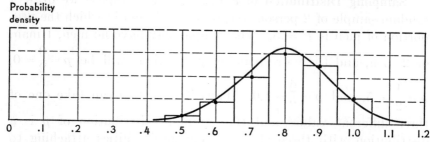

Fig. 15–4 Exact Sampling Distribution for p when $P = .8$ and $N = 10$ and Normal Distribution with Mean $= .8$ and Standard Deviation $= \sqrt{\dfrac{(.8)(.2)}{10}} = .126$.

may be used as approximations for areas of the latter, to simplify computation. Ways in which the approximation can be used effectively will be described below. Methods for exact calculation will also be developed.

Some features of the normal approximation need to be pointed out.

1. The normal approximation improves as sample size increases.

2. For given N the goodness of approximation depends on P. The normal approximation is useful for the distribution of p from samples of 10 when $P = .5$, but is very poor for samples of the

same size when P is near 0 or near 1. A rough rule of thumb is that the normal approximation is satisfactory for given P, if sample size N is such that $NP = 5$ or more when P is equal to or less than 0.5. Thus if P is 0.1, then N should be at least 50. For P more than 0.5, apply the same rule to $Q = 1 - P$.

3. Because the normal approximation involves fitting a curve to a histogram, certain corrections are necessary to improve the fit. These will be introduced as computations are described below.

For use of the normal approximation the following formulas for the mean, variance, and standard deviation of the distribution of p for samples of size N are needed.

$$(15.4) \qquad \text{Mean of } p \qquad\qquad = \mu_p = P$$

$$(15.5) \qquad \text{Variance of } p \qquad\qquad = \sigma_p^2 = \frac{P(1-P)}{N}$$

$$(15.6) \qquad \text{Standard deviation of } p = \sigma_p = \sqrt{\frac{P(1-P)}{N}}$$

The standard deviation of p is usually spoken of as the *standard error of* p.

Point Estimation of a Proportion. When the unknown proportion, P, of a population is to be estimated, the sample value p provides the best single value available, just as a sample mean $\overline{X}$ provides the best single estimate of the parameter μ. Both p and $\overline{X}$ are *unbiased estimates* of their parameters. In other words, repeated samples will yield a variety of values of p, but the average value of p for many samples of the same size will be almost exactly equal to the population value P.

Interval Estimation of a Proportion. A confidence interval for P will be obtained by use of the normal approximation to the distribution of p. The procedure is similar to the one already described in obtaining a confidence interval for μ. The essential difference in the procedure to be described is that it requires a correction for fitting a normal curve to a histogram.

As before, we begin by adopting a confidence coefficient c and reading the values $z_{\frac{1+c}{2}}$ and $z_{\frac{1-c}{2}}$ from a table of normal probability. The confidence limits are then:

$$(15.7) \qquad \text{Upper limit} = p + \frac{1}{2N} + z_{\frac{1+c}{2}} \sqrt{\frac{p(1-p)}{N}}$$

$$(15.8) \qquad \text{Lower limit} = p - \frac{1}{2N} + z_{\frac{1-c}{2}} \sqrt{\frac{p(1-p)}{N}}$$

Here the quantity $\frac{1}{2N}$ is a correction for fitting the normal curve
to a histogram, usually called a *correction for continuity*. The
reader will also note that the quantity, $\sqrt{p(1-p)/N}$, is an estimate of the standard error of p obtained by substituting p for P
in formula (15.6).

As an illustration, suppose a superintendent of schools wants
an estimate of how many persons of voting age in his community
would be in favor of a bond issue for a new school building, and
suppose he selects a random sample of 200 such adults. (This
selection is usually the hardest part of the whole undertaking and
requires a great deal of careful planning.) Suppose an inquiry
to these 200 voters reveals that 140 are in favor of the bond issue.
Then the best single estimate of the proportion of voters who will
vote affirmatively — assuming no major differences between
what a voter says now and what he will do at a later date — is
$\frac{140}{200} = .70$.

If the superintendent wishes to make an interval estimate, he
must choose a confidence coefficient. Suppose he chooses to let
$c = .95$. Then,

$$\text{Upper limit} = .70 + \frac{1}{2(200)} + 1.96 \sqrt{\frac{(.7)(.3)}{200}} = .766$$

$$\text{Lower limit} = .70 - \frac{1}{2(200)} - 1.96 \sqrt{\frac{(.7)(.3)}{200}} = .634$$

With confidence coefficient .95 he can make the statement that
$.634 < P < .766$. If he wants to make a statement in which he
has still greater confidence, he can use a larger value of c. If he
uses $c = .99$, his statement would be $.614 < P < .786$. Certainly
he can feel quite confident that, unless there is a definite shift of
opinion before election day, the vote will carry with a good
majority.

Test of a Hypothesis about a Proportion. To test a hypothesis
about a proportion, we proceed in a manner similar to the one
which was adopted for testing hypotheses about a mean. The
procedure will be modified somewhat because of the necessary
corrections for continuity. We choose a level of significance,
for example, .05 or .01, and set up a region of rejection which may
be in the upper tail, in the lower tail or in both tails.

Suppose now that the hypothetical proportion is P, sample
size is N, and the level of significance is .05. Then, the region of
rejection for an upper-tailed test consists of values of p such that

$$(15.9) \qquad p > P + \frac{1}{2N} + z_{.95} \sqrt{\frac{P(1-P)}{N}}$$

where $z_{.95}$ is the usual value referred to the tables of normal probability. Similarly, for a lower-tailed test, the region of significance would be

$$(15.10) \qquad p < P - \frac{1}{2N} + z_{.05} \sqrt{\frac{P(1-P)}{N}}$$

For the two-tailed region, we have both

$$p > P + \frac{1}{2N} + z_{.975} \sqrt{\frac{P(1-P)}{N}}$$

(15.11)

$$\text{and} \qquad p < P - \frac{1}{2N} + z_{.025} \sqrt{\frac{P(1-P)}{N}}$$

Exact procedures for testing hypotheses will be indicated below.

The Sign Test. An especially interesting and important way to apply tests of hypotheses about proportions is to test the hypotheses on the basis of scores achieved by matched pairs of individuals. The procedure is applicable to problems such as the comparison of deaf and hearing persons discussed in the preceding chapter. The procedure, known as the *sign test*, provides a test of the hypothesis that the median of a population of differences of scores is zero.

The procedure will be described in relation to the scores on balance of deaf and hearing girls appearing in Table 15.1. For all 37 pairs of subjects let us examine the signs of the differences of hearing score minus deaf score. For pair number 1, this difference is plus. For pair number 2, it is minus. As we go through the 37 pairs, we find plus scores 33 times, minus twice, and zero twice. Ignoring the two zeros, the proportion of plus signs is $\frac{33}{35} = .94$.

On the assumption that, in general, the deaf and hearing do not differ in balance, half of the differences would be assumed to be plus and half minus. If P is the proportion of positive differences in the population, then $P = 0.5$. This is the hypothesis to be tested.

Using the .05 level of significance and an upper-tailed region, the region of rejection is

$$p > .5 + \frac{1}{2(35)} + 1.645 \sqrt{\frac{(.5)(1-.5)}{35}}$$

$$\text{or} \qquad p > .65$$

TABLE 15.1 Motor Abilities of 37 Pairs of Deaf and Hearing Girls *

Pair number	Tapping with right hand		Grip		Balance		Tapping with best hand	
	D	H	D	H	D	H	D	H
1	1.3	25.7	10	16	2.0	2.3	18.3	25.7
2	17.0	27.7	14	12	2.0	1.0	17.0	27.7
3	26.3	26.0	12	17	2.7	3.7	26.3	26.0
4	29.7	26.3	21	18	2.7	3.3	29.7	28.7
5	23.0	26.3	19	15	3.0	10.0	23.0	26.3
6	22.7	24.0	12	21	2.7	2.7	22.7	24.0
7	22.0	35.0	19	16	3.7	8.3	22.3	35.0
8	20.7	28.7	17	22	1.3	6.0	30.7	28.7
9	29.0	30.3	19	18	2.0	4.3	29.0	30.3
10	30.0	26.3	25	16	4.3	7.7	30.0	26.3
11	26.7	37.3	23	28	1.0	1.3	26.7	37.3
12	36.0	30.7	25	22	1.7	4.0	36.0	30.7
13	30.7	31.3	24	21	5.0	5.3	30.7	31.3
14	22.3	25.0	15	21	1.0	2.0	22.3	25.0
15	38.3	38.7	25	30	1.7	2.7	38.3	38.7
16	28.7	24.0	13	25	3.3	4.7	28.7	24.0
17	34.3	32.3	25	31	3.0	4.7	34.3	32.3
18	35.7	26.3	23	23	3.3	2.3	35.7	26.3
19	32.3	30.7	23	35	8.0	10.0	32.3	33.0
20	33.0	31.0	15	28	2.3	8.0	33.0	31.0
21	27.3	36.7	18	33	1.7	4.3	29.3	36.7
22	27.7	31.7	19	23	2.0	4.7	27.7	31.7
23	29.0	28.7	34	20	2.0	7.0	34.0	34.0
24	35.3	30.7	32	45	2.7	3.3	35.3	30.7
25	30.3	27.7	29	39	1.0	1.7	32.3	27.7
26	39.0	32.0	26	29	2.0	5.0	39.7	32.0
27	35.7	28.0	35	32	1.3	4.0	35.7	28.0
28	31.7	31.3	31	25	2.3	6.7	31.7	31.3
29	37.7	36.7	29	26	4.3	6.7	37.7	36.7
30	39.3	35.3	31	33	5.3	10.0	39.3	35.3
31	30.7	31.3	31	38	2.3	3.7	30.7	32.0
32	26.7	27.3	22	28	2.0	8.7	26.7	30.7
33	35.7	33.0	34	19	1.7	3.7	35.7	33.0
34	34.0	32.0	22	32	3.0	3.0	34.0	32.0
35	25.3	30.3	27	29	4.0	7.0	25.3	30.3
36	29.7	33.3	31	31	4.7	6.3	29.7	33.3
37	35.3	29.3	29	28	1.3	7.3	35.3	29.3

* Source of data: Long, *op. cit.*

Hence, the hypothesis $P = .5$ is to be rejected if the observed proportion exceeds .65. Since the proportion in the sample is actually .94, the hypothesis is rejected.

Applying a two-tailed test with a .05 level of significance, the region of rejection consists of all points p so that

$$p > .5 + \frac{1}{2(35)} + 1.96 \sqrt{\frac{(.5)(1-.5)}{35}} = .68 \quad \text{and}$$

$$p < .5 - \frac{1}{2(35)} - 1.96 \sqrt{\frac{(.5)(1-.5)}{35}} = .32$$

Consequently, the region of rejection consists of all values of p greater than .680 and less than .320. Since the observed value of $p = .94$ is in the region of rejection, the hypothesis $P = .5$ is rejected on the basis of the two-tailed test as well.

The sign test is an example of a wide variety of tests known as *nonparametric* or *distribution-free*. These tests have the great advantage that they make no assumption such as normality about the distribution of the parent population, and are applicable to populations of any kind. Other nonparametric methods may be found in advanced texts.

Another advantage, though of lesser importance, is that nonparametric tests give, with relatively little work, results closely approximating those obtained by tests based on the assumption of normality.

A Table for Testing Hypotheses about a Proportion. As was pointed out, the methods for testing hypotheses about proportions described to this point have been approximate. Exact methods are available but require extensive tables and mathematical insight. Some help in obtaining exact results is available in Appendix Table XII. This table consists of three parts: A, for the two-tailed test; B, for the upper-tailed test; and C, for the lower-tailed test. All parts are suitable for testing at the 5-percent level of significance only. Each entry in the table indicates a region of rejection corresponding to the number of cases at the left of the row and the value of P at the head of the column in which the entry is located. The entries are stated in terms of number of cases rather than terms of a proportion. Thus, for the sign test one would use the number of differences having a plus sign rather than the corresponding proportion of differences.

As an example of the use of this table, let us apply it to make the sign test of the previous section. The data are $N = 35$, $k = 33$, and $P = 0.5$.

To make a two-tailed test we refer to part A, the column headed .50, and the row for which $N = 35$. The corresponding pair of entries is 11 and 24. This means that the hypothesis $P = .50$ is rejected if the number of positive differences is either as small as, or smaller than, 11 or is as large as, or larger than, 24. Since the observed value of k is 33, the hypothesis is rejected. If the numbers 11 and 24 are reduced to proportions, we have $\frac{11}{35} = .314$ which approximates the value .320 previously obtained and $\frac{24}{35} = .686$ which approximates the value .680.

To develop the corresponding test using a region of rejection in the upper tail, we refer to part B of Table XII. The entry in the column headed .50 and the row for which $N = 35$ is 23. Hence, the hypothesis is again rejected.

Hypothesis that P Is the Same for Two Populations. Suppose that 105 of the 200 adults in the sample described earlier in this chapter have children in school and 95 do not; and suppose that 90 of the 105 parents are in favor of the bond issue, while only 50 of the 95 nonparents are in favor. The situation can be summarized thus:

	Parents	Nonparents	Combined group
Approve	90	50	140
Disapprove	15	45	60
Total	105	95	200

Two populations are under consideration here, a population of parents and one of nonparents. To distinguish these two populations and the samples from them, we shall use the following symbols:

P_1 = proportion of the population of parents who approve the issue

P_2 = proportion of the population of nonparents who approve the issue

p_1 = proportion of the sample of parents who approve the issue; $p_1 = 90/105 = .857$

p_2 = proportion of the sample of nonparents who approve the issue; $p_2 = 50/95 = .526$

The question to be answered is whether the difference $p_1 - p_2 = .857 - .526 = .331$ is so great that it cannot reasonably be presumed to be an outcome of random sampling from two populations which have the same value of P. In other words, do the sample data contradict the hypothesis $P_1 = P_2$?

To answer this question, we need the standard error of the difference $p_1 - p_2$, which is

$$(15.12) \qquad \sigma_{p_1-p_2} = \sqrt{\frac{P_1(1 - P_1)}{N_1} + \frac{P_2(1 - P_2)}{N_2}}$$

In the present situation there is no hypothetical value for either P_1 or P_2. Each of them must be estimated from the data. On the hypothesis that they are equal, so $P_1 = P_2 = P$, the best sample estimate of P is the proportion in the combined group. If we call this estimate p, then for the given data

$$p = \frac{90 + 50}{105 + 95} = \frac{140}{200} = .70$$

Under the hypothesis that $P_1 = P_2$, the standard error is estimated by the value

$$(15.13) \qquad s_{p_1-p_2} = \sqrt{\frac{p(1 - p)}{N_1} + \frac{p(1 - p)}{N_2}}$$

If neither N_1 nor N_2 is very small, tests of the hypothesis $P_1 = P_2$ can be based on the standard normal distribution.

When the alternative is $P_1 > P_2$, use the statistic

$$(15.14) \qquad z = \frac{p_1 - p_2 - \dfrac{N}{2N_1N_2}}{\sqrt{\dfrac{p(1 - p)}{N_1} + \dfrac{p(1 - p)}{N_2}}}$$

and set the region of rejection in the upper tail. When the alternative is $P_2 > P_1$, use the statistic

$$(15.15) \qquad z = \frac{p_2 - p_1 - \dfrac{N}{2N_1N_2}}{\sqrt{\dfrac{p(1 - p)}{N_1} + \dfrac{p(1 - p)}{N_2}}}$$

and set the region of rejection in the upper tail.

When the alternative is $P_1 \neq P_2$, use a two-tailed region. For the upper tail, use the statistic given by formula (15.14). For the lower tail, use the statistic

$$(15.16) \qquad z = \frac{p_1 - p_2 + \dfrac{N}{2N_1N_2}}{\sqrt{\dfrac{p(1 - p)}{N_1} + \dfrac{p(1 - p)}{N_2}}}$$

The term $\dfrac{N}{2N_1N_2}$ is known as *Yates' correction* or the *correction for continuity,* and is usually presented in a somewhat different form. Here, $N = N_1 + N_2$.

In the numerical problem introduced earlier in this section, we found $p_1 = .857$, $p_2 = .526$, $p = .700$, $N_1 = 105$, $N_2 = 95$, $N = 200$. Then, if the alternative is $P_1 > P_2$, we compute

$$z = \frac{.857 - .526 - \dfrac{200}{2(105)(95)}}{\sqrt{\dfrac{(.7)(.3)}{105} + \dfrac{(.7)(.3)}{95}}} = \frac{.321}{.0649} = 4.9$$

This computed z is larger than $z_{.99} = 2.33$ and the hypothesis is rejected. It must be concluded that the parents are more favorable to the bond issue than the nonparents.

EXERCISE 15.1

1. Apply the sign test to the data of Table 14.1, using an upper-tailed test and the .05 level of significance. Use both the normal approximation and Appendix Table XII.

2. Apply the sign test to the difference in the scores of grip recorded in Table 15.1. Are the results consistent with the answer to Question 3 in Exercise 14.1?

3. A group of 50 laboratory animals was divided into two random groups of 25 each, and each group was trained in a complex task by a different method. At the end of a training period, 18 animals in group A and 12 in group B had mastered the task. Test the hypothesis that the two methods are equally effective. (Consider that the two methods of training generate two populations.)

16

Inferences about Correlation Coefficients

The general procedures of statistical inference were developed in Chapters 13 and 14 and applied to problems about means. In Chapter 15, similar methods were applied to proportions. This chapter will introduce problems of statistical inference regarding the correlation coefficient and will deal briefly with its sampling distribution, tests of hypotheses, and interval estimates. It will also provide a discussion of how to interpret the size of a coefficient of correlation.

Bivariate Population. The correlation coefficient, r, which we studied in Chapter 10, is a statistic computed from a sample of pairs of measures. Each pair of measures belongs to the same subject, the two measures being his scores on each of two variables.

In order to set a framework for statistical inference about correlation coefficients, we suppose that there is a population of pairs of measures. This is a population involving two variables and so is called a *bivariate* population. In contrast, the populations which we have considered heretofore may be called *univariate*.

Just as univariate populations differ from each other with respect to mean, spread, flatness, skewness, etc., so bivariate populations differ from each other, and these differences are much more complex, because we must consider not only the characteristics of each variable separately, but also characteristics of the joint variation of the two variables.

We shall discuss briefly only one kind of bivariate population, namely, the *normal bivariate*. In this population each variable, taken separately, is normal, and each is defined separately by its mean and standard deviation. In addition, the joint variation of the two variables is described by a parameter which is the correlation in the population.

Because a bivariate population involves two variables, the means and standard deviations of the population on those variables must be distinguished by appropriate symbols. Thus, if the two variables are called X and Y, the sample statistics would be $\overline{X}$, $\overline{Y}$, s_x, s_y, and r, and the population parameters μ_x, μ_y, σ_x, σ_y, and ρ. If the two variables are called X_1 and X_2, the sample statistics would be $\overline{X}_1$, $\overline{X}_2$, s_1, s_2, and r, and the populations parameters μ_1, μ_2, σ_1, σ_2, and ρ. The Greek letter ρ (rho) corresponds to the English r and so is an appropriate symbol for the correlation coefficient in the population. The reader should be warned that this symbol is also in popular use to mean a coefficient of rank-order correlation.

Distribution of r. The distribution of r, like that of the proportion, is not normal but approaches normality as sample size increases. However, the approach to normality depends not only on sample size, but also on the value of ρ. If samples are drawn from a population for which ρ is at or near zero, the distribution of r is approximately normal for samples even as small as 30. However, when ρ is near $+1$ or -1, the distribution of r is quite skewed even for very large samples. We shall describe below a way of meeting this problem.

Standard Error of r. The standard error of r is given by the formula

$$(16.1) \qquad \sigma_r = \frac{1 - \rho^2}{\sqrt{N - 1}}$$

We may note that the standard error of r, like that of a proportion, depends on its population parameter. This fact and the non-normality of the distribution of r limit the usefulness of the standard error of r.

Tests of the Hypothesis that $\rho = 0$. If $\rho = 0$, the standard error of r given in formula (16.1) reduces to $\dfrac{1}{\sqrt{N - 1}}$ and the standard score for r, which is $\dfrac{r - \rho}{\sigma_r}$, becomes $r\sqrt{N - 1}$. Then, if N is not small, for example, not less than 30, the distribution of $r\sqrt{N - 1}$ will approximate the standard normal.

Suppose we wish to test the hypothesis $\rho = 0$ with a two-sided test and significance level .05. A table of the normal distribution indicates that the region of significance is $z > 1.96$ and $z < -1.96$. Now suppose a sample of 35 cases is drawn, and in this sample r is found to be .30. Therefore, $z = r\sqrt{N - 1} = .30\sqrt{34}$

= 1.75. As this value is not in the region of significance, the hypothesis $\rho = 0$ is tenable, and the observed value of r is *non-significant*.

The test just described is not exact because, even when $\rho = 0$, the distribution of r is not exactly normal. An exact test is available because

$$(16.2) \qquad t = \frac{r\sqrt{N-2}}{\sqrt{1-r^2}}$$

has the t distribution with $N-2$ degrees of freedom. Thus for $N = 35$ and $r = .30$, $t = \dfrac{.30\sqrt{33}}{\sqrt{1-(.30)^2}} = .30\sqrt{\dfrac{33}{.91}} = 1.81$. When we refer this value to Appendix Table V with 30 degrees of freedom (since Table V does not have entries for 33 degrees of freedom), we find it well below $t_{.975} = 2.05$. Again, we cannot reject the hypothesis $\rho = 0$.

Test of Hypothesis $\rho = 0$ by Use of Appendix Table VI. This appendix table enables one to test the null hypothesis about ρ directly from the known value of r without further computation. It is entered with degrees of freedom $n = N - 2$. (For a partial correlation, not discussed here, n would be something else.) By reference to this table, verify the following:

(1) $N = 22$. Then $n = 20$, $r_{.025} = -.423$, $r_{.975} = .423$

     In a sample of 22 cases, any value of r not between $r = -.423$ and $r = .423$ would be significant at the .05 level and would justify rejecting the hypothesis $\rho = 0$.

(2) $N = 52$. Then $n = 52$, $r_{.025} = -.273$, $r_{.975} = .273$

     In a sample of 52 cases, the value of r which is numerically greater than .273 would be significant at the .05 level.

(3) $N = 92$. Any value of r which is numerically greater than .205 would be significant at the .05 level; any value numerically greater than .242, significant at the .02 level; any value numerically greater than .338, significant at the .001 level.

The z_r Transformation. When ρ is different from zero, the sampling distribution of r is skewed, and neither of the tests described in the previous section nor Table VI can be used. A variable, which is usually called z but which we shall call z_r in order to distinguish it from the other variables which have already been denoted by that letter, is related to r by the formula

$$(16.3) \qquad z_r = \frac{1}{2}\log_e \frac{1+r}{1-r}$$

$$(16.4) \qquad = 1.1503 \log_{10} \frac{1+r}{1-r}$$

$$(16.5) \qquad = 1.1503 \left[\log_{10} (1 + r) - \log_{10} (1 - r) \right]$$

This variable, introduced by R. A. Fisher, has two very great advantages. Its distribution is approximately normal even for small samples in which ρ is near 1, and its standard error does not depend on the unknown population value but only on the size of the sample,

$$(16.6) \qquad \sigma_{z_r} = \frac{1}{\sqrt{N-3}}$$

If ζ (zeta) is the population value of z_r corresponding to ρ, then $(z_r - \zeta) \sqrt{N-3}$ may be treated as a normally distributed variable.

The transformation from r to z_r and vice versa can be made easily by reference to Appendix Table VII. For example, suppose $r = .85$. Look in the field of the table for the number nearest to .85. It is .8511, standing in the row headed 1.2 and in the column headed .06. The value of z_r corresponding to $r = .85$ is therefore read as 1.26. Or if $z_r = 2.09$, the corresponding r will stand in a cell in the row 2.0 and column .09. The value found in that cell is $r = .9699$. You will note that small values of r and z_r are very similar, but for large values, z_r is considerably larger than r.

Test of Hypothesis about ρ Using z_r Transformation. Suppose we have $r = .76$ for $N = 228$, and we wish to test the hypothesis that $\rho = .80$ at significance level .05, against the alternative $\rho < .80$. A correct procedure would be as follows:

(1) From Table VII, we find that if $r = .76$, $z = 1.00$;
(2) From the same table we find that if $\rho = .80$, $\zeta = 1.10$;
(3) $\sqrt{N-3} = \sqrt{225} = 15$;
(4) Then the standard score is

$$z = \frac{1.00 - 1.10}{(1/\sqrt{225})} = -1.50$$

(5) As this is a one-sided test, the critical region is $z < z_{.05}$, which is $z < -1.64$;
(6) Since the computed value $z = -1.50$ is not in the critical region, the hypothesis $\rho = .80$ is not rejected.

We may contrast with this the decision which might have been incorrectly obtained by computing $\sigma_r = .024$ and

$$\frac{(r - \rho)}{\sigma_r} = -1.67$$

The computations are not incorrect, but as we have no probability distribution to which the statistic -1.67 can be referred, they lead nowhere. If now we incorrectly refer it to the normal probability distribution and reject the hypothesis $\rho = .80$ because $-1.67 < z_{.05}$, we shall make an incorrect decision.

Confidence Interval for ρ. The z transformation is useful in obtaining a confidence interval for ρ. The procedure is as follows:

(1) In Table VII, find the value of z corresponding to the sample value of r;

(2) Compute a confidence interval for the population value ζ by the formula

(16.7)   Upper limit $= z_r + z_{\frac{1+c}{2}} \Big/ \sqrt{N-3}$

Lower limit $= z_r + z_{\frac{1-c}{2}} \Big/ \sqrt{N-3}$

Here one must remember that z_r and $z_{\frac{1+c}{2}}$ (or $z_{\frac{1-c}{2}}$) are two quite different values represented by the same letter only because of tradition and the brevity of our alphabet.

(3) In Table VII, read the value of ρ corresponding to each of the bounding values of ζ. From these form the interval for ρ.

Thus suppose we have obtained $r = .65$ in a sample of 40 cases, and we want an interval estimate for ρ with confidence coefficient .95. From Table VII we read $z_r = .78$. From the normal probability table we find

$$z_{.025} = -1.96 \quad \text{and} \quad z_{.975} = 1.96. \quad \sqrt{N-3} = \sqrt{37}.$$

Then $.78 - \dfrac{1.96}{\sqrt{37}} < \zeta < .78 + \dfrac{1.96}{\sqrt{37}}$ or $.46 < \zeta < 1.10$

and $.43 < \rho < .80$

Notice that because of the skewness in the distribution of r the confidence limits for ρ are not symmetrically placed about the observed r, but $.80 - .65 = .15$ while $.65 - .43 = .22$.

Test of the Hypothesis that Two Independent Populations Have the Same Correlation. If a sample is drawn from each of two independent, normal bivariate populations the difference $r_1 - r_2$ should fluctuate around $\rho_1 - \rho_2$. If each r is transformed to z, the difference $z_1 - z_2$ will also fluctuate around $\zeta_1 - \zeta_2$ as mean and will have as standard deviation

$$\sqrt{\frac{1}{N_1 - 3} + \frac{1}{N_2 - 3}}$$

Then

$$(16.8) \qquad \frac{(z_1 - z_2) - (\zeta_1 - \zeta_2)}{\sqrt{\dfrac{1}{N_1 - 3} + \dfrac{1}{N_2 - 3}}}$$

may be treated as a normal deviate. If the hypothesis that $\zeta_1 = \zeta_2$ is rejected, the hypothesis $\rho_1 = \rho_2$ must also be rejected. If the hypothesis $\zeta_1 = \zeta_2$ is sustained, the hypothesis $\rho_1 = \rho_2$ must also be sustained.

In his research concerning *Children's Collecting Activity* [1] Durost studied the collections made by 50 boys and 50 girls between the ages of 10 and 14. Among the correlations obtained was a correlation between mental age and the average rating of the child's collections (each of the collections of each child being rated as to quality and the average taken for the child). For boys this correlation was .31 and for girls, .06. Do these figures provide evidence that the relation between mental maturity and quality of collections made is higher for boys than for girls?

	r	z_r	$N - 3$	$\dfrac{1}{N - 3}$
Boys	.31	.32	47	$.021277 = \sigma^2_{z_B}$
Girls	.06	.06	47	$.021277 = \sigma^2_{z_G}$
		$z_B - z_G = .26$		$.042554 = \sigma^2_{z_B} + \sigma^2_{z_G}$

$$z = \frac{.26}{\sqrt{.0426}} = \frac{.26}{.206} = 1.26$$

With so small a value of z, it would be inappropriate to assume that the relationship is higher for boys than for girls.

Test of the Hypothesis that $\rho_{yz} = \rho_{xz}$ when Computed for the Same Population. This situation is quite different from that of the preceding section, though often confused with it. There we had measures on the same two variates, X and Y, for two *different populations*. Here we have for *one population* measures on three variates, X, Y, and Z, and we wish to know whether Z is more highly correlated with X than with Y, or vice versa. This question is particularly important when two predictors are available, but the one showing the higher correlation with the criterion is more expensive, more time consuming, or more difficult to apply. For example, suppose that a prognostic test, long and rather difficult to administer, has yielded a correlation

---

[1] Walter N. Durost, *Children's Collecting Activity Related to Social Factors*, New York. Teachers College, Columbia University, Bureau of Publications, 1932.

of .56 with freshman college marks, while a shorter test, less costly to administer, has yielded a correlation of .43, the two correlations being obtained from the same 100 subjects. If the tests were equally costly, the one yielding the higher correlation would be chosen regardless of whether the difference in the r's was significant or not. Still better, both tests would be used, and prediction made from a multiple regression equation. However, let us suppose the college authorities have decided to use only one test, and to use the more costly test only if its correlation with marks is significantly higher than that of the other test. If the hypothesis $\rho_{yz} = \rho_{xz}$ proves tenable, they have decided to use only the shorter test.

> Let X = score on the longer test
> Y = score on the shorter test
> Z = average mark at end of first semester

A solution of the problem of the significance of the difference between r_{yz} and r_{xz} can be obtained without any assumption as to the form of distribution of X or of Y in the population, but with the limitation that generalization is only to a subpopulation of all possible samples for which X and Y have exactly the same set of values as those in the observed sample. It is assumed that Z has a normal distribution for each value of X and for each value of Y, with common variance.

$$(16.9) \quad \text{Then} \quad t = (r_{xz} - r_{yz}) \sqrt{\frac{(N-3)(1 + r_{xy})}{2(1 - r_{xy}^2 - r_{yz}^2 - r_{xz}^2 + 2r_{xy}r_{xz}r_{yz})}}$$

has Student's distribution with $N - 3$ degrees of freedom.

Obviously it is necessary to know the correlation between the two tests before the question can be answered. Assume that $r_{xy} = .52$.

Then
$$t = (.56 - .43)\sqrt{153.10} = 1.61$$

In view of this small value of t, it would be difficult to make a strong case for the use of the longer test if only one test is to be used. It is, of course, easy to show that the predictive value of $r = .43$ is too low to be of much practical use.

The Size of a Correlation Coefficient. Several different bases exist for interpreting the size of a coefficient of correlation, and much confusion has arisen because what might be termed "large" in one connection would be "small" in another. To draw up a numerical scale and to say that coefficients in one particular range are large and in another negligible only adds to this confusion.

A value of r may be "large" because it is too large to be consistent with the null hypothesis $\rho = 0$; or because it is large enough to be useful for predictive purposes; or because it is larger than values commonly obtained in similar circumstances. To use a single word "large" to cover these three quite disparate meanings is sheer verbal laziness. We shall now look at each in turn.

1. *Interpretation in terms of statistical significance.* To say that a sample value of r is significant at, for instance, the .01 level means that, if a large number of samples of the given size are drawn from an uncorrelated population (i.e., a population in which $\rho = 0$), 1 percent of such samples would be expected to produce a value of r at least as large numerically as the observed value. This is the concept which has been under discussion in the preceding pages. A very small r may be significant if the sample is very large. Thus, for 500 cases, $r = .09$ is significant, but still too small to be useful for most purposes. It must always be kept in mind that the terms "significant" and "nonsignificant" are really comments on the relation of a sample to the hypothesis which is being tested.

2. *Interpretation in terms of usefulness of the regression equation for predictive purposes.* Chapter 9 explained that the usefulness of a regression equation depends upon how closely the estimated and actual values agree. Chapter 10 explained that the correlation coefficient provides the clue to this agreement. Formula (10.1) can be rewritten as

$$(16.10) \qquad 1 - r^2 = \frac{\Sigma(Y - \tilde{Y})^2}{\Sigma(Y - \overline{Y})^2}$$

Here we see that $1 - r^2$ expresses the proportion which the sum of squares of deviations from the regression line is to the sum of squares of deviations from the mean. The smaller this proportion, the better the prediction.

3. *Interpretation in terms of correlations commonly obtained.* Sometimes, when a research worker comments that he obtained a high correlation between two variables, he means only that r was higher than previous experience had led him to anticipate. So many factors affect the size of r that it is well nigh impossible to draw up a list of typical values which would not be misleading. To build up a sense of what is reasonable to expect, a researcher requires experience, familiarity with the research literature in his own field, and careful attention to factors which make one situation different from others with which it is being compared.

TABLE I Ordinates and Areas of the Standard Normal Curve *

(In terms of σ units)

$\frac{x}{\sigma}$	Area	Ordinate	$\frac{x}{\sigma}$	Area	Ordinate	$\frac{x}{\sigma}$	Area	Ordinate
00	.0000	.3989	.50	.1915	.3521	1.00	.3413	.2420
.01	.0040	.3989	.51	.1950	.3503	1.01	.3438	.2396
.02	.0080	.3989	.52	.1985	.3485	1.02	.3461	.2371
.03	.0120	.3988	.53	.2019	.3467	1.03	.3485	.2347
.04	.0160	.3986	.54	.2054	.3448	1.04	.3508	.2323
.05	.0199	.3984	.55	.2088	.3429	1.05	.3531	.2299
.06	.0239	.3982	.56	.2123	.3410	1.06	.3554	.2275
.07	.0279	.3980	.57	.2157	.3391	1.07	.3577	.2251
.08	.0319	.3977	.58	.2190	.3372	1.08	.3599	.2227
.09	.0359	.3973	.59	.2224	.3352	1.09	.3621	.2203
.10	.0398	.3970	.60	.2257	.3332	1.10	.3643	.2179
.11	.0438	.3965	.61	.2291	.3312	1.11	.3665	.2155
.12	.0478	.3961	.62	.2324	.3292	1.12	.3686	.2131
.13	.0517	.3956	.63	.2357	.3271	1.13	.3708	.2107
.14	.0557	.3951	.64	.2389	.3251	1.14	.3729	.2083
.15	.0596	.3945	.65	.2422	.3230	1.15	.3749	.2059
.16	.0636	.3939	.66	.2454	.3209	1.16	.3770	.2036
.17	.0675	.3932	.67	.2486	.3187	1.17	.3790	.2012
.18	.0714	.3925	.68	.2517	.3166	1.18	.3810	.1989
.19	.0753	.3918	.69	.2549	.3144	1.19	.3830	.1965
.20	.0793	.3910	.70	.2580	.3123	1.20	.3849	.1942
.21	.0832	.3902	.71	.2611	.3101	1.21	.3869	.1919
.22	.0871	.3894	.72	.2642	.3079	1.22	.3888	.1895
.23	.0910	.3885	.73	.2673	.3056	1.23	.3907	.1872
.24	.0948	.3876	.74	.2703	.3034	1.24	.3925	.1849
.25	.0987	.3867	.75	.2734	.3011	1.25	.3944	.1826
.26	.1026	.3857	.76	.2764	.2989	1.26	.3962	.1804
.27	.1064	.3847	.77	.2794	.2966	1.27	.3980	.1781
.28	.1103	.3836	.78	.2823	.2943	1.28	.3997	.1758
.29	.1141	.3825	.79	.2852	.2920	1.29	.4015	.1736
.30	.1179	.3814	.80	.2881	.2897	1.30	.4032	.1714
.31	.1217	.3802	.81	.2910	.2874	1.31	.4049	.1691
.32	.1255	.3790	.82	.2939	.2850	1.32	.4066	.1669
.33	.1293	.3778	.83	.2967	.2827	1.33	.4082	.1647
.34	.1331	.3765	.84	.2995	.2803	1.34	.4099	.1626
.35	.1368	.3752	.85	.3023	.2780	1.35	.4115	.1604
.36	.1406	.3739	.86	.3051	.2756	1.36	.4131	.1582
.37	.1443	.3725	.87	.3078	.2732	1.37	.4147	.1561
.38	.1480	.3712	.88	.3106	.2709	1.38	.4162	.1539
.39	.1517	.3697	.89	.3133	.2685	1.39	.4177	.1518
.40	.1554	.3683	.90	.3159	.2661	1.40	.4192	.1497
.41	.1591	.3668	.91	.3186	.2637	1.41	.4207	.1476
.42	.1628	.3653	.92	.3212	.2613	1.42	.4222	.1456
.43	.1664	.3637	.93	.3238	.2589	1.43	.4236	.1435
.44	.1700	.3621	.94	.3264	.2565	1.44	.4251	.1415
.45	.1736	.3605	.95	.3289	.2541	1.45	.4265	.1394
.46	.1772	.3589	.96	.3315	.2516	1.46	.4279	.1374
.47	.1808	.3572	.97	.3340	.2492	1.47	.4292	.1354
.48	.1844	.3555	.98	.3365	.2468	1.48	.4306	.1334
.49	.1879	.3538	.99	.3389	.2444	1.49	.4319	.1315
.50	.1915	.3521	1.00	.3413	.2420	1.50	.4332	.1295

* This table is reproduced from J. E. Wert, *Educational Statistics*, by courtesy of McGraw Hill Book Co.

TABLE I Ordinates and Areas of the Standard Normal Curve. *Concluded*
(In terms of σ units)

$\frac{x}{\sigma}$	Area	Ordinate	$\frac{x}{\sigma}$	Area	Ordinate	$\frac{x}{\sigma}$	Area	Ordinate
1.50	.4332	.1295	2.00	.4772	.0540	2.50	.4938	.0175
1.51	.4345	.1276	2.01	.4778	.0529	2.51	.4940	.0171
1.52	.4357	.1257	2.02	.4783	.0519	2.52	.4941	.0167
1.53	.4370	.1238	2.03	.4788	.0508	2.53	.4943	.0163
1.54	.4382	.1219	2.04	.4793	.0498	2.54	.4945	.0158
1.55	.4394	.1200	2.05	.4798	.0488	2.55	.4946	.0154
1.56	.4406	.1182	2.06	.4803	.0478	2.56	.4948	.0151
1.57	.4418	.1163	2.07	.4808	.0468	2.57	.4949	.0147
1.58	.4429	.1145	2.08	.4812	.0459	2.58	.4951	.0143
1.59	.4441	.1127	2.09	.4817	.0449	2.59	.4952	.0139
1.60	.4452	.1109	2.10	.4821	.0440	2.60	.4953	.0136
1.61	.4463	.1092	2.11	.4826	.0431	2.61	.4955	.0132
1.62	.4474	.1074	2.12	.4830	.0422	2.62	.4956	.0129
1.63	.4484	.1057	2.13	.4834	.0413	2.63	.4957	.0126
1.64	.4495	.1040	2.14	.4838	.0404	2.64	.4959	.0122
1.65	.4505	.1023	2.15	.4842	.0395	2.65	.4960	.0119
1.66	.4515	.1006	2.16	.4846	.0387	2.66	.4961	.0116
1.67	.4525	.0989	2.17	.4850	.0379	2.67	.4962	.0113
1.68	.4535	.0973	2.18	.4854	.0371	2.68	.4963	.0110
1.69	.4545	.0957	2.19	.4857	.0363	2.69	.4964	.0107
1.70	.4554	.0940	2.20	.4861	.0355	2.70	.4965	.0104
1.71	.4564	.0925	2.21	.4864	.0347	2.71	.4966	.0101
1.72	.4573	.0909	2.22	.4868	.0339	2.72	.4967	.0099
1.73	.4582	.0893	2.23	.4871	.0332	2.73	.4968	.0096
1.74	.4591	.0878	2.24	.4875	.0325	2.74	.4969	.0093
1.75	.4599	.0863	2.25	.4878	.0317	2.75	.4970	.0091
1.76	.4608	.0848	2.26	.4881	.0310	2.76	.4971	.0088
1.77	.4616	.0833	2.27	.4884	.0303	2.77	.4972	.0086
1.78	.4625	.0818	2.28	.4887	.0297	2.78	.4973	.0084
1.79	.4633	.0804	2.29	.4890	.0290	2.79	.4974	.0081
1.80	.4641	.0790	2.30	.4893	.0283	2.80	.4974	.0079
1.81	.4649	.0775	2.31	.4896	.0277	2.81	.4975	.0077
1.82	.4656	.0761	2.32	.4898	.0270	2.82	.4976	.0075
1.83	.4664	.0748	2.33	.4901	.0264	2.83	.4977	.0073
1.84	.4671	.0734	2.34	.4904	.0258	2.84	.4977	.0071
1.85	.4678	.0721	2.35	.4906	.0252	2.85	.4978	.0069
1.86	.4686	.0707	2.36	.4909	.0246	2.86	.4979	.0067
1.87	.4693	.0694	2.37	.4911	.0241	2.87	.4979	.0065
1.88	.4699	.0681	2.38	.4913	.0235	2.88	.4980	.0063
1.89	.4706	.0669	2.39	.4916	.0229	2.89	.4981	.0061
1.90	.4713	.0656	2.40	.4918	.0224	2.90	.4981	.0060
1.91	.4719	.0644	2.41	.4920	.0219	2.91	.4982	.0058
1.92	.4726	.0632	2.42	.4922	.0213	2.92	.4982	.0056
1.93	.4732	.0620	2.43	.4925	.0208	2.93	.4983	.0055
1.94	.4738	.0608	2.44	.4927	.0203	2.94	.4984	.0053
1.95	.4744	.0596	2.45	.4929	.0198	2.95	.4984	.0051
1.96	.4750	.0584	2.46	.4931	.0194	2.96	.4985	.0050
1.97	.4756	.0573	2.47	.4932	.0189	2.97	.4985	.0048
1.98	.4761	.0562	2.48	.4934	.0184	2.98	.4986	.0047
1.99	.4767	.0551	2.49	.4936	.0180	2.99	.4986	.0046
2.00	.4772	.0540	2.50	.4938	.0175	3.00	.4987	.0044

TABLE II   Percentile Values of the Standard Normal Distribution *

Area to the left of z	z	Area to the left of z	z	Area to the left of z	z	Area to the left of z	z	Area to the left of z	z
.0001	− 3.719	.045	− 1.695	.280	− .583	.700	.524	.950	1.645
.0002	− 3.540	.050	− 1.645	.300	− .524	.720	.583	.955	1.695
.0003	− 3.432	.055	− 1.598	.320	− .468	.740	.643	.960	1.751
.0004	− 3.353	.060	− 1.555	.340	− .412	.750	.6745	.965	1.812
.0005	− 3.291	.065	− 1.514	.360	− .358	.760	.706	.970	1.881
.001	− 3.090	.070	− 1.476	.380	− .305	.780	.772	.975	1.960
.002	− 2.878	.075	− 1.440	.400	− .253	.800	.842	.980	2.054
.003	− 2.748	.080	− 1.405	.420	− .202	.820	.915	.985	2.170
.004	− 2.652	.085	− 1.372	.440	− .151	.840	.994	.990	2.326
.005	− 2.576	.090	− 1.341	.460	− .100	.860	1.080	.991	2.366
.006	− 2.512	.095	− 1.311	.480	− .050	.880	1.175	.992	2.409
.007	− 2.457	.100	− 1.282	.500	.000	.900	1.282	.993	2.457
.008	− 2.409	.120	− 1.175	.520	.050	.905	1.311	.994	2.512
.009	− 2.366	.140	− 1.080	.540	.100	.910	1.341	.995	2.576
.010	− 2.326	.160	− .994	.560	.151	.915	1.372	.996	2.652
.015	− 2.170	.180	− .915	.580	.202	.920	1.405	.997	2.748
.020	− 2.054	.200	− .842	.600	.253	.925	1.440	.998	2.878
.025	− 1.960	.220	− .772	.620	.305	.930	1.476	.999	3.090
.030	− 1.881	.240	− .706	.640	.358	.935	1.514	.9995	3.291
.035	− 1.812	.250	− .6745	.660	.412	.940	1.555	.9996	3.353
.040	− 1.751	.260	− .643	.680	.468	.945	1.598	.9999	3.719

* Entries in this table are taken from *The Kelley Statistical Tables*, Harvard University Press, 1938, revised 1948, by permission of the author, Truman Lee Kelley.

z is the percentile value named by the area to the left of z. Thus $z_{.30} = -.524$ is the 30th percentile.

TABLE III Squares, Square Roots, and Reciprocals

n	n^2	$\sqrt{n}$	$\sqrt{10n}$	$1/n$	n	n^2	$\sqrt{n}$	$\sqrt{10n}$	$1/n$
1	1	1.000	3.162	1.00000	51	2601	7.141	22.583	.01961
2	4	1.414	4.472	.50000	52	2704	7.211	22.804	.01923
3	9	1.732	5.477	.33333	53	2809	7.280	23.022	.01887
4	16	2.000	6.325	.25000	54	2916	7.348	23.238	.01852
5	25	2.236	7.071	.20000	55	3025	7.416	23.452	.01818
6	36	2.449	7.746	.16667	56	3136	7.483	23.664	.01786
7	49	2.646	8.367	.14286	57	3249	7.550	23.875	.01754
8	64	2.828	8.944	.12500	58	3364	7.616	24.083	.01724
9	81	3.000	9.487	.11111	59	3481	7.681	24.290	.01695
10	100	3.162	10.000	.10000	60	3600	7.746	24.495	.01667
11	121	3.317	10.488	.09091	61	3721	7.810	24.698	.01639
12	144	3.464	10.954	.08333	62	3844	7.874	24.900	.01613
13	169	3.606	11.402	.07692	63	3969	7.937	25.100	.01587
14	196	3.742	11.832	.07143	64	4096	8.000	25.298	.01562
15	225	3.873	12.247	.06667	65	4225	8.062	25.495	.01538
16	256	4.000	12.649	.06250	66	4356	8.124	25.690	.01515
17	289	4.123	13.038	.05882	67	4489	8.185	25.884	.01493
18	324	4.243	13.416	.05556	68	4624	8.246	26.077	.01471
19	361	4.359	13.784	.05263	69	4761	8.307	26.268	.01449
20	400	4.472	14.142	.05000	70	4900	8.367	26.458	.01429
21	441	4.583	14.491	.04762	71	5041	8.426	26.646	.01408
22	484	4.690	14.832	.04545	72	5184	8.485	26.833	.01389
23	529	4.796	15.166	.04348	73	5329	8.544	27.019	.01370
24	576	4.899	15.492	.04167	74	5476	8.602	27.203	.01351
25	625	5.000	15.811	.04000	75	5625	8.660	27.386	.01333
26	676	5.099	16.125	.03846	76	5776	8.718	27.568	.01316
27	729	5.196	16.432	.03704	77	5929	8.775	27.749	.01299
28	784	5.292	16.733	.03571	78	6084	8.832	27.928	.01282
29	841	5.385	17.029	.03448	79	6241	8.888	28.107	.01266
30	900	5.477	17.321	.03333	80	6400	8.944	28.284	.01250
31	961	5.568	17.607	.03226	81	6561	9.000	28.460	.01235
32	1024	5.657	17.889	.03125	82	6724	9.055	28.636	.01220
33	1089	5.745	18.166	.03030	83	6889	9.110	28.810	.01205
34	1156	5.831	18.439	.02941	84	7056	9.165	28.983	.01190
35	1225	5.916	18.708	.02857	85	7225	9.220	29.155	.01176
36	1296	6.000	18.974	.02778	86	7396	9.274	29.326	.01163
37	1369	6.083	19.235	.02703	87	7569	9.327	29.496	.01149
38	1444	6.164	19.494	.02632	88	7744	9.381	29.665	.01136
39	1521	6.245	19.748	.02564	89	7921	9.434	29.833	.01124
40	1600	6.325	20.000	.02500	90	8100	9.487	30.000	.01111
41	1681	6.403	20.248	.02439	91	8281	9.539	30.166	.01099
42	1764	6.481	20.494	.02381	92	8464	9.592	30.332	.01087
43	1849	6.557	20.736	.02326	93	8649	9.644	30.496	.01075
44	1936	6.633	20.976	.02273	94	8836	9.695	30.659	.01064
45	2025	6.708	21.213	.02222	95	9025	9.747	30.822	.01053
46	2116	6.782	21.448	.02174	96	9216	9.798	30.984	.01042
47	2209	6.856	21.679	.02128	97	9409	9.849	31.145	.01031
48	2304	6.928	21.909	.02083	98	9604	9.899	31.305	.01020
49	2401	7.000	22.136	.02041	99	9801	9.950	31.464	.01010
50	2500	7.071	22.361	.02000	100	10000	10.000	31.623	.01000

TABLE IV Four-place Squares of Numbers

N	0	1	2	3	4	5	6	7	8	9
1.0	1.000	1.020	1.040	1.061	1.082	1.103	1.124	1.145	1.166	1.188
1.1	1.210	1.232	1.254	1.277	1.300	1.323	1.346	1.369	1.392	1.416
1.2	1.440	1.464	1.488	1.513	1.538	1.563	1.588	1.613	1.638	1.664
1.3	1.690	1.716	1.742	1.769	1.796	1.823	1.850	1.877	1.904	1.932
1.4	1.960	1.988	2.016	2.045	2.074	2.103	2.132	2.161	2.190	2.220
1.5	2.250	2.280	2.310	2.341	2.372	2.403	2.434	2.465	2.496	2.528
1.6	2.560	2.592	2.624	2.657	2.690	2.723	2.756	2.789	2.822	2.856
1.7	2.890	2.924	2.958	2.993	3.028	3.063	3.098	3.133	3.168	3.204
1.8	3.240	3.276	3.312	3.349	3.386	3.423	3.460	3.497	3.534	3.572
1.9	3.610	3.648	3.686	3.725	3.764	3.803	3.842	3.881	3.920	3.960
2.0	4.000	4.040	4.080	4.121	4.162	4.203	4.244	4.285	4.326	4.368
2.1	4.410	4.452	4.494	4.537	4.580	4.623	4.666	4.709	4.752	4.796
2.2	4.840	4.884	4.928	4.973	5.018	5.063	5.108	5.153	5.198	5.244
2.3	5.290	5.336	5.382	5.429	5.476	5.523	5.570	5.617	5.664	5.712
2.4	5.760	5.808	5.856	5.905	5.954	6.003	6.052	6.101	6.150	6.200
2.5	6.250	6.300	6.350	6.401	6.452	6.503	6.554	6.605	6.656	6.708
2.6	6.760	6.812	6.864	6.917	6.970	7.023	7.076	7.129	7.182	7.236
2.7	7.290	7.344	7.398	7.453	7.508	7.563	7.618	7.673	7.728	7.784
2.8	7.840	7.896	7.952	8.009	8.066	8.123	8.180	8.237	8.294	8.352
2.9	8.410	8.468	8.526	8.585	8.644	8.703	8.762	8.821	8.880	8.940
3.0	9.000	9.060	9.120	9.181	9.242	9.303	9.364	9.425	9.486	9.548
3.1	9.610	9.672	9.734	9.797	9.860	9.923	9.986	10.05	10.11	10.18
3.2	10.24	10.30	10.37	10.43	10.50	10.56	10.63	10.69	10.76	10.82
3.3	10.89	10.96	11.02	11.09	11.16	11.22	11.29	11.36	11.42	11.49
3.4	11.56	11.63	11.70	11.76	11.83	11.90	11.97	12.04	12.11	12.18
3.5	12.25	12.32	12.39	12.46	12.53	12.60	12.67	12.74	12.82	12.89
3.6	12.96	13.03	13.10	13.18	13.25	13.32	13.40	13.47	13.54	13.62
3.7	13.69	13.76	13.84	13.91	13.99	14.06	14.14	14.21	14.29	14.36
3.8	14.44	14.52	14.59	14.67	14.75	14.82	14.90	14.98	15.05	15.13
3.9	15.21	15.29	15.37	15.44	15.52	15.60	15.68	15.76	15.84	15.92
4.0	16.00	16.08	16.16	16.24	16.32	16.40	16.48	16.56	16.65	16.73
4.1	16.81	16.89	16.97	17.06	17.14	17.22	17.31	17.39	17.47	17.56
4.2	17.64	17.72	17.81	17.89	17.98	18.06	18.15	18.23	18.32	18.40
4.3	18.49	18.58	18.66	18.75	18.84	18.92	19.01	19.10	19.18	19.27
4.4	19.36	19.45	19.54	19.62	19.71	19.80	19.89	19.98	20.07	20.16
4.5	20.25	20.34	20.43	20.52	20.61	20.70	20.79	20.88	20.98	21.07
4.6	21.16	21.25	21.34	21.44	21.53	21.62	21.72	21.81	21.90	22.00
4.7	22.09	22.18	22.28	22.37	22.47	22.56	22.66	22.75	22.85	22.94
4.8	23.04	23.14	23.23	23.33	23.43	23.52	23.62	23.72	23.81	23.91
4.9	24.01	24.11	24.21	24.30	24.40	24.50	24.60	24.70	24.80	24.90
5.0	25.00	25.10	25.20	25.30	25.40	25.50	25.60	25.70	25.81	25.91
5.1	26.01	26.11	26.21	26.32	26.42	26.52	26.63	26.73	26.83	26.94
5.2	27.04	27.14	27.25	27.35	27.46	27.56	27.67	27.77	27.88	27.98
5.3	28.09	28.20	28.30	28.41	28.52	28.62	28.73	28.84	28.94	29.05
5.4	29.16	29.27	29.38	29.48	29.59	29.70	29.81	29.92	30.03	30.14
N	0	1	2	3	4	5	6	7	8	9

TABLE IV Four-place Squares of Numbers. *Continued*

N	0	1	2	3	4	5	6	7	8	9
5.5	30.25	30.36	30.47	30.58	30.69	30.80	30.91	31.02	31.14	31.25
5.6	31.36	31.47	31.58	31.70	31.81	31.92	32.04	32.15	32.26	32.38
5.7	32.49	32.60	32.72	32.83	32.95	33.06	33.18	33.29	33.41	33.52
5.8	33.64	33.76	33.87	33.99	34.11	34.22	34.34	34.46	34.57	34.69
5.9	34.81	34.93	35.05	35.16	35.28	35.40	35.52	35.64	35.76	35.88
6.0	36.00	36.12	36.24	36.36	36.48	36.60	36.72	36.84	36.97	37.09
6.1	37.21	37.33	37.45	37.58	37.70	37.82	37.95	38.07	38.19	38.32
6.2	38.44	38.56	38.69	38.81	38.94	39.06	39.19	39.31	39.44	39.56
6.3	39.69	39.82	39.94	40.07	40.20	40.32	40.45	40.58	40.70	40.83
6.4	40.96	41.09	41.22	41.34	41.47	41.60	41.73	41.86	41.99	42.12
6.5	42.25	42.38	42.51	42.64	42.77	42.90	43.03	43.16	43.30	43.43
6.6	43.56	43.69	43.82	43.96	44.09	44.22	44.36	44.49	44.62	44.76
6.7	44.89	45.02	45.16	45.29	45.43	45.56	45.70	45.83	45.97	46.10
6.8	46.24	46.38	46.51	46.65	46.79	46.92	47.06	47.20	47.33	47.47
6.9	47.61	47.75	47.89	48.02	48.16	48.30	48.44	48.58	48.72	48.86
7.0	49.00	49.14	49.28	49.42	49.56	49.70	49.84	49.98	50.13	50.27
7.1	50.41	50.55	50.69	50.84	50.98	51.12	51.27	51.41	51.55	51.70
7.2	51.84	51.98	52.13	52.27	52.42	52.56	52.71	52.85	53.00	53.14
7.3	53.29	53.44	53.58	53.73	53.88	54.02	54.17	54.32	54.46	54.61
7.4	54.76	54.91	55.06	55.20	55.35	55.50	55.65	55.80	55.95	56.10
7.5	56.25	56.40	56.55	56.70	56.85	57.00	57.15	57.30	57.46	57.61
7.6	57.76	57.91	58.06	58.22	58.37	58.52	58.68	58.83	58.98	59.14
7.7	59.29	59.44	59.60	59.75	59.91	60.06	60.22	60.37	60.53	60.68
7.8	60.84	61.00	61.15	61.31	61.47	61.62	61.78	61.94	62.09	62.25
7.9	62.41	62.57	62.73	62.88	63.04	63.20	63.36	63.52	63.68	63.84
8.0	64.00	64.16	64.32	64.48	64.64	64.80	64.96	65.12	65.29	65.45
8.1	65.61	65.77	65.93	66.10	66.26	66.42	66.59	66.75	66.91	67.08
8.2	67.24	67.40	67.57	67.73	67.90	68.06	68.23	68.39	68.56	68.72
8.3	68.89	69.06	69.22	69.39	69.56	69.72	69.89	70.06	70.22	70.39
8.4	70.56	70.73	70.90	71.06	71.23	71.40	71.57	71.74	71.91	72.08
8.5	72.25	72.42	72.59	72.76	72.93	73.10	73.27	73.44	73.62	73.79
8.6	73.96	74.13	74.30	74.48	74.65	74.82	75.00	75.17	75.34	75.52
8.7	75.69	75.86	76.04	76.21	76.39	76.56	76.74	76.91	77.08	77.26
8.8	77.44	77.62	77.79	77.97	78.15	78.32	78.50	78.68	78.85	79.03
8.9	79.21	79.39	79.57	79.74	79.92	80.10	80.28	80.46	80.64	80.82
9.0	81.00	81.18	81.36	81.54	81.72	81.90	82.08	82.26	82.45	82.63
9.1	82.81	82.99	83.17	83.36	83.54	83.72	83.91	84.09	84.27	84.46
9.2	84.64	84.82	85.01	85.19	85.38	85.56	85.75	85.93	86.12	86.30
9.3	86.49	86.68	86.86	87.05	87.24	87.42	87.61	87.80	87.98	88.17
9.4	88.36	88.55	88.74	88.92	89.11	89.30	89.49	89.68	89.87	90.06
9.5	90.25	90.44	90.63	90.82	91.01	91.20	91.39	91.58	91.78	91.97
9.6	92.16	92.35	92.54	92.74	92.93	93.12	93.32	93.51	93.70	93.90
9.7	94.09	94.28	94.48	94.67	94.87	95.06	95.26	95.45	95.65	95.84
9.8	96.04	96.24	96.43	96.63	96.83	97.02	97.22	97.42	97.61	97.81
9.9	98.01	98.21	98.41	98.60	98.80	99.00	99.20	99.40	99.60	99.80
N	0	1	2	3	4	5	6	7	8	9

TABLE V Percentile Values of "Student's" Distribution *

n	t.75	t.80	t.90	t.95	t.975	t.99	t.995	t.9995	n
1	1.00	1.38	3.08	6.31	12.71	31.82	63.66	636.62	1
2	.82	1.06	1.89	2.92	4.30	6.96	9.92	31.60	2
3	.76	.98	1.64	2.35	3.18	4.54	5.84	12.94	3
4	.74	.94	1.53	2.13	2.78	3.75	4.60	8.61	4
5	.73	.92	1.48	2.02	2.57	3.36	4.03	6.86	5
6	.72	.91	1.44	1.94	2.45	3.14	3.71	5.96	6
7	.71	.90	1.42	1.89	2.36	3.00	3.50	5.40	7
8	.71	.89	1.40	1.86	2.31	2.90	3.36	5.04	8
9	.70	.88	1.38	1.83	2.26	2.82	3.25	4.78	9
10	.70	.88	1.37	1.81	2.23	2.76	3.17	4.59	10
11	.70	.88	1.36	1.80	2.20	2.72	3.11	4.44	11
12	.70	.87	1.36	1.78	2.18	2.68	3.05	4.32	12
13	.69	.87	1.35	1.77	2.16	2.65	3.01	4.22	13
14	.69	.87	1.34	1.76	2.14	2.62	2.98	4.14	14
15	.69	.87	1.34	1.75	2.13	2.60	2.95	4.07	15
16	.69	.86	1.34	1.75	2.12	2.58	2.92	4.02	16
17	.69	.86	1.33	1.74	2.11	2.57	2.90	3.96	17
18	.69	.86	1.33	1.73	2.10	2.55	2.88	3.92	18
19	.69	.86	1.33	1.73	2.09	2.54	2.86	3.88	19
20	.69	.86	1.32	1.72	2.09	2.53	2.85	3.85	20
21	.69	.86	1.32	1.72	2.08	2.52	2.83	3.82	21
22	.69	.86	1.32	1.72	2.07	2.51	2.82	3.79	22
23	.69	.86	1.32	1.71	2.07	2.50	2.81	3.77	23
24	.68	.86	1.32	1.71	2.06	2.49	2.80	3.74	24
25	.68	.86	1.32	1.71	2.06	2.48	2.79	3.72	25
26	.68	.86	1.32	1.71	2.06	2.48	2.78	3.71	26
27	.68	.86	1.31	1.70	2.05	2.47	2.77	3.69	27
28	.68	.85	1.31	1.70	2.05	2.47	2.76	3.67	28
29	.68	.85	1.31	1.70	2.04	2.46	2.76	3.66	29
30	.68	.85	1.31	1.70	2.04	2.46	2.75	3.65	30
40	.68	.85	1.30	1.68	2.02	2.42	2.70	3.55	40
60	.68	.85	1.30	1.67	2.00	2.39	2.66	3.46	60
120	.68	.85	1.29	1.66	1.98	2.36	2.62	3.37	120
∞	.6745	.842	1.282	1.645	1.960	2.326	2.576	3.291	∞
	− t.25	− t.20	− t.10	− t.05	− t.025	− t.01	− t.005	− t.0005	

* Reprinted abridged from R. A. Fisher and F. Yates, Statistical Tables, published by Oliver and Boyd Ltd. by permission of the authors and publishers.

TABLE VI Percentile Values of r for n Degrees of Freedom when $\rho = 0$ *

n	$r_{.95}$	$r_{.975}$	$r_{.99}$	$r_{.995}$	$r_{.9995}$	n	$r_{.95}$	$r_{.975}$	$r_{.99}$	$r_{.995}$	$r_{.9995}$
1	.988	.997	.9995	.9999	1.000	30	.296	.349	.409	.449	.554
2	.900	.950	.980	.990	.999	35	.275	.325	.381	.418	.519
3	.805	.878	.934	.959	.991	40	.257	.304	.358	.393	.490
4	.729	.811	.882	.917	.974	45	.243	.288	.338	.372	.465
5	.669	.754	.833	.874	.951	50	.231	.273	.322	.354	.443
6	.622	.707	.789	.834	.925	55	.220	.261	.307	.338	.424
7	.582	.666	.750	.798	.898	60	.211	.250	.295	.325	.408
8	.550	.632	.716	.765	.872	65	.203	.240	.284	.312	.393
9	.521	.602	.685	.735	.847	70	.195	.232	.274	.302	.380
10	.497	.576	.658	.708	.823	75	.189	.224	.264	.292	.368
11	.476	.553	.634	.684	.801	80	.183	.217	.256	.283	.357
12	.458	.532	.612	.661	.780	85	.178	.211	.249	.275	.347
13	.441	.514	.592	.641	.760	90	.173	.205	.242	.267	.338
14	.426	.497	.574	.623	.742	95	.168	.200	.236	.260	.329
15	.412	.482	.558	.606	.725	100	.164	.195	.230	.254	.321
16	.400	.468	.542	.590	.708	125	.147	.174	.206	.228	.288
17	.389	.456	.528	.575	.693	150	.134	.159	.189	.208	.264
18	.378	.444	.516	.561	.679	175	.124	.148	.174	.194	.248
19	.369	.433	.503	.549	.665	200	.116	.138	.164	.181	.235
20	.360	.423	.492	.537	.652	300	.095	.113	.134	.148	.188
22	.344	.404	.472	.515	.629	500	.074	.088	.104	.115	.148
24	.330	.388	.453	.496	.607	1000	.052	.062	.073	.081	.104
25	.323	.381	.445	.487	.597	2000	.037	.044	.016	.058	.074
	$r-_{.05}$	$-_{.025}$	$-r_{.01}$	$-r_{.095}$	$-r_{.0005}$		$-r_{.05}$	$-r_{.025}$	$-r_{.01}$	$-r_{.005}$	$-r_{.0005}$

* Reprinted abridged from R. A. Fisher and F. Yates, *Statistical Tables*, published by Oliver and Boyd Ltd. by permission of the authors and publishers.

TABLE VII Values for Transforming r into $z = \dfrac{1}{2}\log_e\left(\dfrac{1+r}{1-r}\right)$*

	.00	.01	.02	.03	.04	.05	.06	.07	.08	.09
.0	.0000	.0100	.0200	.0300	.0400	.0500	.0599	.0699	.0798	.0898
.1	.0997	.1096	.1194	.1293	.1391	.1489	.1587	.1684	.1781	.1878
.2	.1974	.2070	.2165	.2260	.2355	.2449	.2543	.2636	.2729	.2821
.3	.2913	.3004	.3095	.3185	.3275	.3364	.3452	.3540	.3627	.3714
.4	.3800	.3885	.3969	.4053	.4136	.4219	.4301	.4382	.4462	.4542
.5	.4621	.4700	.4777	.4854	.4930	.5005	.5080	.5154	.5227	.5299
.6	.5370	.5441	.5511	.5581	.5649	.5717	.5784	.5850	.5915	.5980
.7	.6044	.6107	.6169	.6231	.6291	.6352	.6411	.6469	.6527	.6584
.8	.6640	.6696	.6751	.6805	.6858	.6911	.6963	.7014	.7064	.7114
.9	.7163	.7211	.7259	.7306	.7352	.7398	.7443	.7487	.7531	.7574
1.0	.7616	.7658	.7699	.7739	.7779	.7818	.7857	.7895	.7932	.7969
1.1	.8005	.8041	.8076	.8110	.8144	.8178	.8210	.8243	.8275	.8306
1.2	.8337	.8367	.8397	.8426	.8455	.8483	.8511	.8538	.8565	.8591
1.3	.8617	.8643	.8668	.8693	.8717	.8741	.8764	.8787	.8810	.8832
1.4	.8854	.8875	.8896	.8917	.8937	.8957	.8977	.8996	.9015	.9033
1.5	.9052	.9069	.9087	.9104	.9121	.9138	.9154	.9170	.9186	.9202
1.6	.9217	.9232	.9246	.9261	.9275	.9289	.9302	.9316	.9329	.9342
1.7	.9354	.9367	.9379	.9391	.9402	.9414	.9425	.9436	.9447	.9458
1.8	.9468	.9478	.9498	.9488	.9508	.9518	.9527	.9536	.9545	.9554
1.9	.9562	.9571	.9579	.9587	.9595	.9603	.9611	.9619	.9626	.9633
2.0	.9640	.9647	.9654	.9661	.9668	.9674	.9680	.9687	.9693	.9699
2.1	.9705	.9710	.9716	.9722	.9727	.9732	.9738	.9743	.9748	.9753
2.2	.9757	.9762	.9767	.9771	.9776	.9780	.9785	.9789	.9793	.9797
2.3	.9801	.9805	.9809	.9812	.9816	.9820	.9823	.9827	.9830	.9834
2.4	.9837	.9840	.9843	.9846	.9849	.9852	.9855	.9858	.9861	.9863
2.5	.9866	.9869	.9871	.9874	.9876	.9879	.9881	.9884	.9886	.9888
2.6	.9890	.9892	.9895	.9897	.9899	.9901	.9903	.9905	.9906	.9908
2.7	.9910	.9912	.9914	.9915	.9917	.9919	.9920	.9922	.9923	.9925
2.8	.9926	.9928	.9929	.9931	.9932	.9933	.9935	.9936	.9937	.9938
2.9	.9940	.9941	.9942	.9943	.9944	.9945	.9946	.9947	.9949	.9950
3.0	.9951									
4.0	.9993									
5.0	.9999									

* Reprinted abridged from R. A. Fisher and F. Yates, *Statistical Tables*, published by Oliver and Boyd Ltd. by permission of the authors and publishers. The figures in the body of the table are values of r corresponding to z values read from the scales on the left and top of the table.

Code number of student	Section	Prognostic Test Score			Criterion Score		
		Reading	Artificial language	Arithmetic test	Midterm test	Final exam	Semester grade
1	III	33	51	33	58	65	62
2	III	39	50	36	53	51	52
3	I	38	38	39	52	53	53
4	I	23	27	29	47	42	45
*5	I	44	40	41	61	50	56
*6	I	45	54	38	47	53	50
7	I	48	57	42	64	64	64
8	II	38	39	35	64	54	59
9	II	32	46	23	58	50	54
*10	II	28	45	37	44	45	45
11	II	33	53	28	62	63	63
12	II	40	43	25	52	50	51
13	II	34	55	38	50	56	58
14	II	34	57	36	71	68	70
15	II	35	46	37	62	65	64
16	I	32	43	39	52	59	56
17	II	34	44	38	59	57	58
18	II	42	51	35	53	60	57
19	I	32	55	36	62	56	59
*20	III	24	34	17	37	43	40
21	I	39	52	34	55	53	54
22	I	34	25	29	30	42	36
23	II	44	58	35	61	56	59
24	III	27	29	26	49	40	45
25	II	34	52	30	43	38	41
26	II	40	53	29	61	54	58
27	I	37	34	26	47	57	52
28	III	22	40	33	47	50	49
29	I	30	54	40	56	47	52
*30	I	36	58	25	52	39	45
31	I	35	43	40	49	37	43
32	I	39	58	32	49	37	43
33	II	37	28	14	43	36	40
34	II	38	51	26	40	42	41
35	II	36	55	31	59	52	56
36	I	46	52	39	61	63	62
37	II	44	57	32	46	53	50
38		40	56	32	64	49	57
39	III	38	30	18	25	38	32
40	I	50	47	32	58	52	55
41	II	16	49	26	52	36	43
42	I	46	60	43	61	57	59
43	I	42	56	40	59	54	57
*44	III	27	53	26	62	48	55
45	III	33	55	25	55	57	56
46	II	40	54	34	52	57	55
47	I	46	53	37	62	49	56
*48	I	46	58	39	58	56	57

* A woman student.

Methods on Three Prognostic Tests Given at Beginning of Term, Two Course, and the Semester Grade

Code number of student	Section	Prognostic Test Score			Criterion Score		
		Reading	Artificial language	Arithmetic test	Mid-term test	Final exam	Semester grade
*49		25	57	24	46	49	48
*50	III	26	45	18	47	25	36
*51	I	42	46	31	58	56	57
*52	I	34	60	33	62	64	63
53	III	28	37	8	47	46	47
54	II	21	24	16	44	41	43
55	I	44	43	35	58	55	57
56	I	38	47	28	58	56	57
57	III	16	50	27	47	47	47
58	III	40	48	35	56	38	47
59	III	33	42	25	52	46	49
*60	II	35	59	25	52	49	51
61	III	33	40	28	49	47	48
62	III	30	41	30	56	59	58
63	I	38	47	39	62	63	63
*64	III	36	43	26	61	50	56
*65	I	45	57	35	53	46	50
66	III	32	32	21	50	41	46
67	III	36	53	27	49	34	43
*68	III	21	46	39	44	33	39
69	II	30	54	34	47	46	47
70	II	34	49	27	50	44	48
71	II	41	58	39	53	57	55
72	I	44	55	38	47	46	47
*73	II	36	14	20	30	40	35
74	I	58	50	38	68	55	62
75	II	36	41	30	62	56	59
76	III	31	14	18	27	30	29
77	III	40	46	36	58	50	54
78	I	44	60	43	71	45	58
*79	III	36	36	23	49	43	46
80	I	44	51	36	53	47	50
*81	I	34	46	37	43	49	46
*82	I	38	56	36	64	61	63
*83	I	38	52	33	50	56	53
84	I	38	51	33	50	48	49
85	I	46	51	40	62	54	58
86	III	30	42	22	37	33	34
*87	III	26	44	28	58	48	53
*88	I	36	58	42	59	69	64
89	I	36	43	42	46	44	45
*90	III	32	59	36	61	55	58
*91	III	30	23	28	38	38	38
*92	I	31	58	31	44	51	48
93	II	44	34	32	55	49	52
*94	III	14	16	18	40	33	37
95	III	44	26	30	37	19	28
*96	I	30	58	37	61	56	59
97	I	39	34	33	41	46	44
98	I	32	56	30	65	51	58

TABLE IX Scores for 109 Fourth-grade Pupils on the Modern School Achievement Test

Case Number	Age to Nearest Month	I.Q.	Arithmetic Computation	Arithmetic Reasoning	Reading Speed	Language	History-Civics
			Score on Test of				
1*	121	99	12	11	27	17	24
2	124	83	13	4	12	15	13
3*	103	117	5	8	30	26	10
4*	127	83	8	6	30	12	21
5	115	109	7	4	26	27	13
6	108	111	6	3	17	21	20
7*	106	92	9	9	25	30	12
8*	115	95	5	3	28	12	16
9	140	79	8	3	28	23	11
10	111	115	10	8	20	26	4
11	109	120	5	5	26	19	10
12	119	101	6	4	24	14	20
13	119	87	10	5	8	14	17
14	108	106	7	7	10	16	5
15	131	100	6	5	21	20	8
16*	112	120	13	7	21	19	8
17	118	99	4	4	26	16	10
18	96	119	7	7	20	17	12
19	148	66	10	2	16	11	9
20	132	77	5	3	27	19	21
21*	108	124	8	6	29	29	9
22*	96	125	10	5	30	18	16
23	118	104	9	4	18	23	21
24	123	89	6	5	13	19	13
25*	109	97	8	5	28	26	2
26	106	126	11	11	29	30	18
27*	142	68	5	2	7	17	10
28	109	83	6	3	16	23	15
29	150	64	6	1	11	7	7
30	113	96	4	4	25	26	19
31	117	91	6	4	30	19	2
32*	156	75	12	5	30	18	15
33*	119	103	8	5	14	22	18
34*	129	86	9	4	8	14	6
35	114	118	9	3	24	19	10
36	106	140	13	9	40	31	10
37	114	120	12	9	17	21	18
38	134	93	9	3	17	24	12
39*	109	112	7	2	31	24	18
40	115	116	15	5	41	33	22

* All case numbers starred refer to boys, unstarred numbers to girls.

TABLE IX Scores on Achievement Test. *Continued*

Case Number	Age to Nearest Month	I.Q.	Score on Test of				
			Arithmetic Computation	Arithmetic Reasoning	Reading Speed	Language	History-Civics
41	109	123	10	4	34	24	23
42	109	105	11	5	22	25	13
43*	101	121	5	1	35	28	22
44*	108	114	5	4	24	16	10
45*	116	113	13	6	18	20	12
46	111	111	8	4	25	19	12
47*	120	114	9	8	36	23	23
48*	118	99	6	2	33	15	18
49*	109	101	12	2	23	16	18
50*	111	112	12	6	25	15	16
51*	116	125	10	3	33	16	23
52	114	105	13	3	44	20	24
53	129	100	8	6	22	18	20
54	106	144	16	5	40	28	20
55	110	101	10	7	14	17	13
56	125	108	8	4	30	22	18
57*	105	112	6	3	30	14	16
58	124	98	9	7	28	21	12
59	111	105	12	1	24	22	13
60*	118	123	7	3	35	24	22
61*	103	148	9	8	43	32	18
62*	129	93	10	2	24	17	12
63	104	129	8	3	39	25	17
64*	116	106	6	5	45	26	20
65	112	111	8	4	35	17	13
66*	111	121	7	2	45	25	17
67*	109	115	12	7	44	20	20
68*	104	130	8	9	39	29	23
69	107	114	15	7	42	30	21
70	117	118	16	12	49	39	18
71*	114	103	6	7	26	30	19
72	108	108	3	2	21	12	3
73	114	123	1	1	26	31	9
74	112	142	2	8	45	30	5
75*	107	120	2	2	26	25	7
76*	109	136	10	5	34	29	10
77*	113	131	5	7	24	28	8
78	108	141	4	9	23	24	10
79*	116	106	8	5	26	22	3
80*	109	126	4	9	24	19	2

* All case numbers starred refer to boys, unstarred numbers to girls.

TABLE IX Scores on Achievement Test. *Concluded*

Case Number	Age to Nearest Month	I.Q.	Score on Test of				
			Arithmetic Computation	Arithmetic Reasoning	Reading Speed	Language	History-Civics
81	110	125	7	7	24	23	2
82	107	131	6	5	40	36	17
83*	113	104	7	3	28	29	19
84*	109	128	10	9	42	30	18
85	109	133	8	7	31	26	9
86	114	127	9	9	28	24	7
87	107	138	3	6	46	36	4
88*	112	132	4	1	44	31	12
89*	107	136	9	2	29	32	5
90*	113	119	3	7	30	22	9
91	115	106	9	4	24	17	3
92*	108	124	1	5	50	29	23
93	108	124	9	4	48	14	7
94*	122	102	6	2	26	20	5
95*	124	83	8	3	10	15	6
96*	126	93	7	6	16	26	14
97	104	113	8	8	30	23	8
98	115	90	0	2	24	18	5
99*	117	103	8	5	27	17	5
100*	111	88	12	5	10	11	6
101*	115	111	9	7	16	17	10
102	103	130	2	2	41	25	2
103	122	91	4	8	32	9	5
104*	113	106	7	3	15	10	6
105	111	115	6	2	43	28	7
106	114	120	1	3	27	26	8
107*	118	116	11	4	40	19	5
108	109	120	9	2	50	35	4
109	118	123	10	6	41	18	4

* All case numbers starred refer to boys, unstarred numbers to girls.

TABLE X Transformation of Ranks to Standard Scores

Rank	5	6	7	8	9	10	11	12	13	14	15	16	17	18	19	20	21	22	23	24	25	26	27	28	29	30	Rank
1	63	64	65	65	66	66	67	67	68	68	68	69	69	69	69	70	70	70	70	70	71	71	71	71	71	71	1
2	55	57	58	59	60	60	61	62	62	62	63	63	64	64	64	64	65	65	65	65	66	66	66	66	66	66	2
3	50	52	54	55	56	57	57	58	59	59	60	60	60	61	61	62	62	62	62	63	63	63	63	63	64	64	3
4	45	48	50	52	53	54	55	55	56	57	57	58	58	59	59	59	60	60	60	61	61	61	61	62	62	62	4
5	37	43	46	48	50	51	52	53	54	55	55	56	56	57	57	58	58	58	59	59	59	59	60	60	60	60	5
6		36	42	45	47	49	50	51	52	53	53	54	55	55	56	56	56	57	57	57	58	58	58	59	59	59	6
7			35	41	44	46	48	49	50	51	52	52	53	54	54	55	55	55	56	56	56	57	57	57	58	58	7
8				35	40	43	45	47	48	49	50	51	51	52	53	53	54	54	55	55	55	56	56	56	57	57	8
9					34	40	43	45	46	47	48	49	50	51	51	52	52	53	53	54	54	54	55	55	55	55	9
10						34	39	42	44	45	47	48	49	49	50	51	51	52	52	53	53	53	54	54	55	55	10
11							33	38	41	43	45	46	47	48	49	49	50	51	51	52	52	52	53	53	54	54	11
12								33	38	41	43	44	45	46	47	48	49	49	50	51	51	51	52	52	53	53	12
13									32	38	40	42	44	45	46	47	48	48	49	49	50	50	51	51	52	52	13
14										32	37	40	42	43	44	45	46	47	48	48	49	50	50	50	51	51	14
15											32	37	40	41	43	44	45	46	47	47	48	49	49	50	50	50	15
16												31	36	39	41	42	44	45	45	46	47	48	48	49	49	50	16
17													31	36	39	41	42	43	44	45	46	47	47	48	48	49	17
18														31	36	38	40	42	43	44	45	46	46	47	47	48	18
19															31	36	38	40	41	43	44	44	45	46	46	47	19
20																30	35	38	40	41	42	43	44	45	45	46	20
21																	30	35	38	39	41	42	43	44	45	45	21
22																		30	35	37	39	41	42	43	43	45	22
23																			30	35	37	39	40	41	42	43	23
24																				30	34	37	39	40	41	42	24
25																					29	34	37	38	40	41	25
26																						29	34	37	38	40	26
27																							29	34	36	38	27
28																								29	34	36	28
29																									29	34	29
30																										29	30

Number of Persons Ranked

From *Improvement of Grading Practices for Air Training Command Schools*, ATRC Manual 50–900–9.

TABLE XI Random Numbers

Line\Col.	(1)	(2)	(3)	(4)	(5)	(6)	(7)	(8)	(9)	(10)	(11)	(12)	(13)	(14)
1	10480	15011	01536	02011	81647	91646	69179	14194	62590	36207	20969	99570	91291	90700
2	22368	46573	25595	85393	30995	89198	27982	53402	93965	34095	52666	19174	39615	99505
3	24130	48360	22527	97265	76393	64809	15179	24830	49340	32081	30680	19655	63348	58629
4	42167	93093	06243	61680	07856	16376	39440	53537	71341	57004	00849	74917	97758	16379
5	37570	39975	81837	16656	06121	91782	60468	81305	49684	60672	14110	06927	01263	54613
6	77921	06907	11008	42751	27756	53498	18602	70659	90655	15053	21916	81825	44394	42880
7	99562	72905	56420	69994	98872	31016	71194	18738	44013	48840	63213	21069	10634	12952
8	96301	91977	05463	07972	18876	20922	94595	56869	69014	60045	18425	84903	42508	32307
9	89579	14342	63661	10281	17453	18103	57740	84378	25331	12566	58678	44947	05585	56941
10	85475	36857	53342	53988	53060	59533	38867	62300	08158	17983	16439	11458	18593	64952
11	28918	69578	88231	33276	70997	79936	56865	05859	90106	31595	01547	85590	91610	78188
12	63553	40961	48235	03427	49626	69445	18663	72695	52180	20847	12234	90511	33703	90322
13	09429	93969	52636	92737	88974	33488	36320	17617	30015	08272	84115	27156	30613	74952
14	10365	61129	87529	85689	48237	52267	67689	93394	01511	26358	85104	20285	29975	89868
15	07119	97336	71048	08178	77233	13916	47564	81056	97735	85977	29372	74461	28551	90707
16	51085	12765	51821	51259	77452	16308	60756	92144	49442	53900	70960	63990	75601	40719
17	02368	21382	52404	60268	89368	19885	55322	44819	01188	65255	64835	44919	05944	55157
18	01011	54092	33362	94904	31273	04146	18594	29852	71585	85030	51132	01915	92747	64951
19	52162	53916	46369	58586	23216	14513	83149	98736	23495	64350	94738	17752	35156	35749
20	07056	97628	33787	09998	42698	06691	76988	13602	51851	46104	88916	19509	25625	58104
21	48663	91245	85828	14346	09172	30168	90229	04734	59193	22178	30421	61666	99904	32812
22	54164	58492	22421	74103	47070	25306	76468	26384	58151	06646	21524	15227	96909	44592
23	32639	32363	05597	24200	13363	38005	94342	28728	35806	06912	17012	64161	18296	22851
24	29334	27001	87637	87308	58731	00256	45834	15398	46557	41135	10367	07684	36188	18510
25	02488	33062	28834	07351	19731	92420	60952	61280	50001	67658	32586	86679	50720	94953

Taken from the 30-page table of 105,000 random digits prepared by the Bureau of Transport Economics and Statistics of the Interstate Commerce Commission, Washington, D.C., Mr. W. H. S. Stevens, Director. It is used in this text with their permission.

Line\Col.	(1)	(2)	(3)	(4)	(5)	(6)	(7)	(8)	(9)	(10)	(11)	(12)	(13)	(14)
26	81525	72295	04839	96423	24878	82651	66566	14778	76797	14780	13300	87074	79666	95725
27	29676	20591	68086	26432	46901	20849	89768	81536	86645	12659	92259	57102	80428	25280
28	00742	57392	39064	66432	84673	40027	32832	61362	98947	96067	64760	64584	96096	98253
29	05366	04213	25669	26422	44407	44048	37937	63904	45766	66134	75470	66520	34693	90449
30	91921	26418	64117	94305	26766	25940	39972	22209	71500	64568	91402	42416	07844	69618
31	00582	04711	87917	77341	42206	35126	74087	99547	81817	42607	43808	76655	62028	76630
32	00725	69884	62797	56170	86324	88072	76222	36086	84637	93161	76038	65855	77919	88006
33	69011	65795	95876	55293	18988	27354	26575	08625	40801	59920	29841	80150	12777	48501
34	25976	57948	29888	88604	67917	48708	18912	82271	65424	69774	33611	54262	85963	03547
35	09763	83473	73577	12908	30883	18317	28290	35797	05998	41688	34952	37888	38917	88050
36	91567	42595	27958	30134	04024	86385	29880	99730	55536	84855	29080	09250	79656	73211
37	17955	56349	90999	49127	20044	59931	06115	20542	18059	02008	73708	83517	36103	42791
38	46503	18584	18845	49618	02304	51038	20655	58727	28168	15475	56942	53389	20562	87338
39	92157	89634	94824	78171	84610	82834	09922	25417	44137	48413	25555	21246	35509	20468
40	14577	62765	35605	81263	39667	47358	56873	56307	61607	49518	89656	20103	77490	18062
41	98427	07523	33362	64270	01638	92477	66969	98420	04880	45585	46565	04102	46880	45709
42	34914	63976	88720	82765	34476	17032	87589	40836	32427	70002	70663	88863	77775	69348
43	70060	28277	39475	46473	23219	53416	94970	25582	69975	94884	19661	72828	00102	66794
44	53976	54914	06990	67245	68350	82948	11398	42878	80287	88267	47363	46634	06541	97809
45	76072	29515	40980	07391	58745	25774	22987	80059	39911	96189	41151	14222	60697	59583
46	90725	52210	83974	29992	65831	38857	50490	93765	55657	14361	31720	57375	56228	41546
47	64364	67412	33339	31926	14883	24413	59744	92351	97473	89286	35931	04110	23726	51900
48	08962	00358	31662	25388	61642	34072	81249	35648	56891	69352	48373	45578	78547	81788
49	95012	68379	93526	70765	10592	04542	76463	54328	02349	17247	28865	14777	62730	92277
50	15664	10493	20492	38391	91132	21999	59516	81652	27195	48223	46751	22923	32261	85653
51	16408	81899	04153	53381	79401	21438	83035	92350	36693	31238	50649	91754	72772	02338
52	18629	81953	05520	91962	04739	13092	97662	24822	94730	06496	35090	04822	86774	98289
53	73115	35101	47498	87637	99016	71060	88824	71013	18735	20286	23153	72924	35165	43040
54	57491	16703	23167	49323	45021	33132	12544	41035	80780	45393	44812	12515	98931	91202
55	30405	83946	23792	14422	15059	45799	22716	19792	09983	74353	68668	30429	70735	25499
56	16631	35006	85900	98275	32388	52390	16815	69298	82732	38480	73817	32523	41961	44437
57	96773	20206	42559	78985	05300	22164	24369	54224	35083	19687	11052	91491	60383	19746
58	38935	64202	14349	82674	66523	44133	00697	35552	35970	19124	63318	29686	03387	59846
59	31624	76384	17403	53363	44167	64486	64758	75366	76554	31601	12614	33072	60332	92325
60	78919	19474	23632	27889	47914	02584	37680	20801	72152	39339	34806	08930	85001	87820

TABLE XII. Values of $k = Np$ Leading to Rejection of a Hypothesis about a Proportion at .05 Level of Significance

N = Number of cases in sample
k = Number of cases with given characteristic
P = Proportion under hypothesis tested
$p = k/N$

A. Two Tails Region (.025 in each tail)

For $P \leq .5$, reject hypothesis if observed k is less than or equal to left value in cell or is greater than or equal to right value.
For $P > .5$, substitute $1 - P$ for P and $N - k$ for k.

N	.05	.10	.15	.20	.25	.30	.35	.40	.45	.50	N
5	* 2	* 3	* 4	* 4	* 4	* 5	* 5	* 5	* 5	* *	5
6	* 3	* 3	* 4	* 4	* 5	* 5	* 5	* 6	* 6	0 6	6
7	* 3	* 4b	* 4	* 5	* 5	* 6	* 6	* 6	0 7	0 7	7
8	* 3	* 4	* 4	* 5	* 6	* 6	* 7b	0 7	0 7	0 8	8
9	* 3	* 4	* 5	* 5	* 6	* 7b	0 7	0 8b	0 8	1 8	9
10	* 3	* 4	* 5	* 6	* 6	* 7	0 8b	0 8	1 9	1 9	10
11	* 3	* 4	* 5	* 6	* 7	0 7	0 8	0 9	1 9	1 10	11
12	* 3	* 5b	* 5	* 6	* 7	0 8	0 9b	1 9	1 10	2 10	12
13	* 3	* 5	* 6	* 7	0 7	0 8	0 9	1 10	2 10	2 11	13
14	* 4	* 5	* 6	* 7	0 8	0 9	1 9	1 10	2 11	2 12	14
15	* 4	* 5	* 6	* 7	0 8	0 9	1 10	1 11	2 12b	3 12	15
16	* 4	* 5	* 6	* 8	0 9	0 10b	1 11	2 11	2 12	3 13	16
17	* 4	* 5	* 7	0 8	0 9	1 10	1 11	2 12	3 13	4 13	17
18	* 4	* 6	* 7	0 8	0 9	1 10	2 11	2 12	3 13	4 14	18
19	* 4	* 6	* 7	0 8	0 10	1 11	2 12	3 13	3 14	4 15	19
20	* 4	* 6	* 8	0 9	1 10	1 11	2 12	3 13	4 14	5 15	20
21	* 4	* 6	* 8	0 9	1 10	1 12	2 13	3 14	4 15	5 16	21
22	* 4	* 6	* 8	0 9	1 11	2 12	3 13	3 14	4 15	5 17	22
23	* 5b	* 6	0 8	0 10	1 11	2 12	3 14	4 15	5 16	6 17	23
24	* 5	* 7	0 8	0 10	1 11	2 13	3 14	4 15	5 17	6 18	24
25	* 5	* 7	0 9b	0 10	1 12	2 13	3 15b	4 16	5a 17	7 18	25
26	* 5	* 7	0 9	1 10	1a 12	2a 14b	4a 15	5 16	6 18	7 19	26
27	* 5	* 7	0 9	1 11	2 12	3 14	4 15	5 17	6 18	7a 20b	27
28	* 5	* 7	0 9	1 11	2 13	3 14	4 16	5 17	7 19	8 20	28
29	* 5	* 7	0 9	1 11	2 13	3 15	4 16	6 18	7 19	8 21	29
30	* 5	* 8b	0 10	1 12b	2 13	3 15	5 17	6 18	7 20	9 21	30
31	* 5	* 8	0 10	1 12	2 14	4 15	5 17	6 19	8 20	9 22	31
32	* 5	* 8	0 10	1 12	2a 14	4 16	5 18	7 19	8 21	9a 23b	32
33	* 5	* 8	0 10	1 12	3 14	4 16	5 18	7 20	8 21	10 23	33
34	* 6b	* 8	0 10	2 13	3 15	4 17	6 18	7 20	9 22	10 24	34
35	* 6	*c 8	1 11	2 13	3 15	4 17	6 19	7 21b	9 23b	11 24	35

* There is no region of rejection in the indicated tail.
a Increasing this number by 1 will not increase the lower tail to more than .026.
b Decreasing this number by 1 will not increase the upper tail to more than .026.
c Changing * to 0 will not increase the lower tail to more than .026.

For $P \leq .5$, reject hypothesis if observed k is equal to or greater than cell value.
For $P > .5$, substitute $1 - P$ for P and $N - k$ for k; use Table C.

For $P \leq .5$, reject hypothesis if observed k is equal to or less than cell value.
For $P > .5$, substitute $1 - P$ for P and $N - k$ for k; use Table B.

$N \diagdown P$	.05	.10	.15	.20	.25	.30	.35	.40	.45	.50	N
5	2	3	3	4	4	4	5	5	5	5	5
6	2	3	3	4	4	5	5	5	6	6	6
7	2	3	4	4	5	5	6	6	6	7	7
8	3	3	4	5	5	6	6	6	7	7	8
9	3	4	4	5	5	6	7	7	7	8	9
10	3	4	4	5	6	6	7	8	8	9	10
11	3	4	5	6[b]	6	7	8	8	9	9	11
12	3	4	5	6	7	7	8	9	9	10	12
13	3	4	5	6	7	8	8	9	10	10	13
14	3	4	5	6	7	8	9	10	10	11	14
15	3	5	6	7	8	9[b]	9	10	11	12	15
16	3	5	6	7	8	9	10	11	11	12	16
17	4[b]	5	6	7	8	9	10	11	12	13	17
18	4	5	6	8	9	10	11	12	13	13	18
19	4	5	7	8	9	10	11	12	13	14	19
20	4	5	7	8	9	10	12	13	14	15	20
21	4	6	7	8	10	11	12	13	14	15	21
22	4	6	7	9	10	11	12	14	15	16	22
23	4	6	7	9	10	12	13	14	15	16	23
24	4	6	8	9	11	12	13	15	16	17	24
25	4	6	8	9	11	12	14	15	16	18	25
26	4	6	8	10	11	13	14	16	17	18	26
27	4	6	8	10	12	13	15	16	17	19	27
28	4	7	8	10	12	13	15	16	18	19	28
29	5	7	9	10	12	14	15	17	18	20	29
30	5	7	9	11	13[b]	14	16	17	19	20	30
31	5	7	9	11	13	15	16	18	20[b]	21	31
32	5	7	9	11	13	15	17	18	20	22	32
33	5	7	9	12[b]	13	15	17	19	21	22	33
34	5	7	10	12	14	16	18	19	21	23	34
35	5	8	10	12	14	16	18	20	22	23	35

$N \diagdown P$	.05	.10	.15	.20	.25	.30	.35	.40	.45	.50	N
5	*	*	*	*	*	*	*	*	*	0	5
6	*	*	*	*	*	*	*	*	0	0	6
7	*	*	*	*	*	*	0	0	0	0	7
8	*	*	*	*	*	*	0	0	0	1	8
9	*	*	*	*	*	0	0	0	1	1	9
10	*	*	*	*	0	0	0	1	1	1	10
11	*	*	*	*	0	0	0	1	1	2	11
12	*	*	*	*	0	0	1	1	2	2	12
13	*	*	*	*	0	0	1	1	2	3	13
14	*	*	*	0	0	1	1	2	2	3	14
15	*	*	*	0	0	1	1	2	3	3	15
16	*	*	*	0	0	1	2	2	3	4	16
17	*	*	*	0	0[a]	1	2	3	3	4	17
18	*	*	*	0	1	1	2	3	4	5	18
19	*	*	0	0	1	2	2	3	4	5	19
20	*	*	0	0	1	2	3	3[a]	4	5	20
21	*	*	0	0	1	2	3	4	5	6	21
22	*	*	0	1	1	2	3	4	5	6	22
23	*	*	0	1	2	2	3	4	5[a]	7	23
24	*	*	0	1	2	3	4	5	6	7	24
25	*	*	0	1	2	3	4	5	6	7	25
26	*	*	0	1	2	3	4	5[a]	7	8	26
27	*	*	0	1	2	3	4[a]	6	7	8	27
28	*	*	0	1	2	4	5	6	7	9	28
29	*	0	0	1[a]	3	4	5	6	8	9	29
30	*	0	1	2	3	4	5	7	8	10	30
31	*	0	1	2	3	4	6	7	8	10	31
32	*	0	1	2	3	4[a]	6	7	9	10	32
33	*	0	1	2	3	5	6	8	9	11	33
34	*	0	1	2	4	5	6	8	10	11	34
35	*	0	1	2	4	5	7	8	10	12	35

[b] Decreasing this number by 1 will not increase the upper tail to more than .051.

* No region of rejection is available.
[a] Increasing this number by 1 will not increase the lower tail to more than .051.

GLOSSARY OF SYMBOLS

The letters X and Y (and sometimes Z) are here customarily used to denote variables and observations on individuals. Constants are denoted by letters at the beginning of the alphabet. Small letters from the middle of the alphabet, especially i and j, are used as subscripts to indicate reference to specific individuals or groups.

Parameters are customarily denoted by Greek letters and sample statistics by English. Some exceptions are made, as in the use of P and Q to denote proportions in a population.

A bar over a letter indicates the mean of a sample of observations on the variable denoted by the letter.

Greek letters and English letters are listed separately according to their respective alphabets. Symbols of operation are listed separately.

Each definition of a symbol is followed by the page number (in parentheses) which shows the first reference to the symbol in the text.

Symbols used only once for a specific purpose and lacking in general interest are not listed below.

SYMBOL	DEFINITION
A	(1) Arbitrary origin (93).
	(2) Alternative to a hypothesis (236).
a	Constant terms in a regression equation. The first
a_{yx}, a_{xy}	subscript indicates the variable to be predicted; the second indicates the variable which has been observed (127, 145).
b	Regression coefficients used as multipliers of known
b_{yx}, b_{xy}	values in regression equations to compute predicted values. For order of subscripts see a_{xy}, a_{yx} (127, 145).
c	(1) Confidence coefficient (220).
	(2) Subscript for combined groups (101).
d	Difference between two ranks assigned to the same individual (159).
d_i	Difference between the mean of the ith group and the mean of combined groups, $\overline{X}_i - \overline{X}_c$ (101).
e	A constant having a value of approximately 2.718. It has many uses in mathematics but is used in this book only in the equation of the normal curve (184).
f	Frequency in distributions (51).
f_x, f_y	Marginal frequencies of a bivariate distribution (125).
f_{xy}	Frequency in a cell of a bivariate distribution (125).
H	Hypothesis (236).
$H: \mu = k$	Hypothesis that $\mu = k$; k a specific number (236).

SYMBOL	DEFINITION
i	Size of a class interval in scale units (96).
i, j, k	Subscripts used to indicate reference to specific individuals in a group.
I, J	Shapes of curves (115).
k	(1) Number of subgroups of a total group (101). (2) $k = Np$ (253).
$\log_e$	Logarithm to base e (259).
$\log_{10}$	Logarithm to base 10 (260).
N	Number of cases in a sample, sometimes used with a subscript to indicate a subsample (67).
n	Number of degrees of freedom (222).
P	The proportion of cases in one class of a dichotomous population (246).
p	The proportion of cases in one class of a sample from a dichotomous population (245).
Q	$1-P$ (246).
Q_1, Q_L	First quartile or lower quartile (72).
Q_3, Q_U	Third quartile or upper quartile (72).
q	$1-p$ (245).
R	(1) Rank order correlation (159). (2) Correlation derived from a computed correlation (155, 169).
r	Coefficient of correlation; subscripts may be used to indicate variables being correlated (142).
$r_{xy.z}$	Partial correlation between x and y, when variation in z is eliminated (171).
$r_{.05}$	The fifth percentile of the distribution of r (259).
s	Sample standard deviation; may be used with subscript to indicate the variable (90).
S	Sample standard deviation, used when needed to distinguish from small s (169).
$s_{y.x}$	Standard error of estimate (132).
s^2	Variance, or square of standard deviation (90).
$s_{\bar{x}}$	Standard error of a mean estimated from a sample (218).
$s_{\bar{x}_1-\bar{x}_2}$	Standard error of a difference between means (233).
$s_{p_1-p_2}$	Standard error of difference between proportions (255).
T	$50 + 10z$, where z is a scale value of the standard normal distribution (196).

SYMBOL	DEFINITION
t	A scale value of Student's distribution or a variable which has this distribution (221).
X, Y	Variables, or gross scores of variables (87).
$\overline{X}, \overline{Y}$	Means of samples (88).
$\tilde{X}, \tilde{Y}$	Values predicted by regression equations (127).
$X_{.50}$	The 50th percentile; similarly for other percentiles (71).
x, y	$X - \overline{X}, Y - \overline{Y}$ (143).
x', y'	Coded scores (96).
y	Ordinate of normal curve (184).
Z	$50 + 10 \, (X - \overline{X})/s$ (196).
z	Scale value of the standard normal distribution, or standard normal deviate. Also a variable which has this standard normal distribution (181).
z_r	Transformation used in testing the significance of a correlation coefficient (259).
$z_{.05}$	The fifth percentile of the normal distribution (187).
ζ	Population value corresponding to the statistic z_r (260).
μ	Population mean (179, 208).
π	Ratio of circumference of a circle to its diameter; approximately 3.1416.
ρ	Correlation coefficient in a population (258).
Σ	The sum of (87).
σ	Standard deviation in a population (179, 208).
σ^2	Variance in a population (208).
$\sigma_{\overline{x}}, \sigma_p, \sigma_{p_1 - p_2}$ σ_r, σ_{z_r}	Standard error of quantity noted as subscript (213, 249, 255, 258, 260).
ϕ	Measure of relationship between two dichotomous variables (158).
$\neq$	Is not equal to (234).
$a > b$	a is greater than b (228).
$a < b$	a is less than b (228).
$\lvert a \rvert$	The absolute or numerical value of a, the sign being taken as positive (89).
$a \geqq b$	a is greater than or is equal to b (282).
$a \leqq b$	a is less than or is equal to b (282).
$\sqrt{a}$	The positive square root of a (90).
∞	Infinity (271).

LIST OF FORMULAS

(7.17)
$$s^2 = i^2 \left[\frac{\Sigma f(x')^2 - \frac{(\Sigma f x')^2}{N}}{N - 1} \right]$$
97

Raising the arbitrary origin by r intervals:

(7.18) changes $\Sigma x'$ to $\Sigma x' - Nr$ 97

(7.19) and changes $\Sigma (x')^2$ to $\Sigma (x')^2 - 2r\Sigma x' + Nr^2$ 97

Lowering the arbitrary origin by r intervals:

(7.20) changes $\Sigma x'$ to $\Sigma x' + Nr$ 97

(7.21) and changes $\Sigma (x')^2$ to $\Sigma (x')^2 + 2r\Sigma x' + Nr^2$ 97

(7.22)
$$N_c = N_1 + N_2 + \cdots + N_k$$
101

(7.23)
$$\overline{X}_c = \frac{1}{N_c} (N_1 \overline{X}_1 + N_2 \overline{X}_2 + \cdots + N_k \overline{X}_k)$$
101

(7.24)
$$d_i = \overline{X}_i - \overline{X}_c$$
101

(7.25)
$$(N_c - 1)s_c^2 = (N_1 - 1)s_1^2 + (N_2 - 1)s_2^2 + \cdots + (N_k - 1)s_k^2$$
$$+ N_1 d_1^2 + N_2 d_2^2 + \cdots + N_k d_k^2$$
101

(9.1)
$$Y = a + bX$$
122

(9.2)
$$b = \frac{N\Sigma XY - (\Sigma X)(\Sigma Y)}{N\Sigma X^2 - (\Sigma X)^2}$$
127

(9.3)
$$a = \overline{Y} - b\overline{X}$$
127

(9.4)
$$s_{y \cdot x} = \sqrt{\frac{\Sigma (Y - \tilde{Y})^2}{N - 2}}$$
132

(9.5)
$$\Sigma (Y - \tilde{Y})^2 = \frac{1}{N} \left\{ N\Sigma Y^2 - (\Sigma Y)^2 - \frac{[N\Sigma XY - (\Sigma X)(\Sigma Y)]^2}{N\Sigma X^2 - (\Sigma X)^2} \right\}$$
132

(9.6)
$$\Sigma (Y - \overline{Y})^2 = \Sigma (Y - \tilde{Y})^2 + \Sigma (\tilde{Y} - \overline{Y})^2$$
133

(9.7)
$$\bar{\tilde{Y}}_i = a + b\overline{X}_i$$
135

(9.8)
$$b = \frac{\text{vertical segment}}{\text{horizontal segment}} = \frac{v}{h}$$
135

(10.1a)
$$r^2 = 1 - \frac{\Sigma (Y - \tilde{Y})^2}{\Sigma (Y - \overline{Y})^2}$$
142

(10.1b)
$$r^2 = 1 - \frac{\Sigma (X - \tilde{X})^2}{\Sigma (X - \overline{X})^2}$$
142

(10.2a)
$$r = \frac{\Sigma (X - \overline{X})(Y - \overline{Y})}{\sqrt{\Sigma (X - \overline{X})^2 \Sigma (Y - \overline{Y})^2}}$$
143

(10.2b)
$$r = \frac{\Sigma xy}{\sqrt{\Sigma x^2 \Sigma y^2}}$$
143

ANSWERS

Exercise 3.2, page 33

2. (a) 20.8 years; 28.5 years; 24.9 years; 32.1 years; greater for females; greater for nonwhites.　(b) Not if all races are combined.　In 1920 it was slightly higher for nonwhite males than for nonwhite females.　(c) Discrepancy has increased for both whites and nonwhites.　(d) Discrepancy has decreased for both males and females.　(e) No; no.　(f) (1) 1910–20; 1920–30; 1910–20; 1910–20 (2) 1910–20; 1910–20　(g) In 1940–50, increase was 4.5 years.　In 1930–40, increase was 2.4 years.　Time intervals are not constant throughout the table.

3. (a) $0 + 69.6 = 69.6$; $20 + 52.4 = 72.4$; $70 + 11.6 = 81.6$ (b) No.　(c) Ages 65 and 70; age 70

4.

16	33	49
35	14	49

　51　47

Exercise 5.1, page 55

1. (a) 6.5–7.5; 1　(b) 6–8; 2　(c) 6.75–7.25; 0.5　(d) 5.5–8.5; 3　(e) 6.95–7.05; 0.1 (f) $6\frac{7}{8}$–$7\frac{1}{8}$; $\frac{1}{4}$

2. (b) 19.9, 20.0, 20.1, 20.2, 20.3　(c) 17.0, 20.0, 23.0, 26.0, 29.0 (d) 19.99, 20.00, 20.01, 20.02, 20.03

Exercise 5.2, page 57

1. (b)

Scores in interval	Real limits	Score limits	Class index	i
9.5, 10.0, 10.5	9.25–10.75	9.5–10.5	10.0	1.5
8.0, 8.5, 9.0	7.75– 9.25	8.0– 9.0	8.5	1.5
6.5, 7.0, 7.5	6.25–7.75	6.5– 7.5	7.0	1.5

2. (a)

Score limits	Scores in interval	Real limits	Class index	i
17–19	17, 18, 19	16.5–19.5	18	3
14–16	14, 15, 16	13.5–16.5	15	3

(b)

Score limits	Real limits	Class index	i
30–39	29.5–39.5	34.5	10
20–29	19.5–29.5	24.5	10
10–19	9.5–19.5	14.5	10

(c)

70–76	69.5–76.5	73	7
63–69	62.5–69.5	66	7
56–62	55.5–62.5	59	7

3. 35–37 and 38–40; $i = 3$

Exercise 6.1, page 78

2. (a) Not possibly.　(b) No.　　**3.** No; no.　　**4.** III; I; I; I; II.

5. 63.1; a score; *above*, not *in*.

6. In I, nearer to Q_3; in II, a little nearer to Q_1; in III, nearer to Q_1; in combined group, a little nearer to Q_3.

9. B, D, A, C　　　　**10.** C, A, B, E, D　　　**11.** A stands higher.

12. (a) E or OE　(b) D or OD　(c) F or OF　(d) C or OC　(e) CF　(f) Area CFJM (g) Area to right of GI or area GHI　(h) B or OB　(i) BG

13. (a) Vertical　(b) A is the fifth percentile or $X_{.05}$; B is the tenth percentile or $X_{.10}$ (c) Median, 50th percentile, fifth decile, $X_{.50}$　(d) AE is $X_{.95}$–$X_{.05}$; BD is $X_{.90}$–$X_{.10}$ (e) FH is middle 80 percent, and OG is lower 50 percent of the distribution.

Exercise 6.2, page 81

1.

Score:	25	21	18	24	20	21	21
Rank:	1	4	7	2	6	4	4

　　　Sum of ranks = 28 = 7(8)/2

2.

Score:	6	9	13	6	14	8	12	5	2
Rank:	$6\frac{1}{2}$	4	2	$6\frac{1}{2}$	1	5	3	8	9

　　　Sum of ranks = 45 = 9(10)/2

3. Score: 12   8   7   10   6   7   9   7   13   8   14   5

    Rank: 3 $6\frac{1}{2}$ 9   4   11   9   5   9   2 $6\frac{1}{2}$ 1   12

    Sum of ranks $= 78 = 12(13)/2$

4. Score: 5   4   7   9   8   5   3   5   9   12   8   2   13   6

    Rank: 10   12   7 $3\frac{1}{2}$ $5\frac{1}{2}$ 10   13   10 $3\frac{1}{2}$ 2 $5\frac{1}{2}$ 14   1   8

    Sum of ranks $= 105 = 14(15)/2$

Exercise 6.3, page 83

1. \$5840 is the 57th percentile. 57 is the percentile rank of \$5840.

2. 12 is the 87th percentile. 87 is the percentile rank of 12.

3. The 50th percentile is 72.0. The percentile rank of 72.0 is 50.

4. The 95th percentile is \$6850. The percentile rank of \$6850 is 95.

Exercise 7.1, page 88

1. $\overline{X} = 5.7$; $X_{.50} = 5.5$ **2.** $\overline{X} = 16$; $X_{.50} = 18$ **3.** $\overline{X} = 409$; $X_{.50} = 409.5$

Exercise 7.2, page 92

2. Percentile rank of 10.2 is 79 because $\dfrac{17 + .7(4)}{25} = .792$.

3. Percentile rank of 5.4 is 19 because $\dfrac{2 + .9(3)}{25} = .188$.   **5.** $\dfrac{12 - 4}{2.4} = 3.33$

6. and 7.

	$X_{.50}$	$\overline{X}$	s^2	s	Range/s
(a)	9	9	15.8	3.97	3.3
(b)	26	25.4	5.8	2.41	2.5
(c)	10.5	9.1	27.6	5.26	2.7
(d)	1.2	3.5	18.9	4.35	2.5
(e)	2.0	1.0	50.5	7.11	2.4
(f)	-4.0	-2.0	40.7	6.38	2.8

8. The standard deviation can be larger than the mean.

Exercise 7.3, page 99

1. For ungrouped data

	I	II	III	Combined group
$\overline{X}$	55.0	52.8	48.2	52.4
s^2	68.3	80.1	95.4	86.1
s	8.3	8.9	9.8	9.3

For grouped data

$\overline{X}$	54.9	52.7	48.1	52.3
s^2	67.5	78.3	95.1	85.1
s	8.2	8.8	9.8	9.2

3. Yes.

4.

	Grouped	Ungrouped
I	-1.0	-2.6
II	$-.2$	.4
III	$-.1$	$-.8$
Combined group	$-.8$	$-.1$

5. III–II–I

    III–II–I

6.

Section	Grouped	Ungrouped
I	$44/8.2 = 5.4$	$41/8.3 = 4.9$
II	$44/8.8 = 5.0$	$41/8.9 = 4.6$
III	$39/9.8 = 4.0$	$37/9.8 = 3.8$
Combined	$49/9.2 = 5.3$	$46/9.3 = 4.9$

7. $\underline{M}$ (a) $X_{.20} < X_{.40} < X_{.50}$ $\underline{P}$ (h)

  $\underline{P}$ (b) $\underline{M}$ (i) $\Sigma(X - 11) = N + \Sigma(X - 12)$

  $\underline{M}$ (c) $\Sigma(X - 5) = N + \Sigma(X - 6)$ $\underline{P}$ (j)

  $\underline{M}$ (d) $\Sigma(X - \overline{X}) = 0$ $\underline{M}$ (k) $\Sigma(X - \overline{X})^2$ is smaller than

  $\underline{P}$ (e) $\Sigma(X - A)^2$ when $A \neq \overline{X}$.

  $\underline{M}$ (f) $\dfrac{69 - 3}{7.4} = 8.9$ which is unrea- $\underline{P}$ (m)

                sonably large. $\underline{P}$ (n)

  $\underline{P}$ (g)

Exercise 7.4, page 105

	Without interpolation		With interpolation	
1. Range	Number	Percent	Number	Percent
Below $\overline{X} - s$	11	11.2	13.1	13.4
$\overline{X} - s$ to $\overline{X}$	38	38.8	35.9	36.6
$\overline{X}$ to $\overline{X} + s$	32	32.7	34.7	35.4
Above $\overline{X} + s$	17	17.3	14.3	14.6
Below $\overline{X} - 2s$	4	4.1	4.0	4.1
$\overline{X} - 2s$ to $\overline{X}$	45	45.9	45.0	45.9
$\overline{X}$ to $\overline{X} + 2s$	49	50.0	48.2	49.2
Above $\overline{X} + 2s$	0	0.0	.8	.8

2.	Jones	Smith	Brown
A	66	53	41
B	52	48	53
C	51	57	52
D	66	57	45
Mean	59	54	48

3.

	$(X - \overline{X})/s$
English usage	−.95
Algebra	.57
U.S. history	1.28

Exercise 9.1, page 140

2. (a) $\check{Y} = 31.6 + .66(25) = 48.1$ $Y - \check{Y} = 52 - 48.1 = 3.9$
   (b) $\check{Y} = 31.6 + .66(39) = 57.3$ $Y - \check{Y} = 44 - 57.3 = -13.3$

Exercise 10.1, page 149

4. $r = \dfrac{11{,}500}{\sqrt{(177{,}400)(212{,}875)}} = .06$ $b_{yx} = \dfrac{11{,}500}{177{,}400} \cdot \dfrac{5}{3} = .11$ $b_{xy} = \dfrac{11{,}500}{212{,}875} \cdot \dfrac{3}{5} = .03$

Exercise 10.2, page 153

1. No.   **2.** 2 were in both groups.   **3.** No.   **4.** No.   **5.** 7   **6.** 6

Exercise 10.3, page 155

1. $\dfrac{2(.52)}{1.52} = .68$; not necessarily; something not far from .52.

2. $\dfrac{2(.45)}{1.45} = .62$. The result is less likely to be achieved.

Exercise 11.1, page 169

2. All decreased; s_x proportionately more than s_y; b_{xy} proportionately more than b_{yx}.

3. All decreased; s_y proportionately more than s_x; b_{yx} proportionately more than b_{xy}.

4. All increased; s_x proportionately more than s_y; b_{xy} proportionately more than b_{yx}.

5. All increased; s_y proportionately more than s_x; b_{yx} proportionately more than b_{xy}.

Exercise 11.2, page 172

5. (a) r_{26}, r_{27}, r_{34}. (b) (4) is justified (c) (3) is justified
   (e) x_2, x_4, x_5, x_7 are positively related to anxiety. x_3, x_6 are negatively related.
   None are large enough to be of predictive value. None are large enough for
   generalization.

Exercise 12.1, page 186

A. 1. .23   3. .45   5. .48   7. .34   B. 1. .3472   3. .6826   5. .9898
   2. .16   4. .04   6. .46   8. .26   2. .4972   4. .9500   6. .6970
C. 1. .5596   3. .9713   5. .0322   7. .7486   D. 1. .0500   3. .0204   5. .4532
   2. .0934   4. .9525   6. .0495   8. .2514   2. .1010   4. .0098   6. .0050

Exercise 12.2, page 188

A. 1. .07   2. .96   3. .55   4. .31   5. .42
B. 1. .01   2. .95   3. .60   4. .005   5. .05
C. $z_{.07}$, $z_{.81}$, $z_{.42}$, $z_{.05}$, $z_{.40}$
D. 1. .98   2. .99   3. .50   4. .06   5. .95   6. .11
F. 1. .02   2. .01   3. .05   4. .04   5. .10   6. .20

H. 1. $z_{.005}$ and $z_{.995}$ 2. $z_{.01}$ and $z_{.99}$ 3. $z_{.25}$ and $z_{.75}$ 4. $z_{.025}$ and $z_{.975}$
    5. $z_{.05}$ and $z_{.95}$ 6. $z_{.10}$ and $z_{.90}$ 7. $z_{.375}$ and $z_{.625}$ 8. $z_{.0005}$ and $z_{.9995}$
I. 1. 53.7   2. 68.2   3. 23 percent   4. 4 percent
    5. 58.6 and 69.4   6. 48.3 and 79.7   7. 77.2   8. 43.4 and 84.6
J. 1. 71.8   2. 98.9   3. 92 percent   4. 0.3 percent
    5. 80.9 and 101.1   6. 61.6 and 120.4   7. 115.7   8. 52.4 and 129.6
K. 1. 43.6   2. 65.3   3. 18 percent   4. 23 percent
    5. 50.9 and 67.1   6. 35.5 and 82.5   7. 78.7   8. 28.1 and 89.9
L. 1. 0.9   2. 8.1   3. 0 percent   4. 100 percent
    5. 3.3 and 8.7   6. -1.8 and 13.8   7. 12.6   8. -4.3 and 16.3

Exercise 12.4, page 197

2. T scores are 29, 38, 45, 52, 59, 66.

Exercise 13.2, page 214

	Distribution of $\overline{X}$		Range of middle 95 percent of sample means	Range of middle 50 percent of sample means
	Mean	Standard error		
2.	60	1.5	57.1 to 62.9	59.0 to 61.0
3.	40	2.0	36.1 to 43.9	38.7 to 41.3
4.	40	3.0	34.1 to 45.9	38.0 to 42.0
5.	92	.8	90.4 to 93.6	91.5 to 92.5
6.	53	2.5	48.1 to 57.9	51.3 to 54.7
7.	39	.5	38.0 to 40.0	38.7 to 39.3
8.	39	1.25	36.6 to 41.4	38.2 to 39.8

Exercise 13.3, page 218

1. (a) .50   (b) .07   (c) .84   (d) .68   **2.** (a) .98   (b) .87
4. (a) 64.7 and 85.3   (b) 67.3 and 82.7   (c) 69.8 and 80.2
    (d) 71.9 and 78.1   (e) 73.5 and 76.5   (f) 74.0 and 76.0
5. (a) 74.4 to 75.6   (b) 73.6 to 76.4   (c) 73.3 to 76.7
    (d) 72.9 to 77.1   (e) 72.2 to 77.8   (f) 71.7 to 78.3

Exercise 13.4, page 222

2. (a) (1) 1.83   (2) -1.38 (3) $-.88$ (4) -2.82
    (b) (1) 1.75   (2) -1.34 (3) $-.87$ (4) -2.60
    (c) (1) $-.72$ and .72   (2) -1.44 and 1.44   (3) -1.94 and 1.94
       (4) -2.45 and 2.45   (5) -3.71 and 3.71
3. (1) $-.69$ and .69   (2) -1.33 and 1.33   (3) -1.73 and 1.73
    (4) -2.09 and 2.09   (5) -2.86 and 2.86
4. 95 percent. Answer depends only on N.

Exercise 13.5, page 225

1. (a) 14.65 and 32.35   (b) 17.11 and 29.89   (c) 18.25 and 28.75.
2. (a) 22.0 and 25.0   (b) 22.3 and 24.7   (c) 22.5 and 24.5.
3. (a) 20.6 and 26.4   (b) 21.4 and 25.6.

Exercise 14.1, page 234

1. $t = .16$ $t_{.975} = 2.26$ not significant
2. $t = 6.81$ $t_{.99} = 2.43$ significant
3. $t = 1.96$ $t_{.99} = 2.43$ not significant
4. $t = .186$ $t_{.99} = 2.43$ not significant
5. $t = .72$ $t_{.975} = 2.03$ not significant

Exercise 15.1, page 256

1. For normal approximation the region of rejection is $p > .829$, and the hypothesis that deaf and hearing are alike is rejected. Hypothesis is also rejected by Table XIIB.

2. Consistent.   **3.** $z = 1.45$, not significant at .05 level.

INDEX